STRUCTURE, PROCESS, AND PARTY

STRUCTURE, PROCESS, AND PARTY

Essays in American Political History

Peter H. Argersinger

M. E. Sharpe Inc.
ARMONK, NEW YORK
LONDON, ENGLAND

Library of Congress Cataloging-in-Publication Data

Argersinger, Peter H.
    Structure, process, and party : essays in American political history
/ by Peter H. Argersinger.
      p.   cm.
    Includes bibliographical references (p.   ) and index.
    ISBN 0-87332-798-5
    1. United States—Politics and government—1865–1900.
2. Elections—United States—History—19th century. 3. Political parties—
United States—History—19th century. 4. I. Title.
E661.A72 1991
324.973′08—dc20   91–9567
                         324.97308   CIP
                         A691

Printed in the United States of America

MV 10 9 8 7 6 5 4 3 2 1

For My Parents
Marjorie Hayes Argersinger
and
William J. Argersinger, Jr.

Contents

Acknowledgments

I am grateful to a number of persons for their valuable help at various stages in the preparation of this volume. Many scholars gave me the benefit of suggestions and comments on one or more of the essays collected here. Jo Ann E. Argersinger, in particular, provided consistent encouragement, aid, and sound advice. Allan G. Bogue and J. Morgan Kousser also were especially and repeatedly generous in their kind assistance and wise counsel. Others whose support and suggestions proved important include Howard W. Allen, Ballard C. Campbell, Lewis L. Gould, John W. Jeffries, Paul Kleppner, Martin Ridge, David P. Thelen, Philip R. VanderMeer, and James E. Wright. Research grants from the Beveridge Fund of the American Historical Association and the Faculty Development Fund of the University of Maryland, Baltimore County, facilitated my work, as did the professional typing of Carol M. Warner and Linda M. Hatmaker. Michael Weber of M.E. Sharpe first suggested the publication of this volume, and his interest and encouragement made it possible.

Introduction

The "new political history" is now nearly a commonplace, a phrase employed to describe a variety of approaches, methods, concepts, and topics that since the 1960s have significantly transformed the study of past politics. Traditionally, political history focused on particular events, specific campaigns, famous politicians; it relied primarily on literary sources, especially personal manuscripts; its presentation was narrative, as in biographies of presidents and senators. This approach persists, of course, and continues to make contributions, but it has surely been eclipsed by the new political history. The new work emphasizes the systematic analysis of structure and process, draws from the social sciences for both method and theory, exploits new source materials, especially quantitative data, and often focuses on problems and themes, institutions and electorates, rather than on chronological periods and famous individuals. Collectively, it has dramatically expanded and reshaped knowledge of the structure and operation of the American political system, developing new conceptual frameworks to explain political change, revealing the social correlates of electoral behavior, analyzing the evolution of party structure, determining the role of legal and institutional factors, and generally bringing new perspectives to past American politics.[1] The essays collected in this volume are a part of these continuing developments during the past decade.

The scholarly origins and several of the leading concerns of the new political history are discussed in the first essay reprinted in this work. Commissioned for the inaugural volume of a research annual in political science, it surveys the historical literature on popular voting behavior, an undertaking that in itself suggests the interdisciplinary nature of the field. Because of the scope of its subject, I asked my colleague John W. Jeffries, a specialist in twentieth-century American political history, to join me in co-authoring "American Electoral History: Party Systems and Voting Behavior." This essay centers on two major themes that emerge from the early historical work relying on social science perspectives and quantitative analysis. Both emphasize the crucial importance of political parties. The first is the concept of party systems and electoral realignments that portrays American political history as a series of electoral eras or

systems, each with its own characteristic patterns of voting behavior, party identification, and political concerns. Periodically, major social and economic crises
produce elections that realign voters' partisan affiliations, shift party strength,
and revise the saliency of issues, thereby creating another era or party system of
political and governmental stability. The second major analytical concept of the
new political history is the ethnocultural interpretation of voting behavior. Based
on close examination of the local context of political life and analysis of census
records, election returns, church records, and tax lists, this model holds that
partisan cleavages in the United States have been primarily ethnic and religious
rather than economic.

In providing systematic analyses of American political history and drawing
attention to previously ignored issues, these two concepts have proved excep-
tionally influential and continue to shape theory, research, and synthesis in political history. Nevertheless, as our essay indicates, they have also been criticized on
methodological, conceptual, and empirical grounds by a number of scholars. Nor
have such criticisms abated in the years since we wrote our essay in
1983. Moreover, there are other important components of the new political history, some of which in fact provide perspectives useful for critiquing the realignment and ethnocultural models. These other subfields include the analysis of
legislative behavior, the examination of the connections between voting and
policymaking, and especially the investigation of the institutional features of
American politics.[2] The remaining chapters of this volume explore aspects of
these other themes, particularly the last.

Here, too, historians drew from the social sciences. The modern behavioral
approach to the study of politics, in political science as in history, initially
encouraged scholars to devote more substantive and methodological attention to
analyzing individuals, whether in small blocs or large groups, than to the institutional analysis of structural and organizational characteristics. There gradually
developed, however, a reaction against what Rogers Smith has termed "the
treatment of legal and political institutions simply as epiphenomena of self-interested individual and group behavior." This renewed interest in institutions reflected a recognition that they were more than merely arenas within which
political behavior occurred in response to more fundamental factors, such as
ethnocultural interests. In particular, political scientists began to demonstrate a
concern for the institutional framework of the electoral system and its effect
upon what Walter Dean Burnham has described as "the American political
universe."[3]

Among historically inclined political scientists, this "legal-institutionalist"
theory first emerged in an effort to offer an alternative to Burnham's "conspiratorial interpretation" of the transformation in popular voting behavior that occurred after the realignment of the 1890s. Arguing that in their focus on the
social origins of voting behavior scholars had neglected "the institutional or
structural properties of the electoral system itself," political scientists such as

Jerrold Rusk and Philip Converse maintained that ballot- and voting-systems, registration laws, and other electoral mechanics constituted "the framework within which the effects of other independent variables must be judged." In particular, Rusk and Converse asserted that the adoption of the Australian ballot reform and new voter registration procedures were primarily responsible for the increased split-ticket voting and decreased turnout that Burnham had attributed to popular alienation from politics following the establishment of corporate political hegemony.[4]

Although legal-institutionalist theorists usefully redirected scholarly attention and illuminated the political consequences of changing institutional factors, they virtually ignored the political context within which such changes evolved. Thus, structural arrangements appeared as essentially apolitical or nonpartisan determinants shaping politics. Converse even argued that declining turnout and other changes in political behavior were merely "unintended consequences" of the institutional changes in voting rules. Burnham, in fact, complained that the institutionalists treated electoral mechanics as "an uncaused cause" and came close to "excluding politics from the study of political phenomena."[5]

Historians, with their characteristic concern for specific contexts, soon began themselves to investigate the institutional features of the electoral system, exploring their origins as well as their consequences. In the first major such work, J. Morgan Kousser examined in detail the efforts to restrict suffrage in each of the Southern states at the end of the nineteenth century. Methodologically innovative and forcefully argued, Kousser's work rejected V.O. Key's *fait accompli* thesis that the restrictive laws merely legalized conditions already created by other forces and demonstrated how procedural changes reshaped the political system, refuting any contention that the subsequent collapse of white political participation, lack of party competition, limitation of political choice, and other features of twentieth-century Southern politics were "unintended consequences" of black disfranchisement. But, of course, the South has always been regarded as a distinctive case, and some legal-institutionalists among political scientists were themselves willing to argue that Southern Democrats deliberately employed institutional means to dominate politics in their region. What they strongly denied was that Republicans had acted analogously in Northern states, even maintaining that the structural reforms adopted there actually ended the previous practice of manipulating the electoral framework for partisan purposes.[6]

Historians then turned their attention to the electoral structure and procedures of the non-Southern states, explicitly or implicitly attempting to answer the challenges posed by political scientists. "Most important," Converse noted, "is to sort out as clearly as possible, who was doing what to whom with these reforms." Rusk described "legislative intent" as the "paramount" issue in ascertaining the nature of electoral change: "*who* urged the passage of these laws and *why*?" During the 1980s, a number of works appeared, among them those reprinted here as chapters 2–7, which sought to determine the political and electoral environment that reformers wanted to change, the identity and objectives of the reformers, and the effects of the electoral structure upon voting behavior, governance, and public policy.[7]

My own interest in these issues had its origins in my earlier work on Populism. I had been concerned not only with explaining the socioeconomic bases of partisanship and voting behavior in the 1890s but also with the influence of organizational factors, especially that of party structure and procedures, upon the course of the People's Party. I became particularly impressed with the contemporary attention devoted to a ballot law designed to weaken the Populists' political autonomy and influence. Although I only briefly considered the subject in *Populism and Politics*, I subsequently investigated the enactment, implementation, and implications of that and then other election laws. Perhaps because Populism was inherently a challenge to the political system, as much as the People's Party was necessarily a part of it, the political and partisan nature of the electoral structure and its processes was immediately apparent.[8]

Rather than regarding the electoral structure as given and impartial, as exogenous to political behavior and activity, the essays in this volume therefore emphasize the importance of the interaction between the institutional framework and political agents. Rules regulating suffrage, representation, and the voting process fix the parameters of the electoral system and thereby shape political participation, party decisions, election results, and the responsiveness of government. But while productive of such important political consequences, election laws and institutional arrangements are themselves the product of previous political decisions. Their establishment, in fact, was often politically divisive and characterized by partisan, personal, and ideological calculations of their political effects. By analyzing the dynamic relations among the institutional framework, the party system, and the political culture, these essays modify a number of conventional interpretations and demonstrate the complexity of American political history.[9]

The chapter "Electoral Processes in American Politics" introduces the themes and topics that are more fully developed in the subsequent essays. It provides an overview of electoral rules, especially their origins and political implications, drawing from the older descriptive institutional literature in both history and political science as well as from more recent analytical work, including my own specific studies of the nineteenth century and those of political scientists on such contemporary issues as public campaign financing.

The succeeding essays center on the crucial Gilded Age of the late nineteenth century, when states moved from exercising little authority in the electoral process, beyond fixing the broadest boundaries, to establishing control over ballots, the voting process, political parties, and campaign activities. As one representative of the Republicans who shaped Iowa's new rules triumphantly described the system to a dismayed partisan opponent in 1897, "The whole thing is strictly under the dictation of state authority."[10] Although there is some inevitable overlap among these essays, given the interrelationship of the factors and the necessity of focusing on individual states, the similarities as well as the differences are illuminating, pointing up the significance of specific political contexts.

"The Value of the Vote," the third chapter in this volume, calls attention to the study of systems of representation and underscores the usefulness of quantitative analysis in historical scholarship. Despite its significant role in the electoral structure, representation has been neglected by both traditional and social science historians. By examining political developments in several states with varying electoral programs, this essay illustrates the important and sometimes troubling consequences that modes of representation often had for political parties, popular participation, and public policy.

Rules of representation, especially when coupled with a competitive party system, also may have provided an incentive for election fraud, the subject of the fourth chapter. Political scientists have argued vigorously over the existence of election fraud and its possible effects on issues ranging from voter turnout to the nature of the polity. Most new political historians have sided with those who deny the prevalence of massive fraud, while others have documented numerous illegal election practices but disagree as to their meaning and political significance.[11] "New Perspectives on Election Fraud in the Gilded Age" specifies the nature and setting of election fraud and surveys the variety of evidence and sources available for its analysis. Most important, it indicates that election fraud was a product of the interplay of the electoral structure, the party system, and the political culture, demonstrating again that legal and political determinants of the electoral process were often as decisive in election results as the issues, candidates, and attitudes traditionally emphasized.

Election fraud, real or merely perceived, was a major factor in the evolution of the electoral system in the late nineteenth century, as illustrated by the fifth essay in this collection. "From Party Tickets to Secret Ballots" probes Maryland politics to show the consistency with which the search for partisan advantage underlay the shaping of electoral arrangements. Rules for election clerks and poll watchers, for registering voters and casting ballots, all reflected an electoral structure and process dominated by political parties, and any revisions usually derived from competing political efforts to exploit the same system for comparable purposes. The appearance of election fraud generated the popular support for challenges to party control of the electoral process, but that same party control restricted the reality of institutional reform. Even the Australian ballot law was framed by partisan legislators determined to promote party objectives.

One particular partisan use of the Australian system is the subject of the sixth chapter, " 'A Place on the Ballot': Fusion Politics and Antifusion Laws." The adoption of an official, blanket ballot required the state to enact procedures to specify which parties and candidates would be listed on the ballot. In state after state in the North and West, Republicans, their political control tenuous and increasingly challenged, seized this opportunity to manipulate electoral processes to frustrate their opponents and ensure their own hegemony. Under the deceptive cover of ballot regulation, they passed laws that had fateful consequences for traditional nineteenth-century politics, obstructing the common practice of political fusion by which their opponents cooperated against them, undermining the viability of third parties, and discouraging voter turnout.

Antifusion ballot laws are also an important concern of the next essay, "Regulating Democracy," which describes the adoption and implementation of electoral procedures in North and South Dakota. The political volatility of those states in the 1890s makes them an especially valuable setting in which to analyze the interactive nature of the institutional framework and political actors, for as parties alternated in power they also took turns reconfiguring electoral structure and processes. The strictly partisan legislative voting on electoral bills also indicates the common conviction of the political effects of legal regulation. The Dakota experience, moreover, clearly establishes the political role that courts and election officials often played. The product of these various developments, as the essay shows, was an electoral system that many nineteenth-century Americans would not have regarded as democratic.

Legislative behavior also receives attention in the final essay, which similarly suggests the centrality of party in the institutional structure of politics. Organizational rules and procedures certainly shaped legislative behavior and public policy, as I have argued elsewhere,[12] but the focus of "Populists in Power" is more on the systematic analysis of roll-call data to determine the connections between voting, parties, and elections on the one hand, and public policy on the other. Such legislative analysis, an important feature of the new political history, not only demonstrates that the primary determinant of legislative voting was party but also provides important new perspectives on several traditional political questions about Populism. Particularly suggestive is the finding that voting cleavages among Populists within the legislature derived from party decisions adopted in the electoral arena, a significant example of "the dialectical interplay of meaningful decisions and structural constraints."[13]

The essays in this volume are primarily devoted to exploring several major themes of the new political history and to emphasizing the importance of analyzing the connections between political actions and structural factors. By examining the details of different specific contexts, they demonstrate the dynamic nature of factors that all too often are regarded as historical givens. Thus they reveal the complexity, and perhaps the possibilities, of American politics.

Notes

1. For the development of the new political history, see especially Allan G. Bogue, *Clio and the Bitch Goddess: Quantification in American Political History* (Beverly Hills, 1983), and "Systematic Revisionism and a Generation of Ferment in American History,"

Journal of Contemporary History, 21 (April 1986), 135–62. For the continued inclusive nature of the field, see J. Morgan Kousser, "The State of Social Science History in the Late 1980s," *Historical Methods,* 22 (Winter 1989), 13–20, and "Toward 'Total Political History': A Rational-Choice Research Program," *Journal of Interdisciplinary History,* 20 (Spring 1990), 521–60. Richard L. McCormick, *The Party Period and Public Policy: American Politics from the Age of Jackson to the Progressive Era* (New York, 1986), is the most forceful argument for the importance of political parties.

2. Despite its publication date of 1986, we completed this essay in 1983, a discrepancy that may excuse some of its omissions. For a review of recent books, see Phyllis F. Field, "Nineteenth-Century American Voting Studies: The New Generation," *Historical Methods,* 22 (Fall 1989), 164–69. J. Morgan Kousser has been especially important in arguing that "electoral behavior was not the whole of politics" and in directing attention to political institutions, electoral rules, and public policy. See, for example, J. Morgan Kousser, "Are Political Acts Unnatural?" *Journal of Interdisciplinary History,* 15 (Winter 1985), 467–80, esp. 468.

3. Rogers M. Smith, "Political Jurisprudence, the 'New Institutionalism,' and the Future of Public Law," *American Political Science Review,* 82 (March 1988), 89–108, esp. 91; James G. March and Johan P. Olsen, "The New Institutionalism: Organizational Factors in Political Life," *American Political Science Review,* 78 (Sept. 1984), 734–49; Ronald D. Hedlund, "Organizational Attributes of Legislatures: Structure, Rules, Norms, Resources," *Legislative Studies Quarterly,* 9 (Feb. 1984), 51–121; Walter Dean Burnham, "The Changing Shape of the American Political Universe," *American Political Science Review,* 59 (March 1965), 7–28.

4. Jerrold G. Rusk, "The Effect of the Australian Ballot Reform on Split Ticket Voting: 1876–1908," *American Political Science Review,* 64 (Dec. 1970), 1220–38, esp. 1220; Philip E. Converse, "Change in the American Electorate," in Angus Campbell and Philip E. Converse, eds., *The Human Meaning of Social Change* (New York, 1972), 263–337; Converse, "Comment on Burnham's 'Theory and Voting Research,' " *American Political Science Review,* 68 (Sept. 1974), 1024–27; Rusk, "Comment: The American Electoral Universe: Speculation and Evidence," *ibid.,* 1028–49.

5. Walter Dean Burnham, "Theory and Voting Research: Some Reflections on Converse's 'Change in the American Electorate,' " *American Political Science Review,* 68 (Sept. 1974), 1002–23; Burnham, "Rejoinder to 'Comments' by Philip Converse and Jerrold Rusk," *ibid.,* 1050–57, esp. 1054; Burnham, editorial communication in *American Political Science Review,* 65 (Dec. 1971), 1149–52, esp. 1150.

6. J. Morgan Kousser, *The Shaping of Southern Politics: Suffrage Restriction and the Establishment of the One-Party South, 1880–1910* (New Haven, 1974); Jerrold G. Rusk and John J. Stucker, "The Effect of the Southern System of Election Laws on Voter Participation: A Reply to V.O. Key, Jr.," in Joel H. Silbey, Allan G. Bogue, and William H. Flanigan, eds., *The History of American Electoral Behavior* (Princeton, 1978), 198–250; Rusk, "The American Electoral Universe," 1045, 1049.

7. Converse, "Change in the American Electorate," 296; Rusk, "The American Electoral Universe," 1045. In addition to the works cited in the chapter notes, see John F. Reynolds, *Testing Democracy: Electoral Behavior and Progressive Reform in New Jersey, 1880–1920* (Chapel Hill, 1988), the most notable recent examination of institutional and behavioral changes during this period.

8. Peter H. Argersinger, *Populism and Politics: William A. Peffer and the People's Party* (Lexington, Ky., 1974), esp. 289–92. The details of this early election law research were eventually published as "To Disfranchise the People: The Iowa Ballot Law and Election of 1897," *Mid-America,* 63 (Jan. 1981), 18–45. Its analysis was incorporated into an essay of wider focus, " 'A Place on the Ballot': Fusion Politics and Antifusion

Laws," *American Historical Review,* 85 (April 1980), 287–306, reprinted in this volume as chapter 6.

9. As the "new institutionalism" evolved in political science, it sometimes adopted a comparable emphasis on interaction, what Smith has called the "dialectical interplay of meaningful decisions and structural constraints," not only in electoral behavior but also in legislative analysis, jurisprudence, and other areas. See Smith, "Political Jurisprudence," esp. 103; March and Olsen, "The New Institutionalism"; Hedlund, "Organizational Attributes of Legislatures"; and Joseph Cooper and Cheryl D. Young, "Bill Introduction in the Nineteenth Century: A Study of Institutional Change," *Legislative Studies Quarterly,* 14 (Feb. 1989), 67–105.

10. Quoted in Argersinger, "To Disfranchise the People," 30.

11. For the continuing debate over election fraud, see Gerald Ginsburg, "Computing Antebellum Turnout: Methods and Models," *Journal of Interdisciplinary History,* 16 (Spring 1986), 579–611; Walter Dean Burnham, "Those High Nineteenth-Century American Voting Turnouts: Fact or Fiction?" *ibid.,* 613–44; and John F. Reynolds, "A Democratic Vote and a Republican Recount: The Hudson County Election Investigation of 1890," paper presented at the annual meeting of the Social Science History Association, Chicago, Nov. 4, 1988.

12. Peter H. Argersinger, "Ideology and Behavior: Legislative Politics and Western Populism," *Agricultural History,* 58 (Jan. 1984), 43–58, and "No Rights on This Floor: Third Parties and the Institutionalization of Congress," paper presented at the annual meeting of the Social Science History Association, Minneapolis, Oct. 20, 1990.

13. The quoted phrase is from the discussion of the new institutionalism in Smith, "Political Jurisprudence," 103.

STRUCTURE, PROCESS, AND PARTY

1

American Electoral History: Party Systems and Voting Behavior

Theory and Research: Overview

In the past quarter century, the analysis and interpretation of American electoral history have been transformed. The "new political history" responsible for that transformation has itself been part of the larger behavioral revolution in the social sciences, which in the study of history has been characterized by the growing use of social-science and quantitative approaches and methodology (Clubb and Bogue, 1977; Kousser, 1980b; Kammen, 1980; Bogue, 1981a). Developing rapidly since the mid-1960s, the new political history has focused chiefly on electoral behavior, legislative roll-call analysis, and collective biography. Historical patterns in voting have received perhaps the greatest and most fruitful scrutiny (Bogue, 1968, 1980; Bogue et al., 1977; VanderMeer, 1977).

The new political history arose from sources both without and within the historical profession. Although the use of quantitative and social-science methods by political historians goes back nearly a century, their application in recent decades stemmed primarily from the example of and contact with behavioral political scientists. Especially important were the survey-based election and voter studies by P.F. Lazarsfeld and the Columbia University Bureau of Applied Social Research and by A. Campbell and his colleagues at the University of Michigan Survey Research Center and the analyses of aggregate data and time series by such historically minded political scientists as V.O. Key, Jr., and W.D. Burnham. Although it remains true that political scientists look more to general models and paradigms and historians to the particularities of time and place,

From Peter H. Argersinger and John W. Jeffries, "American Electoral History: Party Systems and Voting Behavior," *Research in Micropolitics,* vol. I (1986), pp. 1–33. Reprinted with permission from JAI Press, Inc. and co-author John W. Jeffries.

cross-disciplinary exchange and collaboration have proved increasingly profit-
able in recent decades, especially in the study of parties and voting (Jensen,
1969a, 1969b; Bartley, 1975; Silbey et al., 1978).

Among historians, the encouragement and example of several scholars in the
1950s and 1960s contributed vitally to the development of the new political
history and its application to the study of electoral behavior. The work of Benson
was pivotal. In an enormously influential 1957 essay (collected with other essays
in Benson, 1972), he exposed the weaknesses of traditional political history and
called for the careful specification of hypotheses and the use of "systematic"
data and methods to study time series and group voting. Benson's pathbreaking
book on Jacksonian politics (1961) employed quantitative methods and social-
science concepts to reveal the importance of ethnocultural voting and electoral
cycles. Three historians at the University of Iowa in the late 1950s, Aydelotte,
Bogue, and Hays, were also instrumental in the development and dissemination
of the new political history (see, e.g., Aydelotte, 1971; Bogue, 1968; Hays,
1968).

By the early 1970s, the new political history had direction, momentum, and
achievement. Dissertations, articles, and monographs analyzing electoral history
proliferated; enough important work had been published to support two significant anthologies (Swierenga, 1970; Silbey and McSeveney, 1972); and there was
sufficient interest in quantitative methods to warrant a handbook for analyzing
historical data (Dollar and Jensen, 1971). Moreover, in the area of popular voting
behavior and political parties, the profusion of studies in the 1960s and 1970s
produced what have become the two major analytical constructs of the new
political history: the electoral realignment/party systems framework and the
ethnocultural model of voting.

The electoral realignment/party systems model was developed primarily by
political scientists. Key (1955), Campbell et al. (1960, 1966), Pomper (1967),
and MacRae and Meldrum (1960) were especially important in developing a
typology of elections that designated as "critical" or "realigning" those elections (or periods) that produced major change in voting behavior and party
strength. Burnham (1967, 1970) elaborated the scheme of electoral realignments
and subsequent "party systems" and added to it important issue and policy
dimensions. Sundquist (1973) and W.L. Shade (1973) also offered analytical
syntheses of electoral realignments. Historians did have some part in establishing
the presence of voting cycles (Benson, 1961; Sellers, 1965) and in investigating
critical elections and periods (Rogin and Shover, 1970; Clubb and Allen, 1971).
But the major work in establishing the overall framework was done by political
scientists using both mid-twentieth-century survey data and aggregate historical
voting data in time series; historians typically borrowed the model and applied it
in their studies of specific times and places. Together, the complementary theory
and research of political scientists and historians produced a framework of election types (critical or realigning; maintaining; deviating; reinstating; converting)

and of party systems (those produced by realignments of the early 1800s, 1820s, 1850s, 1890s, and 1930s). In this model, American political history has been cyclical in nature, with electoral realignments periodically disrupting an existing party system and producing another with its own distinctive patterns of voting and turnout, of party strength and functions, and of salient issues and policy agendas.

The second major analytical construct of the new political history is the ethnocultural interpretation of voting. Where the realignment/party systems model provides a longitudinal framework for the American electoral system(s), the ethnocultural model provides an explanation of individual and group voting in the past; and where the realignment model came chiefly from political scientists, the ethnocultural interpretation came primarily from historians—although here too interdisciplinary influences are clear (e.g., Lazarsfeld et al., 1944; Lubell, 1952). Again Hays (1960, 1980) and especially Benson (1961) were central. Rejecting the then-dominant view that class or socioeconomic status had been the principal determinant of American voting, Benson (1961, p. 165) argues "that at least since the 1820's . . . ethnic and religious differences have tended to be *relatively* the most important sources of political differences" (his emphasis). In the next decade (and after) a host of studies employing quantitative and social-science approaches, methods, and theory demonstrated that ethnicity and religion had long been basic to American voting patterns (see Fuchs, 1968; Swierenga, 1971; McSeveney, 1973; Kelley, 1977).

By the 1970s, then, the new political history had developed two complementary frameworks for understanding American electoral history. In place of the "presidential synthesis" for organizing political history (criticized by Cochran, 1948, in an important plea for a new "social science synthesis") was the realignment/party system model; in place of the "progressive" socioeconomic interpretation of voting associated with Charles A. Beard and Frederick Jackson Turner was the ethnocultural interpretation. Based on impressive quantitative and interdisciplinary theory and research, the two frameworks became the reigning paradigms of political historians and have greatly enlarged the understanding of American political history.

Despite their evident strengths and wide acceptance, however, both the realignment and ethnocultural models have been subjected to substantial criticism for methodological, conceptual, and empirical shortcomings. Methodologically, major works in the ethnocultural synthesis, necessarily based primarily on aggregate and areal analysis to determine group voting behavior, have been faulted for usage of homogeneous unit analysis, reliance on ecological correlation coefficients, and failure to employ adequate multivariate or regression analysis (Kousser, 1976; Lichtman and Langbein, 1978). Conceptually, the ethnocultural model has been criticized for inadequate attention to class and status (Green, 1972; Wright, 1973) and for not clearly, consistently, or convincingly specifying and demonstrating the relationships between ethnic or religious group membership, values, or behavior on the one hand and voting on the other (Wright, 1973;

R.L. McCormick, 1974; Bogue et al., 1977). Empirical findings have revealed times and places where class or socioeconomic status seem clearly more important than ethnocultural factors in voting. Nor does the ethnocultural synthesis sufficiently explain change or realignment (Bogue et al., 1977; Lichtman, 1976, 1983); as Bogue (1980, p. 250) notes, "There is surely some logical inconsistency in displaying strong correlations between ethnocultural groups and party during periods of political stability and failing to show that realignment was effected by fundamental shifts in the allegiance of such groups." Finally, the ethnocultural model has seemed to focus too narrowly on but one aspect of politics, voting, and too little on acquiring and using power or making policy (Green, 1972; R.L. McCormick, 1974).

The realignment/party systems model has encountered equally broad and in some respects even fiercer criticism. Scrutiny of its problems has left the character, causes, and consequences of electoral realignment in doubt and not just the formulation but the very validity of the party systems framework open to serious question (Sternsher, 1975; Lichtman, 1976, 1982, 1983; Bogue et al., 1977; Chubb, 1978; Ladd with Hadley, 1978; Prindle, 1979; Kousser, 1980a; Clubb et al., 1980; R.L. McCormick, 1982). Conceptually, the realignment/party systems model has been criticized for being too narrowly taxonomic and descriptive, i.e., for establishing a complicated classification system without adequate theory or explanation of change and with insufficient attention to the whole political system and to the role of public policy in electoral change. The classification system itself has been faulted for lacking sufficiently precise and well-defined specification of the amount and rate of change needed for "critical" realignment, of the length a "critical period" may extend, and indeed of the very mechanics and nature of realigning change. Methodological problems include identifying and measuring realignments, ascertaining the amount of change produced by mobilization of new voters vs. conversion of old ones, and gauging behavioral (voting) as against deeper attitudinal change in partisan identification. Empirically, the results of the many studies of realignment have tended to be conflicting, confusing, and noncumulative. Substantial local, group, and temporal variations have been found in the extent, rate, and nature of realigning electoral change; surprising continuity has appeared in "realigning" periods, as has variability in "stable" phases; and a complicated and at times contradictory array of periods and phases within party systems has emerged. Twenty-one of the 39 presidential elections from 1824 to 1976 have been labeled "critical" by one study or another (Lichtman, 1982).

Beyond such criticisms and caveats as these, there is even more fundamental objection to the realignment/party systems framework. Chubb (1978) has maintained that the very notion of an ongoing cycle of periodic critical realignments is faulty—that there is no necessary relation between one party system and its successor and that change occurs because of unpredictable exogenous factors rather than internal, periodic, systemic ones. A similar argument (Ladd with

Hadley, 1978, p. 376) holds that there is "no realignment cycle, no striking rhythm," no one pattern or model of electoral change, that realignments result from broad sociopolitical change and consequent change in political agendas. Furthermore, scholars have identified not only "critical" realigning change but also secular electoral change (Key, 1959) and nonperiodic change (Burnham, 1965, 1970) in the electoral system.

Influenced by Burnham's analysis of the declension of parties in the twentieth century, some political historians have begun to sketch out an alternative periodization of electoral history to the five-party-system division of the realignment model. R.L. McCormick (1979) has termed the nineteenth century the "party period" of American political history, in which parties had electoral and policy roles far greater than in the twentieth century, while Lichtman (1976, p. 347) has suggested that perhaps "a qualitatively different era of electoral politics" marked by the declining importance of parties and partisanship began around the turn of the century (see also Benson et al., 1978, for a related analysis). R.L. McCormick and others (Clubb et al., 1980; Kleppner, 1982a) have linked such major changes in party functions to the social and economic modernization of American life, which transformed the political universe in which party systems developed and functioned and thus divided electoral history into periods fundamentally different from those of the party systems framework.

Such criticism and reconsideration of the realignment/party systems model led R.L. McCormick to declare "realignment theory in disarray" (1982, p. 94) and political history in "crisis" (1979, p. 279) by the late 1970s and another major political historian (Kousser, 1980a, p. 895) to call for a "new synthetic idea." Political scientists, too, have recognized the need to strengthen or reformulate realignment theory and to connect electoral change with policymakers and policymaking (e.g., Campbell and Trilling, 1980). Yet even the recent major work of synthesis and revision by Clubb et al. (1980; considerably foreshadowed by Burnham et al., 1978), refining the conceptualization, measurement, and analysis of electoral change and linking voting behavior to elite behavior and policymaking, does not satisfy the most forceful critics of the realignment/party systems model, who want it supplemented or replaced (R.L. McCormick, 1982; Lichtman, 1982).

Beyond seeking further to improve and refine existing explanations and to employ better research designs and quantitative techniques for aggregate electoral data (Kousser, 1973; McCarthy and Tukey, 1978; Hammond, 1979; Clubb et al., 1980, 1981; VanderMeer, 1981; W.G. Shade, 1981a; Hammarberg, 1983), political historians are embarking in new directions. Two seem especially important: the study of voting-policy linkages and the analysis of voter participation. As noted above, the narrow focus on mass electoral behavior and the failure to investigate the connections between voting and policy have increasingly been recognized as weaknesses of both the ethnocultural and the realignment models (see especially R.L. McCormick, 1974, 1982; Lichtman, 1976, 1982; Kousser, 1980a, 1982). Political historians have gone far in illuminating the social bases of voting but not in specifying the electoral causes and consequences of public policy. In addition to analyzing the role of issues in voting and realignment (Key, 1966; Burnham, 1970; Ginsberg, 1972; Sundquist, 1973; Bennett and Haltom, 1980), political scientists much more than historians have investigated the question of voting-policy linkages (Schattschneider, 1960; Key, 1966; Burnham, 1970; Ginsberg, 1976; Brady, 1978; Beck, 1979; Brady with Stewart, 1982). But historians increasingly are addressing those matters (Clubb et al., 1980; R.L. McCormick, 1979, 1981, 1982; Kousser, 1982) and are providing important new studies of legislative behavior (Campbell, 1980; Bogue, 1981b).

The second significant area of new theory and research in electoral history involves voter participation and turnout. Historians have increasingly recognized that aggregate electoral data can reveal illuminating patterns not only of partisan distributions but also of voter participation—that the question of who voted can be as important as the question of who voted for whom (e.g., Kousser, 1974; Argersinger, 1980; Kleppner, 1982a; Winkle, 1983). Here again, historians enter territory scouted by political scientists and where significant debate already exists (Burnham, 1965, 1970, 1974a, 1974b; Rusk, 1970, 1974; Converse, 1972, 1974; Rusk and Stucker, 1978). Related to the issues of both turnout and partisan realignment is the recent attention given to the role in realignments of mobilizing new voters. Developed chiefly by political scientists (Beck, 1974; Andersen, 1976, 1979; Petrocik, 1981), the thesis that mobilization has been the fundamental mechanism of realignments seems certain to command increasing scrutiny in historical scholarship.

Despite the criticisms and revisions of the ethnocultural and realignment/party systems models and despite the new directions in political historiography, the ethnocultural and realignment frameworks have been extraordinarily fruitful and continue to shape theory, research, and synthesis in electoral history (Clubb et al., 1980; Kleppner et al., 1981). Adopting the realignment/party systems framework as its fundamental organizing device, the remainder of this essay will discuss in more depth the literature on party systems and voting patterns in American history. The varying emphases in our treatment of the several realignments and party systems discussed below follow those of the literature, which has been shaped by the varieties of historical data and historiographic questions specific to each period. Inclusion of the relevant work of political scientists, with concerns, data, and methods sometimes quite distinct from those of historians, both reflects the interdisciplinary nature of the new political history and further structures our discussion, especially for the recent period.

Party Systems and Voting Behavior:
History and Historiography

Although the original formulations of the realignment/party systems framework posited five party systems, the first beginning around 1800, it now seems that there have been only three true party systems. The first party era, that of the Federalists and Jeffersonians, has been aptly described as a "preparty" system, for—as Formisano (1981) has shown—it never had completely developed or institutionalized parties or consistent partisan behavior by its electorate. Nor does the succeeding Jacksonian era of Whigs and Democrats seem to qualify as a party system, even though it was the subject of much of the earliest important research of the new political history (Benson, 1961; R.P. McCormick, 1959, 1960, 1966). W.G. Shade (1981b) has concluded that, even in its most developed phase, the second party era exhibited significantly lower levels of party development, partisan identification, and political integration than did the subsequent third party system, and that its origins in the transition period of the 1830s do not fit critical election theory. Hence our discussion of the history and historiography of party systems and voter behavior will begin with the realignment of the 1850s.

Realignment of the 1850s

The political crisis of the 1850s has long attracted great attention, but the voting behavior studies of the new political history have provided important and productive new perspectives. Although Holt (1969), Formisano (1971), and Hansen (1980) have presented detailed discussions of local phases of the realignment of the 1850s, the most succinct and integrated is that of Kleppner (1979). The change from the second, or Jacksonian, to the third party system involved much more than a simple replacement of the Whigs by the Republicans. By using measures of central tendency and dispersion in analyzing partisan voting, Kleppner determined that the dissolution of the second electoral era came in stages: first, the nationally based Whig party was destroyed; second, and quite distinct from the first, the sectionally based Republican party developed in its place; and third, the Democratic party underwent sectional polarization. The second stage of realignment can be further divided into two phases (Shortridge, 1976), involving first the 1856 combination of Free Soilers and many Whigs into a firm Republican core and then the shift of many 1856 Know-Nothings and nonvoters into the Republican coalition by 1860. Although the realigning phase was complete in the North by 1860, Kleppner maintained that from a national perspective it extended into the 1870s and the end of Reconstruction, when the stable phase of the third party system finally began. This diverges from the usual view of short periods of electoral change dividing longer periods of electoral continuity, but it may reflect Kleppner's choice of measurement techniques.

In explaining the social dynamics of the realignment of the 1850s, the new studies of voting behavior (Kleppner, 1979; Formisano, 1971; Holt, 1969; Silbey, 1967; Sweeney, 1976) depart from traditional interpretations (e.g., that of Sundquist, 1973) that stress national issues, particularly slavery and the Kansas-Nebraska Act, in the disruption of the political system and the coming of the Civil War. Instead they emphasize local nativist and anti-Catholic agitation which in the early 1850s produced ethnocultural conflict in the North and weakened existing partisan attachments. Volatile and divisive issues involving alien suffrage, temperance, and Sabbatarian legislation drove native Protestants out of the Democratic and Whig parties into the emerging Republican organization, which came to represent political evangelicalism and Protestant moralism. Kleppner (1981b, p. 124) described this "coalitional reshuffling" as "set in motion by a religious enthusiasm unleashed on electoral politics." The Republican party's antisouthernism appears as but an additional part of an evangelical Protestant outlook that already included nativism, anti-Catholicism, and temperance. Holt (1969, p. 312), for instance, describes anti-Catholic and nativist groups, not those motivated by larger sectional issues, as "the fundamental blocs of Republican coalitions."

Far less is known about partisan realignment among Democrats or within the South than about the formation of the Republican party in the North. While many Northern Protestant Democrats apparently shifted into the developing opposition party, Shortridge (1976) has cautioned that Democratic voting choices were remarkably stable. In the South, declining Whig strength by the early 1850s suggests an increasing sectional self-consciousness and identification with the Democratic party in reaction to what Kleppner has termed "Yankee-cultural imperialism," but realignment in the sense of voters switching parties was apparently a more delayed and complex development (McCrary et al., 1978).

In addition to the general methodological and analytical criticisms of the ethnocultural model noted above, its application to the realignment of the 1850s has provoked specific criticism. Most importantly, the focus on local and cultural issues has not provided a satisfactory explanation for the sectional conflict culminating in civil war (Latner and Levine, 1976). Other historians have disputed the claims that the anti-Catholic and nativist elements that initially produced the Know-Nothing movement in the mid-1850s became essential elements in the Republican coalition that later emerged. By using ecological regression estimation to identify the sources of Republican support, Baum (1978) has found that the Republican party, in Massachusetts at least, was not dependent on former Know-Nothing voters and represented antislavery more than nativist sentiment. By examining turnout rates, as other historians had not, Baum also concluded that nativism was losing its political salience in the late 1850s, thereby challenging the assumption that local ethnocultural issues mobilized voters more effectively than did national issues. Similarly, Kamphoefner (1975) has determined that the formation of the Republican party in St. Louis depended on German and even, for a time, Irish voters and not on nativists or prohibitionists, a finding that further cautions against uncritically accepting the ethnocultural interpretation of national political realignment.

Baum's reassertion of the importance of antislavery sentiments in the Republican party has received limited endorsement from Rozett (1976) and Field (1982). The ethnocultural interpretation, in deemphasizing the slavery issue, has

depicted Republicans as racist as well as nativist. If that amalgam seemed har-
monious, it also pointed to a larger inconsistency: that the allegedly pietistic
reformers who formed the Republican party would forsake the most important
moral cause. By analyzing voting behavior on referenda in Illinois and New
York, respectively, Rozett and Field have demonstrated that Republican voters
were more in sympathy with black rights than were other groups, particularly
when those voters came from areas of "Yankee" culture. But this subject is
complex and remains but one of a number of disputed facets of the realignment
of the 1850s (Holt, 1978).

Finally, it seems clear that virtually all historians seeking to explain the apparent changes in partisan cleavages and coalitions in the 1850s have failed to
consider how dramatically the electorate itself changed during the decade.
Through analysis of individual-level data provided by poll books, Winkle (1983)
has discovered extreme turnover within local electorates, casting considerable
doubt on prevailing interpretations of electoral behavior; and Petrocik (1981) has
concluded that the great growth of the electorate, in conjunction with a stable
Democratic vote, indicates that Republican ascendancy depended less on converting Democrats to a new party than on mobilizing new voters who had not
previously participated in the electorate.

The Third Party System

As would be expected from the foregoing description of the realignment process,
the prevailing ethnocultural interpretation of voting behavior during the period of
the third electoral system holds that partisan cleavages were primarily ethnic and
religious rather than economic. Major works that, in varying degree, posit this
interpretation for the late nineteenth century include those of Kleppner (1970,
1979), Jensen (1971), Luebke (1969), McSeveney (1972), and Wyman (1968).
Partisanship reflected both the conflict between the Yankee and Southern subcul-
tures that underlay the basic sectionalism of the third party system between the
Democratic South and the more Republican North, as well as the religious conflict between pietistic Republicans and antipietistic Democrats within the North,
where voting pivoted more on issues involving prohibition and parochial schools
than the tariff or currency (Kleppner, 1979).

The party system based on that division endured until the 1890s but of course
not without fluctuations. Because the partisan division lay along ethnoreligious
and sectional lines, the party system could not express class interests, resulting in
"deviating" elections in such times of depression as the 1870s. A second consequence of the partisan division was a secular decline in Republican strength, for
demographic changes in immigration, natural increase, and sectional distribution
of the population all benefited the Democrats. As the size and consequent activity of antipietist groups increased, moreover, pietist enthusiasm for prohibition
and other moralistic campaigns was stimulated, thereby provoking political quar-

rels resulting in Republican defeats or shrinking margins of victory over time (Kleppner, 1979).

Such ethnocultural analysis has clarified many aspects of late nineteenth-century politics, and certainly there is now impressive evidence of a strong relationship between ethnocultural attributes and popular voting behavior, particularly in the Midwest and East, with their large ethnic populations and divisive cultural politics. But many scholars remain unconvinced of the validity of the complete ethnocultural interpretation. The thesis that a coherent belief system linked theological, social, and political principles, however logically argued, cannot be empirically demonstrated but only inferred from incomplete and imperfect data, including (in terms of theological principles and clerical dicta) types of evidence that the ethnoculturalists find suspect in the political sphere. Moreover, the early studies, despite their pioneering status, often rested on a wobbly methodological basis provided by analysis of homogeneous units and simple correlation coefficients. Kleppner (1979) does furnish regression estimates of the partisan voting of ethnocultural groups, but there remains some dissatisfaction with his use, presentation, and even interpretation of this data.

The concentration of the ethnocultural studies on the Northeast and Midwest raises questions as to whether theories of voter behavior generated from observations in regions characterized by a volatile ethnic mixture are applicable elsewhere. The convoluted efforts of ethnocultural historians to account for the Democratic allegiance of Southern evangelicals is suggestive of this problem. Moreover, many scholars analyzing voting behavior in the West and South (Parsons, 1973; Wright, 1974; Argersinger, 1974; Kousser, 1974; Hart, 1975; Allen and Austin, 1979; Cherny, 1981; Williams, 1981) have found instances, especially in the 1890s, when economic and social factors were clearly more important than ethnocultural ones. Even Kleppner himself (1983) has recently concluded that in the West ethnocultural factors and religious issues had little salience in partisan voting. Despite its contributions to the new political history, then, ethnocultural theory is less than a complete explanation of mass voting behavior in the third party system.

Even for the Midwest during the 1870s, Hammarberg (1977) has proposed an alternative explanation, one based on the concepts developed by the Michigan Survey Research Center in analyzing contemporary voting behavior. But unlike other scholars who have applied such concepts to the analysis of aggregate voting in the past without considering their historical validity (see Burnham, 1965), Hammarberg carefully determined their relevance. The product is a sophisticated mixture of data, theory, and quantitative methods that enabled Hammarberg to avoid the ecological fallacy that confronts historians required to work with aggregate data. Voter behavior emerges as far more complex than suggested by either the traditional economic or the more recent ethnocultural interpretation. The fundamental political division was defined by a combination of social and structural characteristics of Indiana society. On one side were town dwellers,

who tended toward Republican affiliation; on the other were farmers, who because of geographic and occupational isolation had weaker partisan ties and
whose voting was thus more volatile, responding to short-term forces such as
agricultural depressions. The concept of partisan attachment thus had an important influence, distinct from social and economic correlates of voting behavior,
though occupational status did emerge as an important indicator of political
affiliation. Religion was relevant politically but less for its doctrinal content as
emphasized by ethnoculturalists than for the opportunities churches provided for
the personal interaction necessary in maintaining partisan norms.

Other characteristics of the third party system involve the size and shape of
the electorate itself. First described in Burnham's influential article (1965), these
include "awesome rates of turnout," minimal drop-off in voting between presidential and succeeding off-year elections, virtually no roll-off or split-ticket voting, and low levels of mean partisan swing. To Burnham this indicated a
democratic party system with a completely and intensely involved electorate tied
to the polity by close attachments to responsive political parties. Jensen (1969c,
1971) and Kleppner (1979, 1981b, 1982a) reached similar conclusions: high
rates of turnout and partisan competition, stability in partisan percentages over
time, and low rates of drop-off and defection reflected the voters' genuine identification with the political parties and the values they represented as well as the
parties' ability to shape voting behavior.

With few exceptions (Shortridge, 1980, 1981a, 1981b), scholars have accepted this description of electoral behavior, but there is considerable controversy over the origins and meanings of these characteristics. Converse (1972)
and Rusk (1974) have argued that nineteenth-century elections were marked by
extensive fraud, which inflated turnout statistics and made the polity less democratic than Burnham believed. Some historians (Allen and Allen, 1981; Kleppner
and Baker, 1980) have vigorously denied the existence of massive fraud. Others
(Reynolds, 1980; Cox and Kousser, 1981; Argersinger, 1985/86) have documented a variety of fraudulent election practices but differ from Converse and
Rusk as to their meaning and effects. A complex and difficult problem, the
subject of election fraud requires more study and systematic analysis.

The issue of fraud is also related to the "legal-institutional" theory that
attributes aspects of voting behavior to the institutional framework of the electoral system (Converse, 1972; Rusk, 1974; Rusk and Stucker, 1978). Rusk
(1970), for instance, has maintained that the low levels of split-ticket voting that
Burnham believed reflected intense partisan identification really were an artifact
of the party ballot system of the time and that only with the "reform" of the
Australian ballot in the 1890s was it possible for voters to split their tickets and
vote their own personal choices. Historians have recognized the importance of
institutional factors in shaping voting but have warned against ignoring the specific political context within which they developed. Kousser (1974) refuted the
belief that the low turnout, absence of party competition, and other features that

characterized Southern politics were simply "unintended consequences" of electoral changes. He also rejected V.O. Key's *"fait accompli"* thesis that the restrictive laws merely legalized conditions already created by other forces. Other historians (Argersinger, 1980, 1981, 1983; R.L. McCormick, 1981; Reynolds, 1983) have reached similar conclusions about the legal parameters of Northern politics: they were generally created by partisan politicians seeking to protect or advance their own interests by manipulating the rules of the game to suppress opposition (and turnout) and party competition.

Realignment of the 1890s

Historians have always regarded the election of 1896 as crucial, even before political scientists incorporated it into critical election theory, and it is the subject of an immense body of historical literature. Although many studies have focused on specific issues, events, or personalities prominent in the election, historians have also recognized the larger significance of the election (together with that of 1894) as ending the political equilibrium of previous decades and ushering in an era of Republican hegemony. That transformation has usually been attributed to the effects of the 1890s depression, which caused voters to turn against the incumbent Democrats, and the free silver campaign of William Jennings Bryan, which attracted the agricultural regions of the South and West but seemed to offer little to the urban, industrial Northeast.

The new political history has produced two additional explanations that attempt to describe the underlying processes at work in the 1890s. Building on the foundation of the economic interpretation, Burnham (1965, 1970, 1981) constructed a general theory of the relationships between the economic and political systems. He maintained that the volatile and divisive issues arising from the developing economic system polarized political choices in 1896 and forced voters to change their voting patterns permanently. Nationally this resulted in a sectional realignment as the "colonial" South and West merged in the Bryanized Democracy against the Northeastern "Metropole" which aligned with the GOP. The practical result of these conversion movements was to entrench the Republicans (and the corporate capitalist elite they represented) in national power, safe from significant challenge for decades to come.

The other major interpretation of the realignment of the 1890s stems from the ethnocultural historians. It portrays the Republican ascendancy in 1894–1896 not only in terms of a general voter reaction against the Democrats as the party in power during the depression but also in terms of a two-way movement of voters along ethnocultural lines. There was a reshuffling of partisan allegiances among ethnoreligious groups as Republican managers pragmatically deemphasized the party's pietistic thrust, and as the Democratic nomination and campaign of the evangelical Bryan alienated traditional Democratic ethnic groups while attracting formerly Republican pietistic voters (Jensen, 1971; Kleppner, 1970, 1979).

These descriptions have come under a number of attacks. As noted before, the ethnocultural model seems weakest in its ability to explain realignment, and many studies have stressed the importance of economic factors in the 1890s. Other historians, looking at individual states or regions, have rejected the conclusion of interactive change and maintained that virtually every group in the electorate shifted toward the Republican party (McSeveney, 1972; Benson et al., 1978; Brye, 1979). In some areas, on the other hand, traditional Democratic ritualistic groups remained loyal to the Bryanized Democratic party (McSeveney, 1972; Cherny, 1981). Moreover, the initial descriptions of a permanent realignment of the social bases of partisanship failed to examine voting behavior in subsequent elections. Scholars who have analyzed such elections (Brye, 1979; Allen and Austin, 1979; Zanjani, 1979; Clubb et al., 1980; Cherny, 1981) have generally reported that for a number of states the election of 1896 was more "deviating" than "realigning," for there was no lasting alteration in partisan attachments among the electorate. In addition, the conflict between ethnoreligious groups that supposedly faded away with the new Republican commitment to pluralism and "social harmony" (Kleppner, 1978) frequently reoccurred in subsequent years, over the same issues and with the same partisan divisions as before (Folsom, 1981; Cherny, 1981).

Most recently, and most forcefully, Lichtman (1983) has denied virtually all aspects of both ethnocultural and realignment theory as applied to the election of 1896. Employing ecological regression to estimate how the behavior of both voters and nonvoters changed in the national electorate between 1892 and 1896, Lichtman concluded that there was no realignment, no changing coalitions of party voters, and certainly no major two-way transfer of voters along ethnocultural lines. Instead Democrats retained virtually (but not) all their 1892 voters while attracting most 1892 Populist voters; Republicans retained their 1892 voters and were more successful than Bryan in gaining the support of those who had not voted in 1892. This process did of course shift the balance of power to the GOP and, with the exception of Democratic losses of some of their temporary Populist recruits, there was considerable continuity in voting coalitions for the next three decades. Strikingly, however, in terms of voting patterns the 1888 election resembled those subsequent elections more than did the election of 1896. Lichtman therefore concluded that voting coalitions were both more stable and more volatile than critical election theory would predict and that voters were more responsive to campaign issues and economic conditions than ethnocultural theory would predict (for the latter, see also Bennett and Haltom, 1980).

Other studies have similarly suggested the importance of new voters to the Republicans' successful 1896 coalition. Petrocik (1981) has estimated that the electorate increased about 15 percent between 1892 and 1896 and that nearly all of the 2 million new voters joined the Republicans, more than compensating for the 1 million Populists who voted Democratic. Wanat and Burke (1982) have attempted in more detail to specify the degree and relative importance of mobilization and conversion. Focusing primarily on the crucial Midwest, they calculated that demographic changes (including naturalization of immigrants, attainment of voting age by the native-born, death, and outmigration) resulted in nearly one-fourth of the region's 1896 electorate being composed of new voters. Rejecting the "grand conversion" thesis, they concluded that Republican victory stemmed not from shifts in partisan allegiance by Democrats but from the GOP's greater success in mobilizing new voters. Ironically, the intensity of partisan identification that Burnham, Kleppner, and Jensen describe as characteristic of the period became for Wanat and Burke a reason why the major conversion of voters posited by these authors did not occur: "Conversion in 1896 would require the rejection of a political affiliation that was near to a primary allegiance. . . . It was far easier to bring in new voters whose political allegiance was perhaps unformed" (1982, p. 369). Thus the 1896 election may have brought a major and decisive shift in American politics, but by most definitions it does not constitute a critical election.

Finally, historians have found little evidence of policy transformations in government as a direct consequence of the elections of the 1890s (R.L. McCormick, 1979, 1981, 1982; Zanjani, 1979). Indeed a focus on policy and the mechanisms of governance has suggested to R.L. McCormick that American political history can be effectively periodized into eras fundamentally different from those provided by the concept of partisan realignment. Historians have thus discovered enough contradictions and inconsistencies to question the validity of the realignment model or at least its applicability to the 1890s (see also Benson et al., 1978; Clubb et al., 1980).

The System of 1896

The uncertainty as to whether a classic realignment actually occurred obviously complicates analysis of the fourth party system and the classification of the period's elections. Despite its dramatic name, the chronological boundaries of the "System of 1896" are unclear. State and regional variations, differences at the presidential, congressional, and state levels, and ambiguities arising from different definitions and measuring techniques all suggest a diffuse beginning and an uncertain end (Burnham, 1970, 1981; Clubb et al., 1980; Zanjani, 1979; Zingale, 1978; Sundquist, 1973). Moreover, some elections of the fourth party system show clear relationships to voting patterns in both the third and fifth party systems, and some major characteristics such as the Democratic nature of the South stretch consistently across all three eras (Lichtman, 1976, 1983; Clubb et al., 1980; Key and Munger, 1959; Gould, 1978). There is at least general agreement that there were two stable phases, divided by a deviating phase or "subcritical realignment" (Burnham, 1981) roughly from 1910 through 1916. Democratic victories in those years were essentially artifacts of Republican divisions, and the elections after 1918 indicated that little permanent change had occurred in the distribution of partisan affiliations (Clubb, 1978; Allen and Austin, 1979; Allen and Clubb, 1974; Burnham, 1981). Many ethnic voters, for instance, sharply repudiated the Democrats from 1918 through 1924 in reaction to Wilson's policies and to nativist hostility but returned to their usual patterns of partisan identifications in 1928, leading some later observers who focused narrowly on the 1920s to conclude that the Al Smith campaign produced a realigning election (Nelson, 1972; Lichtman, 1976, 1979; Brye, 1979; Burner, 1968; Lorence, 1982). Indeed, the actual nature of the voting alignments in the 1920s forms a key element in the scholarly debate over the origins of the fifth party system and is better discussed in that connection below.

Longstanding historiographic emphases further limit analysis of the fourth electoral era. Compared to their extensive investigation of nineteenth-century electorates, historians have devoted relatively little attention to identifying the social determinants of party voting in the early twentieth century. Many of the voting studies available, moreover, focus primarily on variations of traditional historical topics. Some, for example, attempt to identify Progressive voters but without always clearly and logically specifying who were Progressive candidates or what constituted a Progressive vote (Rogin and Shover, 1970; Wyman, 1974; Allen and Clubb, 1974; Dykstra and Reynolds, 1978; Brye, 1979; Cherny, 1981). Others seek to differentiate between Populists and Progressives (Hackney, 1969; Cherny, 1981) or to trace the political behavior of various ethnic groups (Allswang, 1971; Nelson, 1972). Studies that have investigated party voting determinants disclose, as noted above, considerable similarity to those of the earlier third system (Lichtman, 1983; Folsom, 1981; Cherny, 1981; Allen and Austin, 1979).

For all the electoral continuity, however, there were important ways in which the political universe of the early twentieth century differed from that of the preceding decades, suggesting that whatever "realignment" occurred was but part of a larger political transformation. The close election outcomes gave way to Republican domination; the distribution of partisan strength became intensely sectional, eliminating most party competition within sections even more than nationally; turnout dropped dramatically, especially among lower-class elements; and there was a sharp increase in split-ticket voting, roll-off, drop-off, and other indexes of partisan volatility and voter marginality (Burnham, 1965, 1970). These enduring changes in the nature and behavior of the electorate were obviously related to political developments rooted in the 1890s (R.L. McCormick, 1981; Cherny, 1981), but the precise connection is not yet clear.

Petrocik (1981) has contended that the turnout decline in the fourth party system did not involve a reduction in voting by previously active voters so much as a rapid increase in the number of newly eligible voters who failed to participate fully in the electorate. This noninvolvement was especially characteristic of ethnic and lower-class groups, and the subsequent mobilization of these groups helped shape the New Deal coalition. Kleppner (1982a) has also noted a partisan bias in the turnout patterns of this era. The size of the Democratic off-year electorate declined sharply more than its presidential-year electorate, suggesting again that marginally involved voters were more often Democrats. Rusk (1974) and Converse (1972) have argued that such indications of demobilization and electoral instability derived largely from a new legal context in the early twentieth century that added such "reforms" as personal registration requirements and the enfranchisement of women to the earlier adoption of the secret ballot. Burnham (1981) has maintained that these and other institutional changes (including such "antipartisan" legislation as the direct primary and direct election of senators) were part of a deliberate attack on political parties and their influence over the mass electorate in order to protect the corporate capitalist order represented by the Republican party. They did have their influence in demobilizing the potential electorate, but he also emphasized that systemic features (especially increasing political sectionalism and declining party competition) had analogous behavioral consequences by loosening voters' partisan attachments and incentive to vote.

Except for Kousser (1974), historians have not yet carefully examined the question of legislative intent in these rule changes in the early twentieth century. But at least in his evaluation of consequences Burnham has received recent support. Multiple regression analysis reveals that while personal registration requirements, residency requirements, and woman suffrage depressed turnout, these legal factors were separately and cumulatively less important predictors of turnout than was electoral competitiveness. In particular, new age cohorts, entering the less competitive, less intensely partisan political system, proved less likely to vote than older cohorts socialized under previous conditions or than their own age-cohort counterparts had in the third party system. "That age-structured electoral demobilization was primarily a behavioral response to the 'System of 1896' " (Kleppner and Baker, 1980, p. 205; Kleppner, 1982a, 1982b).

Realignment of the 1930s

The New Deal realignment and party system, the former especially, have been the subjects of much study and much debate. Because they have obvious present as well as historical importance and can be analyzed with both survey and aggregate electoral data, they have been studied far more intensively than earlier realignments and party systems by political scientists. There exists general agreement that at the presidential level the New Deal realignment was substantially completed by 1936, that the core of the new majority Democratic coalition comprised urban, ethnic, Catholic, Jewish, black, white Southern, working-class, and liberal voters, and that the New Deal party system fell into serious, perhaps terminal, disrepair after the early 1960s (Sternsher, 1984). But beyond that consensus lies important disagreement.

The modern era of New Deal political historiography began in the 1950s with studies by Lubell (1952) and Key (1955). In complementary analyses, Lubell and Key maintained that before the "Roosevelt revolution" of the 1930s came an "Al Smith revolution" in the presidential election of 1928. According to their accounts, the Democrats by nominating Smith, a foreign-stock, Catholic New Yorker, lost the election but won new support that began the urban, ethnic, working-class shift to the Democratic party which culminated in the New Deal coalition of the 1930s. Lubell focused especially on the urban-ethnic component of the coalition, Key on his thesis that 1928 was, at least in New England, a "critical election." Historians soon reinforced and supplemented those findings. Major studies of Massachusetts (Huthmacher, 1959), the urban vote (Degler, 1964), the Democratic party (Burner, 1968), and Chicago (Allswang, 1971) demonstrated the central importance of ethnocultural conflict, issues, and voting patterns in the 1920s and underscored the significance of the 1928 election.

The view that ethnic voting and the 1928 election were crucial in forging the new majority Democratic coalition of the 1930s quickly attracted close scrutiny and revision. The result has been a rich and still-growing literature, one eluding consensus but shedding light not only on the New Deal realignment but also on the electoral realignment/party systems model and the ethnocultural interpretation of voting. In their modification of Key's critical election thesis, MacRae and Meldrum (1960) found that in Illinois there had been instead a "critical period" extending from 1924 to 1936. Similarly, Shover (1967) held that California's realignment had occurred in a critical period, while Stave (1967) maintained that in Pittsburgh a "La Follette revolution" in 1924 had preceded the Al Smith revolution in shaping a new urban, ethnic, working-class coalition that prefigured Roosevelt's of the 1930s.

There is in fact suggestive evidence that origins of the New Deal coalition and party system lie as far back as the Progressive era—or even before (Cherny, 1981; Lichtman, 1983). Gould (1978, p. v) has termed the 1916 election "a contest whose issues and alignments anticipated the battles of the New Deal"; and there are other indications that antecedents of both the farmer-labor-ethnic-reformer Roosevelt coalition (Burner, 1968; Rogin and Shover, 1970; Hammond, 1976; Lichtman, 1976; Cherny, 1981) and the class-based and ideological voting and the interest-group politics of the New Deal party system (Wyman, 1974; Cherny, 1981; R.L. McCormick, 1981) can be found in the Progressive era. Pointing to long-term continuities spanning party systems, such analyses suggest that after deviating elections in 1920 and 1924, the 1928 contest was not a critical election but rather renewed old patterns and secular trends (Rogin and Shover, 1970; Alvarez and True, 1973; Lichtman, 1979). (Lichtman goes further still: criticizing critical election theory, he maintains that there was no critical election or critical period in the presidential elections from 1916 to 1940.)

The designation of 1928 as a critical election has also been challenged from the perspective of post-1928 developments. In an influential essay, Clubb and Allen (1969) concluded that nonpresidential electoral data better supported interpretations of either a critical period beginning in 1928 or a realignment confined to the 1930s and produced by the Great Depression and the New Deal. The latter suggestion presaged a fundamental reevaluation of the place of the 1928 election in the New Deal realignment. For even as the idea of a critical period in which the 1928 election played a major role gained prominence (Sternsher, 1975), two important studies (Sundquist, 1973; Lichtman, 1976) argued that the 1928 election had no very important connection at all to the realignment. In such a view, the 1920s are better seen as the last stages of the fourth party system than as the first stages of the fifth, with agrarian protest and Al Smith's 1928 candidacy producing minor, geographically limited electoral change that at most prefigured the realignment of the 1930s (Clubb, 1978; Sundquist, 1983). The most recent major work on the 1928 election, Lichtman's sophisticated interdisciplinary study (1979), finds that the election pivoted on religion (as do Levine, 1976; Hammond, 1976, 1979; Zingale, 1978) and that its salient issues and voting patterns made it essentially an aberrant election. "Smith's candidacy," Lichtman (p. 201) argues, "generated an intense conflict between Catholics and Protestants that only marginally affected subsequent patterns of politics."

In explaining the realignment producing the new majority Democratic coalition and the New Deal party system, the studies cited above and other recent works, in various ways and with varying emphases, point to the 1930s, not the 1920s, to the impact of the Great Depression and especially the New Deal, not Al Smith's candidacy, and to the primacy of socioeconomic and ideological, not ethnocultural, voting (see also: Key, 1966; Rogin and Shover, 1970; Ladd with Hadley, 1978; Allen and Austin, 1979; Clubb et al., 1980; Burnham, 1981; Kleppner, 1982a). As in the 1890s, so again in the 1930s, economic collapse in this view demolished one party system, triggered realignment producing its successor, and revealed the dominance of class and ideology over ethnicity and religion in crisis times. In the 1930s, an affirmative majority response to New Deal policies cemented the realignment.

But the idea of a realignment period originating in the 1920s and having significant ethnocultural dimensions cannot yet be dismissed. The most recent full-scale studies of the New Deal realignment (Allswang, 1978; Andersen, 1979) date the beginning of the realignment in the 1920s and ascribe large importance to ethnic groups in the creation of the majority Democratic coalition. By Andersen's account, the remobilization of the electorate that was part of the realignment began in 1928 as well, and other recent studies (Shively, 1971/72; Shover, 1974; Jeffries, 1979) further support the view that the realignment occurred in a series of elections beginning in the 1920s and that ethnic voting figured prominently in it.

The composition of the New Deal coalition has tended to receive rather less scholarly discussion than the chronology of the realignment. Yet the question of "who" not only has its own intrinsic importance but also bears directly on the question of "when." If voting patterns, electoral change, and resulting party coalitions can be explained essentially in socioeconomic terms, the case for a realignment confined to the 1930s is strengthened, whereas a dominant or even significant ethnocultural dimension would suggest including the 1928 election in the realignment process.

Class, ethnicity and religion, and region and residence were the principal social correlates of voting in the realignment and the New Deal coalition (Allswang, 1978; Ladd with Hadley, 1978). Not all the voting patterns were new, of course; the Democratic allegiance of white Southerners, for example, went well back into the nineteenth century, as did such ethnocultural political divisions as the Republican proclivities of Protestant Yankees and the Democratic leanings of Catholic immigrants. But while the new Democratic majority evidently came largely from a tidal surge across groups to the Democrats instead of through massive interactive change (Clubb et al., 1980), the realignment did include important new patterns. Much more than before, politics turned on issues of government regulation and assistance, and (with regional and ethnic variations) party coalitions reflected socioeconomic and ideological polarities. Democrats had particular strength among such groups as blue-collar workers and union members, the unemployed, marginal farmers and farm workers, and liberals; Republicans, among conservatives and the affluent middle and upper classes (Allswang, 1978; Ladd with Hadley, 1978; Sundquist, 1983; Kleppner, 1982a; Jensen, 1981b).

But the New Deal coalition comprised ethnic as well as socioeconomic groups, and not only working- and lower-class voters but also blacks, Jews, and such Catholic immigrant groups as the Italians and Poles shifted decisively toward the Democrats in the realignment (Collins, 1956; Gordon, 1969; Allswang, 1978; Ladd with Hadley, 1978; Andersen, 1979; Jeffries, 1979). Ethnocultural voting patterns, moreover, were not spurious; the black and working-class ethnic votes were not just socioeconomic, for example, nor was the Jewish vote simply ideological. A variety of statistical and analytical techniques for a variety of groups and places reveals that ethnicity, religion, and race had significant independent effects on voting in the New Deal years, effects typically as strong or stronger than socioeconomic ones (Lazarsfeld et al., 1944; Allswang, 1971, 1978; Shover, 1973; Ladd with Hadley, 1978; Jeffries, 1979; Brye, 1979; Jensen, 1981a, 1981b). And the ethnic and religious voting patterns were more than statistical artifacts or relics of earlier party systems. Ethnic and racial concerns were present, if usually secondary, in the 1930s, and politicians and office-holders understood the ethnic as well as the economic bases of politics and tailored political strategies accordingly (Allswang, 1971, 1978; Jeffries, 1979; Lubell, 1952).

Such evidence cautions against emphasizing too exclusively the economic and ideological causes of the realignment. No doubt the Depression and the New Deal were the decisive factors producing the profound transformations in voting patterns and the political system; without them there likely would have been no electoral realignment. But such speculation quickly becomes counterfactual history and overlooks complexities and connections. As events transpired from the late 1920s on, Al Smith's candidacy, the Great Depression, and the New Deal evidently worked together, reinforcing one another, to produce the interconnected socioeconomic and ethnocultural voting patterns of the 1930s and the new Democratic majority coalition with its distinctive urban–ethnic–working-class base.

What further confounds generalization about chronology and composition in the New Deal realignment is the great variety of patterns in different areas and at different political levels. Significant divergence characterized presidential, congressional, and local coalitions and trends (Burnham, 1970; Sundquist, 1983; Allswang, 1978). Geography, the third major voting determinant, entailed more than the Democratic voting of Southerners and urbanites or the Republican strength in suburbs, small towns, and rural areas outside the South. Distinct local and regional variations marked voting patterns and the pace and timing of realignment. In the Northeast, for example, the 1928 election was apparently part of the realignment sequence, while in the South the anti-Smith vote among normally Democratic white Protestants made the election deviant; non-Southern farm areas, especially in the Midwest, as another example, moved toward the GOP in 1936, counter to the national trend; and not before the late 1930s was the realignment firm in the West (Allswang, 1978; Clubb et al., 1980). Contributing to the complex multiplicity of findings—and, like the many local variations, reflecting general problems of the realignment/party systems model—have been the different approaches and methods of different scholars. [See, for example, the varying accounts of Pennsylvania's New Deal realignment in Burnham (1970), Chubb (1978), Prindle (1979), and McMichael and Trilling (1980).]

Recently debate has also arisen about the "how" of the New Deal realignment. Denying that conversion of Republicans to the Democratic party produced the realignment, Andersen (1976, 1979) has maintained that the Democrats became the majority party because they mobilized far more new voters than did the GOP. Supplemented by Prindle (1979) and Petrocik (1981), Andersen's mobilization thesis complements Beck's generational explanation of realignment (1974) and finds support in Kleppner's analysis of electoral turnout (1982a). In this view, demographic change (especially immigration and natural increase) and woman suffrage greatly expanded the potential electorate by the 1920s, while at the same time the noncompetitive and legal-institutional characteristics of the System of 1896 and the failure of both major parties to appeal to the urban, ethnic working class served to inhibit voting. The result was the extraordinarily low turnout rate of the 1920s and a large pool of latent voters, particularly among young people, the working class, and urban ethnic groups. The Democrats' success in mobilizing such newly eligible and previously abstaining voters produced the realignment and the New Deal coalition. But while the mobilization thesis has much to commend it and has influenced historical accounts of the realignment, the idea that demographic change and the activation of new voters were important is not new (e.g., see Lubell, 1952; Key, 1955; Campbell et al., 1960; Rogin and Shover, 1970), nor is the primacy of mobilization over conversion uncontested among political scientists (Ladd with Hadley, 1978; Erickson and Tedin, 1981; Sundquist, 1983) or historians (Lichtman, 1979, 1982; Sternsher, 1984). And although more attention deservedly will be given the question of mobilization, for the 1930s as for other realignments, it seems likely that both mobilization and conversion will be found important to the New Deal realignment, with variation by election, place, and group.

The New Deal Party System

Despite the debate about the chronology, composition, and causes of the New Deal realignment, there is substantial agreement (and much less historical literature) on the nature and course of the New Deal party system down to the 1960s. The realignment of the 1930s was a systemic one, involving major changes in salient issues and public policy as well as in mass electoral behavior and extending from presidential coalitions and the federal government to state and local politics and government (Allswang, 1978; Clubb et al., 1980). Local realignment often lagged behind realignment in the presidential vote, resulting in a two-stage process before convergence (Sundquist, 1983).

Significant if limited partisan remobilization marked the early phase of the New Deal party system. Outside the South, the regional one-party domination of the fourth party system ended. Party loyalty increased, split-ticket voting declined, Democratic organizations at all levels were strengthened (Stave, 1970; Allswang, 1978), and voter participation rose. But the demobilization and disaggregation of the System of 1896 were only temporarily halted and not fundamentally reversed, partly because the restrictive legal-institutional framework still existed, and the turnout increase was noticeable chiefly in presidential elections, reflecting growth in the marginal more than in the core electorate (Burnham, 1965, 1970; Kleppner, 1982a).

The New Deal coalition proved to be a particularly durable one, with its lineaments persisting strongly until at least the 1960s. Party coalitions were never perfectly stable, to be sure (Key, 1966), for there were both short-term and secular changes, but the essential ethnocultural, socioeconomic, and geographic voting determinants and patterns evident in the 1930s remained at the heart of politics decades later (Axelrod, 1972; Knoke, 1976); and post-1930s changes in voting patterns appear in some analyses as extensions of the 1930s realignment and the New Deal party system (Ladd with Hadley, 1978; Sundquist, 1983). The "maintaining" period from 1936 to 1948—even the eventful era of World War II—was one of fundamental continuity in voting patterns and the salience of New Deal issues (Key, 1966; Jeffries, 1979). So, too, if less so, were the 1950s. Despite the deviating 1952 and 1956 presidential elections, Democrats remained the majority party and New Deal era party images and party loyalties persisted (Campbell et al., 1960; Sternsher, 1982).

Even so, some scholars stress the evidence of change (or "midsequence adjustment") and decay in the New Deal coalition and party system by the late 1940s (Clubb et al., 1980; Boylan, 1981). The partisan remobilization and the Democratic coalition of the New Deal realignment began to erode. Prosperity and international concerns altered the political context, New Deal issues lost salience, and after 1948 class effects declined in voting. But the South provided the most important early change in the New Deal party system. White Southern disaffection with Democratic policy, especially but not only with regard to race, built during the 1940s (Garson, 1974; Barnard, 1974) and in ensuing decades produced substantial shifts, regional and national, in party coalitions (Bartley and Graham, 1975). The end of the Democratic Solid South in the presidential elections after 1944 spelled a major break not just in the New Deal party system but in a fundamental characteristic of party systems going back to the Civil War.

The change and deterioration of the New Deal party system apparent by the 1950s accelerated dramatically after the early 1960s. Nor surprisingly, given the particular concerns of their discipline, study of the post-1960 era has come predominantly from political scientists. The principal works (Nie et al., 1976; Ladd with Hadley, 1978; Petrocik, 1981; Sundquist, 1983) are not of a piece with respect to focus, definitions, methodology, and conclusions (more evidence of the imprecision and variability in realignment/party systems study), but their chief findings are broadly consistent.

Major changes in parties, issues, and voting have marked the past two decades. Democrats have lost their normal majority in the presidential vote but have not been supplanted by the GOP and retain majority status below the presidential level. Both parties, but the Republicans especially, have lost ground in partisan identification as independents have become far more numerous. As that suggests, the roles, functions, and strength of the parties have declined precipitously from the early 1960s, when the twentieth-century trend of partisan declension and disaggregation resumed vigorously (see also Kleppner, 1982a). Except for blacks, who entered the electorate in large numbers as a result of the civil rights movement (Bartley and Graham, 1975; Lawson, 1976; Kleppner, 1982a), voter participation has declined along with party strength and partisan allegiance. Salient issues veered away from New Deal economic issues and toward sociocultural, racial, and foreign-policy issues; and particularly in presidential elections, issues came to have more effect on voting decisions. On lifestyle and sociocultural issues especially, there has occurred a striking degree of class "inversion" from the early stages of the New Deal party system, with the upper socioeconomic strata taking more liberal positions, the lower strata more conservative ones (Ladd with Hadley, 1978). Significant shifts in party coalitions, connected to the rise of new issues and the ideological class inversion, have occurred. Republicans have made gains among white Southerners; Catholic ethnic groups and the working class remain predominantly Democratic, but less reliably so; and Democrats have won new strength among blacks and the non-Southern old-stock middle and upper classes. New, especially young, voters and independents have further rearranged the social correlates of politics. Significantly for the ethnocultural model, ethnicity, religion, and race proved the best predictors of partisanship in the 1970s (Bartley and Graham, 1975; Knoke, 1976; Jensen, 1981b; Petrocik, 1981).

Scholars do not agree whether those changes amount to realignment, transformation, dealignment—or something else. The difference between voter behavior and partisan identification, always a problem in assessing electoral change, has become all the more vexing because of the volatility, disaggregation, and increased independency in recent politics. But clearly the changes spell a fundamental alteration, perhaps even the end, of the New Deal party system. Indeed, if depoliticization, demobilization, and the decline of parties continue apace, some scholars believe, there may be no successor to the New Deal party system, no new partisan realignment; the New Deal party system may be the "last party system" (Jensen, 1981b).

References

Allen, H.W., and Allen, K.W. Vote fraud and data validity. In J.M. Clubb, W.H. Flanigan, and N.H. Zingale (Eds.), *Analyzing electoral history*. Beverly Hills, CA: Sage, 1981.

Allen, H.W., and Austin, E.W. From the Populist era to the New Deal: A study of partisan realignment in Washington state, 1889–1950. *Social Science History, 1979, 3,* 115–143.

Allen, H.W., and Clubb, J. Progressive reform and the political system. *Pacific Northwest Quarterly,* 1974, *65,* 130–145.

Allswang, J.M. *A house for all peoples: Ethnic politics in Chicago, 1890–1936.* Lexington: University Press of Kentucky, 1971.

Allswang, J. M. *The New Deal and American politics: A study in political change.* New York: Wiley, 1978.

Alvarez, D.J., and True, E.J. Critical elections & partisan realignment: An urban test-case. *Polity,* 1973, *5,* 563–576.

Andersen, K. Generation, partisan shift, and realignment: A glance back to the New Deal. In N.H. Nie, S. Verba, and J.R. Petrocik (Eds.), *The changing American voter.* Cambridge, MA: Harvard University Press, 1976.

Andersen, K. *The creation of a Democratic majority, 1928–1936.* Chicago: University of Chicago Press, 1979.

Argersinger, P.H. *Populism and politics: William Alfred Peffer and the People's party.* Lexington: University Press of Kentucky, 1974.

Argersinger, P.H. "A place on the ballot": Fusion politics and antifusion laws. *American Historical Review,* 1980, *85,* 287–306, reprinted in this volume as chapter 6.

Argersinger, P.H. To disfranchise the people: The Iowa ballot law and election of 1897. *Mid-America,* 1981, *63,* 18–35.

Argersinger, P.H. Regulating democracy: Election laws and Dakota politics, 1889–1902. *Midwest Review,* 1983, *5,* 1–19, reprinted in this volume as chapter 7.

Argersinger, P.H. New perspectives on election fraud in the Gilded Age. *Political Science Quarterly,* 1985/86, *100,* 669–687, reprinted in this volume as chapter 4.

Axelrod, R. Where the votes come from: An analysis of electoral coalitions, 1952–1968. *American Political Science Review,* 1972, *66,* 11–20.

Aydelotte, W.O. *Quantification in history.* Reading, MA: Addison-Wesley, 1971.

Barnard, W.D. *Dixiecrats and Democrats: Alabama politics, 1942–1950.* University, AL: University of Alabama Press, 1974.

Bartley, N.V. Voters and party systems: A review of the recent literature. *The History Teacher,* 1975, *8,* 452–469.

Bartley, N.V., and Graham, H.D. *Southern politics and the Second Reconstruction.* Baltimore: Johns Hopkins University Press, 1975.

Baum, D. Know-Nothingism and the Republican majority in Massachusetts: The political realignment of the 1850s. *Journal of American History,* 1978, *64,* 959–986.

Baum, D. The "Irish vote" and party politics in Massachusetts, 1860–1876. *Civil War History,* 1980, *26,* 117–141.

Beck, P.A. A socialization theory of partisan realignment. In R.G. Niemi (Ed.), *The politics of future citizens.* San Francisco: Jossey-Bass, 1974.

Beck, P.A. The electoral cycle and patterns of American politics. *British Journal of Political Science,* 1979, *9,* 129–156.

Bennett, W.L., and Haltom, W. Issues, voter choice, and critical elections. *Social Science History,* 1980, *4,* 379–418.

Benson, L. Research problems in American political historiography. In M. Komarovsky (Ed.), *Common frontiers of the social sciences.* New York: Free Press, 1957.

Benson, L. *The concept of Jacksonian Democracy: New York as a test case.* Princeton, NJ: Princeton University Press, 1961.

Benson, L. *Toward the scientific study of history: Selected essays.* Philadelphia: Lippincott, 1972.

Benson, L., Silbey, J.H., and Field, P.F. Toward a theory of stability and change in American voting patterns: New York state, 1792–1970. In J.H. Silbey, A.G. Bogue, and W.H. Flanigan (Eds.), *The history of American electoral behavior.* Princeton, NJ: Princeton University Press, 1978.

Berelson, B.R., Lazarsfeld, P.F., and McPhee, W.N. *Voting: A study of opinion formation in a presidential campaign.* Chicago: University of Chicago Press, 1954.

Bogue, A.G. United States: The "new" political history. *Journal of Contemporary History,* 1968, *3,* 5–27.

Bogue, A.G. The new political history in the 1970s. In M. Kammen (Ed.), *The past before us: Contemporary historical writing in the United States.* Ithaca, NY: Cornell University Press, 1980.

Bogue, A.G. Numerical and formal analysis in United States history. *Journal of Interdisciplinary History,* 1981a, *12,* 137–175.

Bogue, A.G. *The earnest men: Republicans of the Civil War Senate.* Ithaca. NY: Cornell University Press, 1981b.

Bogue, A.G., Clubb, J.M., and Flanigan, W.H. The new political history. *American Behavioral Scientist,* 1977, *21,* 201–220.

Boylan, J. *The New Deal coalition and the election of 1946.* New York: Garland, 1981.

Brady, D.W. Critical elections, congressional parties and clusters of policy changes. *British Journal of Political Science,* 1978, *8,* 79–99.

Brady, D., with Stewart, J., Jr. Congressional party realignment and transformations of public policy in three realignment eras. *American Journal of Politcal Science,* 1982, *26,* 333–360.

Brye, D.L. *Wisconsin voting patterns in the twentieth century, 1900 to 1950.* New York: Garland, 1979.

Burner, D. *The politics of provincialism: The Democratic party in transition, 1918–1932.* New York: Knopf, 1968.

Burnham, W.D. The changing shape of the American political universe. *American Political Science Review*, 1965, *59*, 7–28.

Burnham, W.D. Party systems and the political process. In W.N. Chambers and W.D. Burnham (Eds.), *The American party systems: Stages of political development*. New York: Oxford University Press, 1967.

Burnham, W.D. *Critical elections and the mainsprings of American politics*. New York: Norton, 1970.

Burnham, W.D. Theory and voting research: Some reflections on Converse's "Change in the American Electorate." *American Political Science Review*, 1974a, *68*, 1002–1023.

Burnham, W.D. Rejoinder to "Comments" by Philip Converse and Jerrold Rusk. *American Political Science Review*, 1974b, *68*, 1050–1057.

Burnham, W.D. The System of 1896: An analysis. In P. Kleppner et al., *The evolution of American electoral systems*. Westport, CT: Greenwood Press, 1981.

Burnham, W.D., Clubb, J.M., and Flanigan, W.H. Partisan realignment: A systemic perspective. In J.H. Silbey, A.G. Bogue, and W.H. Flanigan (Eds.), *The history of American electoral behavior,* Princeton, NJ: Princeton University Press, 1978.

Campbell, A., Converse, P.E., Miller, W.E., and Stokes, D.E. *The American Voter*. New York: Wiley, 1960.

Campbell, A., Converse, P.E., Miller, W.E., and Stokes, D.E. *Elections and the political order*. New York: Wiley, 1966.

Campbell, B.A., and Trilling, R.J. (Eds.). *Realignment in American politics: Toward a theory*. Austin: University of Texas Press, 1980.

Campbell, B.C. *Representative democracy: Public policy and Midwestern legislatures in the late nineteenth century*. Cambridge, MA: Harvard University Press, 1980.

Cherny, R.W. *Populism, Progressivism, and the transformation of Nebraska politics, 1885–1915*. Lincoln: University of Nebraska Press, 1981.

Chubb, J.E. Systems analysis and partisan realignment. *Social Science History*, 1978, *2*, 144–171.

Claggett, W. Turnout and core voters in the nineteenth and twentieth centuries: A reconsideration. *Social Science Quarterly*, 1981, *62*, 443–449.

Clubb, J.M. Party coalitions in the early twentieth century. In S.M. Lipset (Ed.), *Emerging coalitions in American politics*. San Francisco: Institute for Contemporary Studies, 1978.

Clubb, J.M., and Allen, H.W. The cities and the election of 1928: Partisan relignment? *American Historical Review*, 1969, *74*, 1205–1220.

Clubb, J.M. and Allen, H.W. (Eds.). *Electoral change and stability in American political history*. New York: Free Press, 1971.

Clubb, J.M., and Bogue, A.G. History, quantification, and the social sciences. *American Behavioral Scientist*, 1977, *21*, 167–185.

Clubb, J.M., Flanigan, W.H., and Zingale, N.H. *Partisan realignment: Voters, parties, and government in American history*. Beverly Hills, CA: Sage, 1980.

Clubb, J.M., Flanigan, W.H., and Zingale, N.H. *Analyzing electoral history: A guide to the study of American voter behavior*. Beverly Hills, CA: Sage, 1981.

Cochran, T.C. The "presidential synthesis" in American history. *American Historical Review*, 1948, *53*, 748–759.

Collins, E.M. Cincinnati Negroes and presidential politics. *Journal of Negro History*, 1956, *41*, 131–137.

Converse, P.E. Change in the American electorate. In A. Campbell and P.E. Converse (Eds.), *The human meaning of social change*. New York: Russell Sage Foundation, 1972.

Converse, P.E. Comment on Burnham's "Theory and Voting Research." *American Political Science Review*, 1974, *68*, 1024–1027.

Cox, G.W., and Kousser, J.M. Turnout and rural corruption: New York as a test case. *American Journal of Political Science*, 1981, *25*, 646–663.

Degler, C.N. American political parties and the rise of the city: An interpretation. *Journal of American History*, 1964, *51*, 41–59.

Dollar, C.M., and Jensen, R.J. *Historian's guide to statistics: Quantitative analysis and historical research*. New York: Holt, Rinehart and Winston, 1971.

Dykstra, R.R., and Reynolds, D.R. In search of Wisconsin Progressivism, 1904–1952: A test of the Rogin scenario. In J.H. Silbey, A.G. Bogue, and W.H. Flanigan (Eds.), *The history of American electoral behavior*. Princeton, NJ: Princeton University Press, 1978.

Erikson, R.S., and Tedin, K.L. The 1928–1936 partisan realignment: The case for the conversion hypothesis. *American Political Science Review*, 1981, *75*, 951–962.

Field, P.F. *The politics of race in New York: The struggle for black suffrage in the Civil War era*. Ithaca, NY: Cornell University Press, 1982.

Folsom, B.W. Tinkerers, tipplers, and traitors: ethnicity and democratic reform in Nebraska during the Progressive era. *Pacific Historical Review*, 1981, *50*, 53–75.

Formisano, R.P. *The birth of mass political parties: Michigan, 1827–1861*. Princeton, NJ: Princeton University Press, 1971.

Formisano, R.P. Federalists and Republicans: Parties, yes—system, no. In P. Kleppner et al., *The evolution of American electoral systems*. Westport, CT: Greenwood Press, 1981.

Fuchs, L.H. (Ed.). *American ethnic politics*. New York: Harper & Row, 1968.

Garson, R.A. *The Democratic party and the politics of sectionalism, 1941–1948*. Baton Rouge: Louisiana State University Press, 1974.

Ginsberg, B. Critical elections and the substance of party conflict, 1844–1968. *Midwest Journal of Political Science*, 1972, *16*, 603–625.

Ginsberg, B. Elections and public policy. *American Political Science Review*, 1976, *70*, 41–49.

Gordon, R.W. The change in the political alignment of Chicago's Negroes during the New Deal. *Journal of American History*, 1969, *56*, 584–603.

Gould, L.L. *Reform and regulation: American politics, 1900–1916*. New York: Wiley, 1978.

Green, J.R. Behavioralism and class analysis: A review essay on methodology and ideology. *Labor History*, 1972, *13*, 89–106.

Hackney, S. *Populism to Progressivism in Alabama*. Princeton, NJ: Princeton University Press, 1969.

Hammarberg, M. *The Indiana voter: The historical dynamics of party allegiance during the 1870s*. Chicago: University of Chicago Press, 1977.

Hammarberg, M. An analysis of American electoral data. *Journal of Interdisciplinary History*, 1983, *13*, 629–652.

Hammond, J.L. Revival religion and anti-slavery politics. *American Sociological Review*, 1974, *39*, 175–186.

Hammond, J.L. Minor parties and electoral realignments. *American Politics Quarterly*, 1976, *4*, 63–85.

Hammond, J.L. New approaches to aggregate electoral data. *Journal of Interdisciplinary History*, 1979, *9*, 473–492.

Hansen, S.L. The making of the third party system: Voters and parties in Illinois, 1850–1876. Ann Arbor: UMI, 1980.

Hart, R.L. *Redeemers, Bourbons, and Populists: Tennessee, 1870–1896*. Baton Rouge: Louisiana State University Press, 1975.

Hays, S.P. History as human behavior. *Iowa Journal of History*, 1960, *58*, 193–206.

Hays, S.P. Political parties and the community-society continuum. In W.N. Chambers and

W.D. Burnham (Eds.), *The American party systems: Stages of political development.* New York: Oxford University Press, 1967.

Hays, S.P. New possibilities for American political history: The social analysis of politcal life. In S.M. Lipset and R. Hofstadter (Eds.), *Sociology and history: Methods.* New York: Basic Books, 1968.

Hays, S.P. *American political history as social analysis.* Knoxville: University of Tennessee Press, 1980.

Holt, M.F. *Forging a majority: The formation of the Republican party in Pittsburgh, 1848–1860.* New Haven, CT: Yale University Press, 1969.

Holt, M.F. *The political crisis of the 1850s.* New York: Wiley, 1978.

Huthmacher, J.J. *Massachusetts people and politics, 1919–1933.* Cambridge, MA: Harvard University Press, 1959.

Jeffries, J.W. *Testing the Roosevelt coalition: Connecticut society and politics in the era of World War II.* Knoxville: University of Tennessee Press, 1979.

Jensen, R. History and the political scientist. In S.M. Lipset (Ed.), *Politics and the social sciences.* New York: Oxford University Press, 1969a.

Jensen, R. American election analysis: A case history of methodological innovation and diffusion. In S.M. Lipset (Ed.), *Politics and the social sciences.* New York: Oxford University Press, 1969b.

Jensen, R. Armies, admen, and crusaders: Types of presidential election campaigns. *The History Teacher,* 1969c, *2,* 33–50.

Jensen, R. *The winning of the Midwest: Social and political conflict, 1888–1896.* Chicago: University of Chicago Press, 1971.

Jensen, R. The cities reelect Roosevelt: Ethnicity, religion, and class in 1940. *Ethnicity,* 1981a, *8,* 189–195.

Jensen, R. The last party system: Decay of consensus, 1932–1980. In P. Kleppner et al., *The evolution of American electoral systems.* Westport, CT: Greenwood Press, 1981b.

Kammen, M. (Ed.). *The past before us: Contemporary historical writing in the United States.* Ithaca, NY: Cornell University Press, 1980.

Kamphoefner, W.D. St. Louis Germans and the Republican party. *Mid-America,* 1975, *57,* 69–88.

Kelley, R. Ideology and political culture from Jefferson to Nixon. *American Historical Review,* 1977, *82,* 531–562.

Key, V.O., Jr. A theory of critical elections. *Journal of Politics,* 1955, *17,* 3–18.

Key, V.O., Jr. Secular realignment and the party system. *Journal of Politics,* 1959, *21,* 198–210.

Key, V.O., Jr. *The responsible electorate: Rationality in presidential voting, 1936–1960.* Cambridge, MA: Harvard University Press, 1966.

Key, V.O., Jr., and Munger, F. Social determinism and electoral decision: The case of Indiana. In E. Burdick and A. Brodbeck (Eds.), *American voting behavior.* New York: Free Press, 1959.

Kleppner, P. Lincoln and the immigrant vote: A case of religious polarization. *Mid-America,* 1966, *48,* 176–195.

Kleppner, P. *The cross of culture: A social analysis of midwestern politics, 1850–1900.* New York: Free Press, 1970.

Kleppner, P. From ethnoreligious conflict to ''social harmony'': Coalitional and party transformations in the 1890s. In S.M. Lipset (Ed.), *Emerging coalitions in American politics.* San Francisco: Institute for Contemporary Studies, 1978.

Kleppner, P. *The third electoral system, 1853–1892: Parties, voters, and political cultures.* Chapel Hill: University of North Carolina Press, 1979.

Kleppner, P. Critical realignments and electoral systems. In P. Kleppner et al., *The evolution of American electoral systems*. Westport, CT: Greenwood Press, 1981a.

Kleppner, P. Partisanship and ethnoreligious conflict: The third electoral system, 1853–1892. In P. Kleppner et al., *The evolution of American electoral systems*. Westport, CT: Greenwood Press, 1981b.

Kleppner, P. *Who voted? The dynamics of electoral turnout, 1870–1980*. New York: Praeger Publishers, 1982a.

Kleppner, P. Were women to blame? Female suffrage and voter turnout. *Journal of Interdisciplinary History*, 1982b, *12*, 621–643.

Kleppner, P. Voters and parties in the western states, 1876–1900. *Western Historical Quarterly*, 1983, *14*, 49–68.

Kleppner, P., and Baker, S.C. The impact of voter registration requirements on electoral turnout, 1900–1916. *Journal of Political and Military Sociology*, 1980, *8*, 205–226.

Kleppner, P., Burnham, W.D., Formisano, R.P., Hays, S.P., Jensen, R., and Shade, W.G. *The evolution of American electoral systems*. Westport, CT: Greenwood Press, 1981.

Knoke, D. *Change and continuity in American politics: The social bases of political parties*. Baltimore: Johns Hopkins University Press, 1976.

Kousser, J.M. Ecological regression and the analysis of past politics. *Journal of Interdisciplinary History*, 1973, *4*, 237–262.

Kousser, J.M. *The shaping of southern politics: Suffrage restriction and the establishment of the one-party South, 1880–1910*. New Haven, CT: Yale University Press, 1974.

Kousser, J.M. The "new political history": A methodological critique. *Reviews in American History*, 1976, *4*, 1–14.

Kousser, J.M. History QUASSHed: Quantitative social scientific history in perspective. *American Behavioral Scientist*, 1980a, *23*, 885–904.

Kousser, J.M. Quantitative social scientific history. In M. Kammen (Ed.), *The past before us: Contemporary historical writing in the United States*. Ithaca, NY: Cornell University Press, 1980b.

Kousser, J.M. Restoring politics to political history. *Journal of Interdisciplinary History*, 1982, *12*, 569–595.

Ladd, E.C., Jr., with Hadley, C.D. *Transformations of the American party system: Political coalitions from the New Deal to the 1970s* (2nd ed.). New York: Norton, 1978.

Latner, R.B., and Levine, P. Perspectives on antebellum pietistic politics. *Reviews in American History*, 1976, *4*, 15–24.

Lawson, S.F. *Black ballots: Voting rights in the South, 1944–1969*. New York: Columbia University Press, 1976.

Lazarsfeld, P.F., Berelson, B., and Gaudet, H. *The people's choice: How the voter makes up his mind in a presidential campaign*. New York: Duell, Sloan and Pearce, 1944.

Levine, M.V. Standing political decisions and critical realignment: The pattern of Maryland politics, 1872–1948. *Journal of Politics*, 1976, *38*, 292–325.

Lichtman, A.J. Critical election theory and the reality of American presidential politics, 1916–40. *American Historical Review*, 1976, *81*, 317–351.

Lichtman, A.J. *Prejudice and the old politics: The presidential election of 1928*. Chapel Hill: University of North Carolina Press, 1979.

Lichtman, A.J. The end of realignment theory? Toward a new research program for American political history. *Historical Methods*, 1982, *15*, 170–188.

Lichtman, A.J. Political realignment and "ethnocultural" voting in late nineteenth century America. *Journal of Social History*, 1983, *16*, 55–82.

Lichtman, A.J., and Langbein, L.I. Ecological regression versus homogeneous units: A specification analysis. *Social Science History*, 1978, *2*, 172–193.

Lorence, J.J. Socialism in northern Wisconsin, 1910–1920: An ethnocultural analysis. *Mid-America*, 1982, *64*, 25–51.

Lubell, S. *The future of American politics*. New York: Harper & Row, 1952.

Luebke, F.C. *Immigrants and politics: The Germans of Nebraska, 1880–1900*. Lincoln: University of Nebraska Press, 1969.

McCarthy, J.L., and Tukey, J.W. Exploratory analysis of aggregate voting behavior: Presidential elections in New Hampshire, 1896–1972. *Social Science History*, 1978, *2*, 292–331.

McCormick, R.L. Ethno-cultural interpretations of nineteenth-century American voting behavior. *Political Science Quarterly*, 1974, *89*, 351–377.

McCormick, R.L. The party period and public policy: An exploratory hypothesis. *Journal of American History*, 1979, *66*, 279–298.

McCormick, R.L. *From realignment to reform: Political change in New York state, 1893–1910*. Ithaca, NY: Cornell University Press, 1981.

McCormick, R.L. The realignment synthesis in American history. *Journal of Interdisciplinary History*, 1982, *13*, 85–105.

McCormick. R.P. Suffrage classes and party alignments: A study in voter behavior. *Mississippi Valley Historical Review*, 1959, *46*, 397–410.

McCormick, R.P. New perspectives on Jacksonian politics. *American Historical Review*, 1960, *65*, 288–301.

McCormick, R.P. *The second American party system: Party formation in the Jacksonian era*. Chapel Hill: University of North Carolina Press, 1966.

McCrary, P., Miller, C., and Baum, D. Class and party in the secession crisis: Voting behavior in the Deep South, 1856–1861. *Journal of Interdisciplinary History*, 1978, *8*, 429–457.

McMichael, L.G., and Trilling, R.J. The structure and meaning of critical realignment: The case of Pennsylvania, 1928–1932. In B.A. Campbell and R.J. Trilling (Eds.), *Realignment in American politics: Toward a theory*. Austin: University of Texas Press, 1980.

MacRae, D., Jr., and Meldrum, J.A. Critical elections in Illinois: 1888–1958. *American Political Science Review*, 1960, *54*, 669–683.

McSeveney, S.T. *The politics of depression: Political behavior in the Northeast, 1893–1896*. New York: Oxford University Press, 1972.

McSeveney, S.T. Ethnic groups, ethnic conflicts, and recent quantitative research in American political history. *International Migration Review*, 1973, *7*, 14–33.

Nelson, C.L. *German-American political behavior in Nebraska and Wisconsin, 1916–1920*. Lincoln: University of Nebraska Press, 1972.

Nie, N.H., Verba, S., and Petrocik, J.R. *The changing American voter*. Cambridge, MA: Harvard University Press, 1976.

Parker, A.C.E. Beating the spread: Analyzing American election outcomes. *Journal of American History*, 1980, *67*, 61–87.

Parsons, S.B. *The Populist context: Rural versus urban power on a Great Plains frontier*. Westport, CT: Greenwood Press, 1973.

Petrocik, J.R. *Party coalitions: Realignment and the decline of the New Deal party system*. Chicago: University of Chicago Press, 1981.

Pomper, G. Classification of presidential elections. *Journal of Politics*, 1967, *29*, 535–566.

Prindle, D.F. Voter turnout, critical elections, and the New Deal realignment. *Social Science History*, 1979, *3*, 144–170.

Reynolds, J.F. "The silent dollar": Vote buying in New Jersey. *New Jersey History*, 1980, *98*, 191–211.

Reynolds, J.F., and McCormick, R.L. An honest and a straight party vote: Ballot reform and split-ticket voting in New Jersey and New York, 1880–1910. Paper presented at the meeting of the Organization of American Historians, Cincinnati, April 1983.

Rogin, M.P., and Shover, J.L. *Political change in California: Critical elections and social movements, 1890–1966*. Westport, CT: Greenwood Publishing Corporation, 1970.

Rozett, J.M. Racism and Republican emergence in Illinois, 1848–1860: A reevaluation of Republican Negrophobia. *Civil War History*, 1976, *22*, 101–115.

Rusk, J.G. The effect of the Australian ballot reform on split ticket voting, 1876–1908. *American Political Science Review*, 1970, *64*, 1220–1238.

Rusk, J.G. Comment: The American electoral universe: Speculation and evidence. *American Political Science Review*, 1974, *68*, 1028–1049.

Rusk, J.G., and Stucker, J.J. The effect of the southern system of election laws on voting participation: A reply to V.O. Key, Jr. In J.H. Silbey, A.G. Bogue, and W.H. Flanigan (Eds.), *The history of American electoral behavior*. Princeton, NJ: Princeton University Press, 1978.

Salisbury, R.H., and MacKuen, M. On the study of party realignment. *Journal of Politics*, 1981, *43*, 523–530.

Schattschneider, E.E. *The semisovereign people: A realist's view of democracy in America*. New York: Holt, Rinehart and Winston, 1960.

Sellers, C. The equilibrium cycle in two-party politics. *Public Opinion Quarterly*, 1965, *29*, 16–38.

Shade, W.G. "New political history": Some statistical questions raised. *Social Science History*, 1981a, *5*, 171–196.

Shade, W.G. Political pluralism and party development: The creation of a modern party system, 1815–1852. In P. Kleppner et al., *The evolution of American electoral systems*. Westport, CT: Greenwood Press, 1981b.

Shade, W.L. *Social change and the electoral process*. Gainesville: University of Florida Press, 1973.

Shively, W.P. A reinterpretation of the New Deal realignment. *Public Opinion Quarterly*, 1971/72, *25*, 621–624.

Shortridge, R.M. The voter realignment in the Midwest during the 1850s. *American Politics Quarterly*, 1976, *4*, 193–222.

Shortridge, R.M. Voter turnout in the Midwest, 1840–1872. *Social Science Quarterly*, 1980, *60*, 617–629.

Shortridge, R.M. Nineteenth century turnout: A rejoinder. *Social Science Quarterly*, 1981a, *62*, 450–452.

Shortridge, R.M. Estimating voter participation. In J.M. Clubb, W.H. Flanigan, and N.H. Zingale (Eds.), *Analyzing electoral history*. Beverly Hills, CA: Sage Publications, 1981b.

Shover, J.L. Was 1928 a critical election in California? *Pacific Northwest Quarterly*, 1967, *58*, 196–204.

Shover, J.L. Ethnicity and religion in Philadelphia politics, 1924–1940. *American Quarterly*, 1973, *25*, 499–515.

Shover, J.L. The emergence of a two-party system in Republican Philadelphia, 1924–1936. *Journal of American History*, 1974, *60*, 985–1002.

Silbey, J.H. *The transformation of American politics, 1840–1860*. Englewood Cliffs, NJ: Prentice-Hall, 1967.

Silbey, J.H., and McSeveney, S.T. (Eds.). *Voters, parties, and elections: Quantitative essays in the history of American popular voting behavior*. Lexington, MA: Xerox College Publ., 1972.

Silbey, J.H., Bogue, A.G., and Flanigan, W.H. (Eds.). *The history of American electoral behavior*. Princeton, NJ: Princeton University Press, 1978.

Stave, B.M. The "La Follette revolution" and the Pittsburgh vote, 1932. *Mid-America*, 1967, *49*, 244–251.

Stave, B.M. *The New Deal and the last hurrah: Pittsburgh machine politics*. Pittsburgh: University of Pittsburgh Press, 1970.

Sternsher, B. The emergence of the New Deal party system: A problem in historical analysis of voter behavior. *Journal of Interdisciplinary History*, 1975, *6*, 127–149.

Sternsher, B. Reflections on politics, policy, and ideology. In R.H. Bremner and G.W. Reichard (Eds.), *Reshaping America: Society and institutions, 1945–1960*. Columbus: Ohio State University Press, 1982.

Sternsher, B. The New Deal party system: A reappraisal. *Journal of Interdisciplinary History*, 1984, *15*, 53–81.

Sundquist, J.L. *Dynamics of the party system: Alignment and realignment of political parties in the United States*. Washington, DC: Brookings Institution, 1973.

Sundquist, J.L. *Dynamics of the party system: Alignment and realignment of political parties in the United States* (rev. ed.). Washington, DC: Brookings Institution, 1983.

Sweeney, K. Rum, romanism, representation, and reform: Coalition politics in Massachusetts, 1847–1853. *Civil War History*, 1976, *22*, 116–137.

Swierenga, R.P. *Quantification in American history: Theory and research*. New York: Atheneum, 1970.

Swierenga, R.P. Ethnocultural political analysis: A new approach to American ethnic studies. *Journal of American Studies*, 1971, *5*, 59–79.

VanderMeer, P.R. The new political history: Progress and prospects. *Computers and the Humanities*, 1977, *2*, 265–278.

VanderMeer, P.R. Religion, society, and politics. *Social Science History*, 1981, *5*, 3–24.

Wanat, J., and Burke, K. Estimating the degree of mobilization and conversion in the 1890s: An inquiry into the nature of electoral change. *American Political Science Review*, 1982, *76*, 360–371.

Williams, J.C. Economics and politics: Voting behavior in Kansas during the Populist decade. *Explorations in Economic History*, 1981, *18*, 233–256.

Winkle, K.J. A social analysis of voter turnout in Ohio, 1850–1860. *Journal of Interdisciplinary History*, 1983, *13*, 411–435.

Wright, J.E. The ethnocultural model of voting: A behavioral and historical critique. *American Behavioral Scientist*, 1973, *16*, 653–674.

Wright, J.E. *The politics of Populism: Dissent in Colorado*. New Haven, CT: Yale University Press, 1974.

Wyman, R.E. Wisconsin ethnic groups and the election of 1890. *Wisconsin Magazine of History*, 1968, *51*, 269–293.

Wyman, R.E. Middle-class voters and progressive reform: The conflict of class and culture. *American Political Science Review*, 1974, *68*, 488–504.

Zanjani, S.S. A theory of critical realignment: The Nevada example, 1892–1908. *Pacific Historical Review*, 1979, *49*, 259–280.

Zingale, N.H. Third party alignments in a two party system: The case of Minnesota. In J.H. Silbey, A.G. Bogue, and W.H. Flanigan (Eds.), *The history of American voting behavior*. Princeton, NJ: Princeton University Press, 1978.

2

Electoral Processes in American Politics

Scholars analyze elections and political history in terms of the issues and constituencies involved, but the contests themselves took place within, and were shaped by, the parameters of election laws and procedures regulating parties, nominations, ballots, and voting. Although historians ignore or regard as givens many of these now standard electoral parameters, they were often critical matters of great concern at the time of their adoption and during the political campaigns that followed. For however equitable the procedures might seem, they are rarely impartial in their effects within a specific political context. As Austin Ranney has observed, "decisions on rules are never politically neutral. . . . In politics as in all other forms of human conflict, the rules make a difference in determining who wins and who loses."

The establishment of electoral processes, therefore, has nearly invariably been characterized by discord and by partisan and ideological calculations. Indeed, after analyzing several decades of legislation detailing electoral procedures in New Jersey, Richard P. McCormick (1953) concluded that virtually all such laws "were intended for no other purpose than to insure the supremacy of the temporarily dominant party." But if parties and political considerations have consistently shaped electoral processes, the converse also is true: electoral processes have shaped parties, voting behavior, campaign strategies, and other features of the political system. This dual theme is evident throughout the history of American electoral processes.

In creating a new form of government for the United States, the Constitution drawn up in 1787 necessarily had to develop the broad electoral processes appropriate to the type of government envisaged. For historical and practical reasons, considerable control over questions of suffrage and election administration was left with the state governments, guaranteeing diversity and subsequent conflict. But the constitutional convention in Philadelphia also drew up electoral rules as part of its efforts to strengthen the central government, restrict democratic possibilities, establish a stable republic, and balance different interests through political compromises. Indeed, the need for balance preoccupied the Framers, and they eventually seized on the idea of the separation of powers as the method to preserve both freedom and order. They constructed a political system to balance the interests of small and large states, the need for a vigorous national government with the preservation of active state governments, the necessity for popular support with the clamor for protection of property rights. Within the federal government they created a bicameral legislature in which each house would reflect different interests and constituencies and constitute a check on the power of the other. Members of the House of Representatives were apportioned according to population, satisfying the demands of the larger states, while equal representation by state was established for the Senate, accommodating the smaller states seeking to protect their position. Members of the House were to be elected every two years directly by the people—the only federal officers to be popularly elected. Members of the Senate, on the other hand, would be chosen for six-year terms by their state legislatures and were expected to be more conservative and sympathetic to propertied classes. This divided national legislature would be further balanced by an independent executive branch whose chief magistrate would have a term of four years.

The most complex problem that the delegates faced involved the process by which this president should be elected. Most delegates originally favored his election by Congress, but that course became untenable when the separation of powers had been established as the major principle guiding the organization of the new government. Direct popular election was also rejected for several reasons. Some delegates vigorously expressed their fear and distrust of the people's capacity to make such an important decision. Others objected to direct election for the advantage it would give the larger states. Some delegates believed that the insularity of the general population would prevent the election of a truly national figure and result in native sons receiving most of the votes—still another advantage for the larger states. Implicit in this last argument was the inability of the Framers to imagine national political parties developing in response to the creation of national offices.

Ironically, the system finally established for the selection of the president, the electoral college, ultimately proved of great importance in shaping national party organization. Each state was to select electors (equal in number to the total of its representatives and senators) by any method that its legislature chose to adopt. These electors would then vote for two persons, at least one of whom could not be an inhabitant of the elector's state. The person receiving a majority of the votes would become president. If no one received a majority, the House of

Representatives (voting by states) would select the president from the five candidates with the largest number of votes. The candidate with the second largest number of votes would become vice-president.

This ingenious compromise was designed to make the presidency independent of Congress; to balance the interests of the large and small states, by incorporating some consideration of population in allocating electors while mandating equal state voting power in the contingent election in the House of Representatives; to appease states' rights advocates, by reserving to the state legislatures the power to determine how the electors should be chosen; to provide a limited element of popular participation while assuring that the election itself would be by men of special "information and discernment," as Alexander Hamilton described the electors; and to minimize the possibility of faction or intrigue. This method of election also literally created the position of vice-president in order to ensure that electors did not throw away their second vote on improbable candidates and thereby again threaten the influence of the smaller states. As convention delegate Hugh Williamson of North Carolina later declared, "such an officer as vice-president was not wanted. He was introduced only for the sake of a valuable mode of election which required two to be chosen at the same time."

Despite the ingenuity of the Framers, however, the electoral college was unrealistic and dangerously flawed, and the early elections shattered the complex plan. The provision leaving the decision on the method of selecting electors to the various state legislatures proved to be one source of great difficulty. The convention had not even debated the possibilities—whether the legislatures would choose the electors themselves, have them chosen by popular vote in districts, or mandate statewide popular vote on general tickets. As factional and partisan conflict developed in the 1790s, politicians in every state realized that variations in electoral procedure could influence the election's outcome. Initially, most states selected electors by the legislature. In 1792, for example, in nine of fifteen states the legislature chose the electors, three states chose electors by popular vote using the district system, and only Pennsylvania, Vermont, and New Hampshire employed the general-ticket system with popular election. But the partisan manipulation of such arrangements became a common feature in each presidential election. For the election of 1800, for instance, six of sixteen states changed their laws for selecting electors in order to advance the interests of the dominant party. Massachusetts was notorious in this practice, changing its mode of election according to the partisan calculations of its legislators in seven consecutive presidential elections, adopting legislative choice of electors on the eve of the elections of 1800, 1808, and 1816, and establishing varying forms of the district system for 1804, 1812, and 1820.

The trend in the partisan manipulation of selection modes was for states to maximize their political influence by consolidating the entire electoral vote of the state, either through having the legislature appoint the electors or through the adoption of a general-ticket system. Simultaneously, the belief became common that the elector should not express his individual preference but should vote according to his party's dictates. Most partisan leaders favored legislative choice because it guaranteed that the dominant party would appoint and control all of the state's electors. The general-ticket system also produced a winner-take-all result that commended this arrangement to party leaders as well. Certainly there was a close relationship between these two electoral modes and the rise of political parties. As Richard P. McCormick (1982) has noted, "parties found such modes most adaptable to their purposes, and such modes, in turn, were dependent on parties." The importance of state elections for controlling legislative decisions as to the mode of choosing electors encouraged the development of partisan organization on the state and local level, so that political parties became much less "factions" or national "parties of notables" centered about individuals like Jefferson or Hamilton. And the adoption of the general ticket, in particular, stimulated far more than did the district system the development of statewide political organizations. Thus the evolution of electoral rules and the course of political parties were interactive.

Gradually, the general-ticket system came to prevail. It retained the partisan winner-take-all feature of legislative choice while responding to the growing demand for increased popular participation in politics. The number of states employing this system increased from only two in 1800 to twelve by 1824; six more adopted it by 1828; and by 1836 the only holdout remaining was South Carolina, which retained legislative choice until the Civil War. This acceptance of the general-ticket system profoundly shaped American politics. Its ultimate significance is that the president is elected not by a national electorate but by the electorates of the several states, and this procedure ensures that presidents can be elected by a minority of the popular vote. Assigning the entire electoral vote of a state to the candidate with the largest popular vote in that state means that the minority of the state's voters are effectively disenfranchised. As Senator Thomas Hart Benton of Missouri noted in 1824, "To lose their votes is the fate of all minorities, and it is their duty to submit; but this is not a case of votes lost, but of votes taken away, added to those of the majority, and given to a person to whom the minority is opposed." It is this electoral process that largely explains the election of fifteen presidents with a minority of the popular votes since 1824. The Constitution's failure to apportion electors strictly according to population or to the vote cast is a second reason why a majority in the electoral college is not always secured by the candidate receiving a majority or even a plurality of the popular vote. Woodrow Wilson in 1912, for example, gained more than 80 percent of the electoral vote with less than 42 percent of the popular vote.

The election of one of these minority presidents was also made possible by the lack of procedures for settling contests in the counting of electoral votes and resulted in the last occasion when the election of a president devolved upon Congress. In 1876, Democratic candidate Samuel Tilden won a popular majority, but disputed returns from four states left him one vote short of a majority in the electoral college; his Republican opponent, Rutherford Hayes, needed all of the disputed electoral votes. Congress had to determine which of the double sets of returns should be accepted but had no established procedure to guide its deliberations. To resolve the predicament Congress adopted the extraordinary expedient of creating an electoral commission to consider the disputed returns. The electoral commission consisted of fifteen members, five each from the Senate, the House, and the Supreme Court; eight members were Republican and seven Democratic. Acting on the premise that presidential electors are state, not federal, officials, the commission accepted the returns as certified by the states despite obvious irregularities. On strict party lines, the commission awarded all of the disputed electoral votes to Hayes, giving him the presidency by one electoral vote despite Tilden's popular majority.

To avoid such dangerous situations in the future, Congress in 1887 passed the Electoral Count Act, which made each state responsible for determining which electors were legally chosen and required Congress to accept the returns as certified by the states. For Congress to reject an electoral vote, a concurrent majority of both houses was required. Congress implemented this law only once, in 1969, when it considered the vote cast for George Wallace by a North Carolina Republican elector pledged to Richard Nixon. Neither house, however, voted to sustain the protest.

Despite such electoral crises, the formal structure and procedure of the electoral college have remained largely unchanged, although there have been nearly constant attempts to reform this system. Most have been directed against the general-ticket mode of election. In the early nineteenth century scores of constitutional amendments were proposed to establish a uniform and equitable method of election. On four occasions, proposed amendments to establish the more democratic district system of choosing electors received the required two-thirds vote in the Senate, only to fail in the House in the face of opposition from such large states as Virginia and Pennsylvania, reluctant to lose the disproportionate power they enjoyed through the general-ticket mode. The absence of uniformity on the district plan virtually compelled uniformity on the general ticket, for noncompliant states would lose their political influence. Thus, as Lucius Wilmerding has noted, the question of reform was decided on the basis of state power and political forces rather than national principle. Another plan, to divide each state's electoral votes among the candidates in proportion to their popular votes, has attracted support since the 1870s, when twenty proportional-system amendments were proposed. In 1950, the Senate passed one such amendment, its first endorsement in 130 years of a constitutional revision in the electoral college, but the House rejected the measure. After being an object of public controversy in the 1950s and 1960s, the proportional plan faded as a significant alternative. More recently, there has been support for the direct popular election of the president, with no intermediate electors at all. More than 100 amendments have been proposed in Congress since 1816 to adopt direct election. None of them made much progress because of the common belief that such an amendment would never be ratified by the states, for the majority of them would lose some of the influence provided by the prevailing electoral college apportionment. But beginning in the 1960s pressure developed for direct election, and in 1969 the House approved a direct-vote amendment. A filibuster prevented Senate action, and in 1979 the Senate voted down the proposal, despite support for it from President Jimmy Carter.

Despite these continued rebuffs to significant reform, there was one earlier change in the format of the electoral college to correct what Hamilton termed the "defect in the Constitution." This was the requirement that each elector vote for two persons without differentiating between his choice for president and his choice for vice-president. But the particulars of the very first election guaranteed that electors had definite preferences in mind. As Neal Peirce and Lawrence Longley note, "no one thought of Washington as a possible vice-president, and no one at this point (except perhaps Adams himself) thought of Adams as a candidate for president." But if all the electors had voted for both Washington and Adams, the two would have received the same electoral vote. Even worse was the possibility that through some quirk there might not be complete unanimity on Washington. Then, as Hamilton concluded in horror, "the man intended for Vice-President may in fact turn up President." To prevent such an outcome, Hamilton urged some electors to withhold their votes from Adams, a course that led to lasting hostility between the two Federalist leaders. When Washington retired, and with the rise of political parties, a third unexpected consequence of the dual-vote system became apparent. The possibility emerged that if the winning party diverted some of its electoral votes from its vice-presidential candidate in order to prevent a tie in the electoral college, the opposing party's presidential candidate might be elected vice-president. Indeed, this is precisely what happened in 1796, with the Federalist Adams elected president and the Republican Jefferson chosen his vice-president.

After the 1796 election, several Federalists proposed constitutional amendments requiring distinct votes for president and vice-president, but secured no effective action. In 1800, a major governmental crisis arose from the dual-vote provision of the Constitution. The two Republican candidates, Jefferson, again clearly intended for the presidency, and Aaron Burr, explicitly nominated for the vice-presidency, received the unified support of their majority party's electors and thus tied in the electoral college, causing the election to be thrown into the House of Representatives, which the Federalists controlled. Only with difficulty—and great Federalist reluctance—were the rules not used to defeat the known intent of the electors and did Jefferson emerge as president. The rise of the party system had completely changed the situation from what the Framers had desired. Before the next presidential election, Congress passed a constitutional amendment requiring electors to vote separately for president and vice-president. The states promptly ratified the measure in 1804. In a constitutional sense, this Twelfth Amendment—like the adoption of the general ticket for presidential electors—represented the adaptation of the electoral process to the needs of political parties.

In other ways, too, the unexpected rise of political parties altered the format of presidential elections as envisaged by the Framers of the Constitution. To prevent the confusion over candidates, party strategy, and electoral-vote divisions that had accompanied the election of 1796, both Federalists and Republicans held congressional caucuses in 1800 and nominated candidates for president and vice-president. A significant innovation in the electoral process, these congressional caucuses established the procedure for nominating presidential candidates that survived until the 1820s. By making partisan nominations, moreover, the caucuses clearly sought to direct the electors rather than leaving them to their own discretion, thereby destroying the founding fathers' vision of the disinterested elector. Henceforth the electors were scarcely more than the tools of the political parties that had already determined the nominees. Moreover, the practical effect of the caucuses was to place the nomination of the president exactly where the constitutional convention had resolved not to place it—in Congress.

Although denounced as "King Caucus," the congressional nominating caucus was never a particularly strong institution and served mainly to articulate the consensus already existing among Republicans as to their logical candidates. When that consensus disappeared, so did the caucus. As an institution, it lacked popular support, failed to represent states that had no Republican congressmen, ignored influential state party leaders, and ultimately could not even compel the participation of the eligible congressmen. The final caucus was held in 1824, and its nomination of William H. Crawford perhaps more injured than advanced his candidacy. In 1822 and 1823 various state legislatures had already "nominated" John Quincy Adams and Andrew Jackson. Their supporters described these nominations as more expressive of popular sentiment than the decision of the congressional caucus. Then in 1828 the delegate convention began to replace even these legislative caucuses as a state-level device to make nominations. Such conventions were a practical necessity as much as a democratic development, for Jacksonians in New England (and Adams' supporters in the South and West) were so little represented in legislatures that they had to create an alternative means of expressing their candidate preferences. Partisan ambitions had thus again led to an important innovation in electoral procedures.

For similar reasons, the national nominating convention developed. The Anti-Masons held the first national party convention in 1831. Because their support was limited to only a few states, they could not depend upon state-sponsored nominations, and they sought as well the added visibility that they thought a national convention would provide. The National Republicans and the Jacksonian Democrats soon followed suit, adopting the practice of holding national conventions primarily to reconcile the various groups that only gradually were coalescing into modern parties. Within a decade, national nominating conventions had become an essential part of a presidential electoral process that reflected partisan influences more than constitutional intentions. As Richard P. McCormick (1982) has written: "Its basic rules were that pledged electors would be chosen by popular vote on general tickets, that the contest would be waged by two major political parties, that the selection of candidates would be arranged by national conventions, that campaigns would be designed to arouse committed partisans, that candidates would play decidedly subordinate roles. . . . Every element . . . was at variance with the republican ideology that had shaped the actions of the Framers when they contrived their process of presidential selection."

Although the Constitution carefully defined the electoral process for choosing the president, it devoted far less attention to the election of other federal officeholders. Article I stated simply that representatives should be popularly elected, by voters qualified to vote for members of the "most numerous Branch of the State Legislature," and that senators should be chosen by the state legislatures. This difference in constituencies reflected the Framers' concern for a balanced government, as did their decision to leave to the individual states the important question of suffrage requirements. All other aspects of the electoral process also were left up to the individual states: "The Times, Places, and Manner of holding Elections for Senators and Representatives, shall be prescribed in each State by the Legislature thereof; but the Congress may at any time by Law make or alter such Regulations. . . ." And of course states altogether determined electoral procedures for state offices.

One particular matter that would significantly shape the political system was initially of little concern. As much as the method of electing the president operated to establish the two-party system, the constitutional requirement of an electoral majority functioning to restrict practical competition to two contestants, so too did the system of representation underlying legislative elections, both state and national. The Constitution apportioned representatives to states on the basis of population but ignored the question of intrastate allocation of representatives. As they did for their own legislatures, states chose to elect representatives by geographical districts. Representation on a territorial or geographical basis reflected, among other things, the process by which the American colonies had been settled and by which representation was gradually extended to new areas. In New England, for example, representation in the colonial and then state legislatures was based on the town, while most other states based representation on the county. Indeed, most early state governments stressed geographical diffusion of representation more than representation proportional to population and sometimes provided for equal representation by political subdivisions regardless of population. This frequently provoked discontent but was in a systematic way perhaps less important than the unappreciated fact that elections were on the basis on single-member legislative districts in which the plurality formula determined the results.

Under such a system, as E.E. Schattschneider has observed, the electoral success of parties is determined not just by the total vote cast for their candidates but especially by the geographical distribution of their voting strength. Partisan representation in legislatures proportionate to the popular vote distribution would occur in a single-member district system only if the voting strength of all the parties were in every case concentrated perfectly by districts. If the vote of each party were, however, distributed uniformly throughout the state, the strongest party would win all the legislative seats. Thus even a minor change in the geographical distribution of the party vote in an election held under the single-member district system can produce great variations in electoral outcomes. This reality led to the development of gerrymandering, a partisan effort to manipulate artificially the geographical distribution of various constituencies in order to maximize representation out of proportion to popular vote.

The single-member district system, as compared to a system of proportional representation characteristic of most European governments, has two further effects. It exaggerates the representation of the winning party relative to its popular vote, and the greater the victory the more the exaggeration. In 1932, for example, the Democrats received 57 percent of the popular vote but 72 percent of the House seats and 89 percent of the votes in the electoral college, which, because of the general ticket, is an elective functional equivalent of a legislature based on single-member districts. Second, the single-member district system has a bipolarizing effect on parties. Since only one candidate can win in each district, this electoral form encourages coalitions and discourages multiple parties. It discriminates against smaller parties (unless their voting strength is geographically concentrated, like that of the Populists of the 1890s) to the point of their virtual elimination. By encouraging the tendency for the defeated major party to secure and retain a monopoly of the opposition, however, this electoral mode guarantees its perpetuation and thus establishes the two-party system, one of the most prominent and firmly established features of American politics.

There has been little effective variation from this basic system of representation. Some states did elect their representatives at large in early years, but in 1842 Congress mandated the system of single-member districts for the whole country. A rare attempt to secure representation of parties in accordance with their proportional strength within a state's electorate occurred in 1870, when Illinois adopted a system of cumulative voting for the election of members of its lower house. They are elected in three-member districts, and each voter possesses three transferable votes, which can be cast for separate candidates or cumulated on one or two. In practice, the stronger major party in each district generally nominates only two candidates and the weaker major party one, virtually assuring the election of all nominees. Illinois's system of cumulative voting thus maintains the two-party tendency of the district system but modifies that system's characteristic majority-party dominance.

State Regulation of Election Procedures

The states created greater variety in the electoral processes reflecting the "Times, Places, and Manner of holding Elections." Initially, the times of holding elections differed considerably. In the colonial period, elections were generally called at the discretion of the governor and were held both infrequently and irregularly. In reaction to this practice, the new state constitutions provided for regular and frequent elections of state officials, which required in turn the establishment of specific rather than arbitrary times for holding elections. But such times varied by states and, sometimes, by office within individual states, often reflecting local customs and climate. Most northern states scheduled their state elections for spring. Massachusetts, for instance, set the first Monday in April for electing the governor and May for electing representatives. Middle Atlantic states like Maryland, Delaware, and Pennsylvania staged their contests at different times in the early fall; while southern states like South Carolina and Georgia chose November or December. Many states held annual or even semiannual elections for state officials, and even most upper houses had relatively short terms of two to three years.

The period for the actual balloting also varied considerably. The New England states, where people voted on a township basis, restricted balloting to one day. In North Carolina and South Carolina, however, polls generally were open two days; New York allowed up to five days at the discretion of the presiding officials. New Jersey initially failed to specify any particular period, and during the first congressional election partisans kept the ballot box open for three weeks in some counties and for almost ten weeks in Essex County. Nor was there much consistency concerning the precise hours for the polls to be open on election days. Frequently, the decision was left to the whim of local election officials, but some states did establish regulations. Georgia, for instance, required the polls to remain open from 9:00 A.M. to 6:00 P.M., while New York mandated a period from one hour after sunrise until sunset. Some states adopted different rules for different communities or varied them with the nature of the election. Pennsylvania, for example, allowed polls in Philadelphia to remain open an additional hour in order that workingmen might be able to vote.

The development of temporal uniformity in holding elections was itself an irregular process, reflecting the authority of the different states, not the national government, over some of the particulars. One important early innovation was the increased number of polling places. In the colonial period, voters outside New England had to travel to the county seat to vote. Beginning in the late eighteenth century, however, many state governments began to create new voting districts, usually at the township level, and new polling places. In addition to the county courthouse, now taverns, mills, and churches were used as polling places, greatly facilitating access to the ballot box and reducing the necessity for holding elections over a span of several days to accommodate voters coming from long distances. Well into the nineteenth century, however, New York and several other states still held elections over periods of up to three days. Although election districts coincident with townships long proved satisfactory in rural areas, the larger population in urban areas soon led to the use of smaller geographical areas such as wards. But by the mid-nineteenth century even wards contained far too many voters to serve as convenient election districts, and states gradually developed regulations for establishing election districts, usually by specifying the maximum number of voters permitted at any one poll.

Polling hours also became more regularized, but with frequent fluctuations as partisan legislatures manipulated statutes in accordance with expected voter behavior. "Sunset laws" closing the polls at sunset were favorite devices of Whigs and Republicans to disenfranchise workingmen, according to Democrats, or to enable employers to control the ballots of the working class by having employees vote under supervision of plant foremen. New Jersey saw a constant struggle over sunset laws. The Republicans enacted such a law in 1866 to reduce the opportunities for the largely Democratic working class to vote; the Democrats repealed the law in 1868. Several years later the legislature, again under Republican control, enacted another sunset law only to have the Democrats repeal it again the following year. By the mid-twentieth century, most states had enacted legislation requiring employers to give their workers time off for voting, often without deductions from wages, and polling hours were generally long enough to enable people to vote before or after work.

Gradually, also, there was some consolidation of election days. Some of this stemmed from federal actions to which states responded. In 1792, Congress designated the first Wednesday in December as the day when electors were to vote for president and stipulated that they be chosen within thirty-four days of that date. In response, the states named a number of different days in November to choose electors: fourteen states selected the first Monday, two the first Tuesday, two the second Monday, two the second Tuesday, two the Friday nearest 1 November, one state the Tuesday after the first Monday. As long as most states appointed electors through their legislatures this diversity was no major problem, but the increasing popular election of electors led to difficulties. With elections scheduled on different days in different states, illegal voting by repeaters became common, and in 1840 and 1844 both parties organized gangs of voters who went from state to state. To reduce such fraud, Congress in 1845 established the date for electing electors as the first Tuesday after the first Monday in November for all states. Similarly, in 1872, Congress adopted the same date for the election of representatives unless a state's constitution prescribed a different day. To lessen confusion and expense, the states progressively adopted that date for election of state officials as well. Thus many of the "October states," the early elections of which had attracted great attention as possible indicators of the November federal results, consolidated their election days, with Iowa taking the step in 1878, Indiana in 1880, and Ohio in 1885. Maine, however, persisted in its September elections until 1960. Other states lacked complete consonance between state and federal elections because they continued to hold annual elections. Maine adopted biennial elections in 1879 and Wisconsin in 1882; but Massachusetts, Connecticut, and other states repeatedly rejected such proposals. Finally, in 1920, Massachusetts changed its gubernatorial election from every year to every other year and then, in 1966, to every four years, joining the other states in a national trend toward longer terms for officials.

Only rarely were local elections consolidated with federal ones, and there was often a concerted effort to keep the two separate. Partisan motives frequently underlay the decision for either alternative. In New Jersey, for instance, the 1889 Democratic legislature prohibited scheduling municipal elections on general election day. While allegedly designed to separate local from state and national issues, this measure increased the influence of the Democratic "machine vote" in the cities. When the Republicans gained power, they sought to dominate local contests with the greater strength that they achieved on national issues by consolidating municipal and general elections in all cities in 1901 and then, in 1905, in all townships and villages. South Dakota Republicans, too, used this tactic to weaken their Populist opponents, requiring in 1901 that local elections coincide with general elections, the larger Republican turnouts of which were expected to overwhelm dissidents even on issues of intense interest to certain communities. The Populists denounced this law as "denying the minority in each county from any representation whatever." Generally, the push for Progressive municipal reform, however, involved the separation of municipal from state and national elections and an attempt to replace partisanship with the "business principles" of "good government." Such a movement was no less biased than those promoting partisan goals, for it sought to advance the self-interested objectives of its members through the destruction of the "machine" as an agency of mass mobilization.

Though state control of the times and places of elections was thus of both partisan and public concern, the third prescribed area of state authority over electoral processes has been of most importance, "the Manner of holding Elections." This subject involved a number of apparently mundane matters, such as choosing election officials, managing the polls, identifying qualified voters, overseeing the method of voting, and counting the ballots; but the development of election machinery and the rules of election administration have in important ways both reflected and shaped American politics.

In designating election officials to oversee the polls, states originally followed a variety of practices. In New England, the town selectmen generally served as election officials; in South Carolina, the parish church wardens presided, but in most southern states the sheriff remained in control. New York and other states replaced sheriffs with a group of local judges and inspectors to conduct elections. In some cases, these officials were elected by, and from among, the voters assembled as the polls opened; in other instances, such township officials as assessor, commissioner of tax appeals, and town clerk served, *ex officio,* as election officials as well. In either case conflict and partisanship characterized the conduct of elections, for invariably these men were all members of the political party dominant locally. They were required impartially to judge the qualifications of voters, maintain order at the polls, count the ballots, and prepare the election certificates, but frequently partisan sentiments influenced their actions. The behavior of such officials was a frequent source of controversy, particularly their refusal to prevent illegal voting by members of their own party.

Quite apart from the partisan manipulation of election machinery, there were other problems as well. Even if the election officials were conscientious, they had no satisfactory procedure for determining who met the various age, residence, property, citizenship, and other requirements for suffrage. Originally there had been little felt need for such a system: communities were relatively small, stable, and homogeneous, and election officials could literally recognize those eligible to vote. Beginning with Massachusetts in 1800, however, states gradually began to enact laws to register voters and thereby provide a list of qualified voters in election districts. These initial efforts to establish registration systems focused on urban areas, where the smaller scale of community life had dissolved; and they reflected the growing concern about urbanization, immigration, and the development of urban political machines and election frauds (rural Americans stoutly resisted the expense and inconvenience of—and denied the necessity for—such safeguards in their own areas). Such registration systems also received a partisan impetus from those who believed that the votes of the growing urban, ethnic electorate were cast for their opponents. As early as the 1830s, Whigs managed to enact registry laws in several eastern states, both to prevent repeating and to restrict balloting by social groups that voted Democratic. Registration based on a tax, for instance, served to reduce voter turnout in Philadelphia, New York City, and Rhode Island. Such laws, not surprisingly, were attacked as partisan, antiurban, and antipoor. Such attributes were so flagrant in New York's 1840 law that it was repealed in 1842, and few states outside New England made a serious effort to enact registration laws.

Beginning in the 1860s, however, interest in adopting voter registration requirements developed significantly. Some of the registry laws then enacted, in Maryland and Missouri, for example, represented efforts by the temporarily dominant Republicans to reinforce their ascendancy over the state government; others, such as that passed by Illinois in 1865, were legislative responses to widespread election fraud in major cities. Frequently, the partisan motive was indistinguishable from the announced hostility to election fraud and urban social evils. In Ohio, for instance, the Republican-controlled 1877 legislature reacted to alleged ballot-box stuffing by Cincinnati Democrats by passing a registry law with a lengthy residence requirement to minimize the "floating" vote. Democrats demanded the repeal of the registry law because it was "burdensome and expensive, and discriminates unjustly against the poorer class of voters," the mobile working-class population that, not incidentally, constituted a major Democratic constituency.

By 1880, most states had enacted some form of registration law. There were, however, important exceptions. The key state of Indiana, for instance, did not have a valid registration law until 1911, and a number of state courts struck down registration laws as prescribing suffrage qualifications beyond those constitutionally established. The registration laws that were adopted in the Gilded Age, moreover, were invariably weak and ineffectual. They generally provided for nonpersonal registration. That is, the burden of establishing eligibility to vote was not imposed on the individual voter but was assumed by election officials, usually chosen on a partisan basis, or by the political parties themselves. New Jersey even permitted any legal voter to present names for the registry by affidavit. This meant, as Richard P. McCormick (1953) has observed, "that local party workers could save their constituents—real or imaginary—the trouble and inconvenience of appearing before the [election] board in person." Registries so compiled were no better than general guides to voter eligibility, and their utility was further weakened by the failure of many registry laws even to restrict voting to those registered. Instead there were provisions to enable unregistered persons to vote if they "swore in" their ballot by avowing their eligibility on election day. The registration laws of this period, then, had little immediate effect and were more important as an innovation that would later be refined into a significant procedural factor shaping American politics.

Modes of Voting

One of the most important electoral processes involved the actual mode of voting. During the colonial and early national periods, voting was usually conducted openly and orally. After swearing to his qualifications, the voter would call out the names of the candidates he preferred and a clerk would record his preferences against his name on the public poll books. The use of ballots had not been altogether unknown in the colonial period, and beginning with the new state constitutions of the 1770s there was a shift from oral voting to paper ballots. But Virginia and Maryland retained *viva voce* (oral) voting, and this mode was subsequently adopted by additional states, including Kentucky, Illinois, Missouri, Arkansas, Texas, and Oregon.

Certainly there was little firm commitment to the principal of using ballots, and their adoption did not definitively end support for the traditional voting form of *viva voce;* electoral "reform" was rarely linear, for nearly all electoral processes had recognizably dissimilar effects on different parties and constituencies. In Connecticut in 1801, for example, the Federalist legislature passed the so-called Stand Up Law, which abolished the ballot and required voters to stand up when publicly polled. Designed to intimidate Republican voters, this system of open voting favored the reelection of the traditional elite. Illinois similarly shifted its mode of voting, adopting *viva voce* voting in 1818, rejecting it in 1819, restoring it in 1821 only to abandon it in 1823, and then using it again from 1829 until 1848.

To some extent, the spread of *viva voce* voting derived from the practice of western states' copying the constitutional provisions of older states. Virginia had retained the English practice of *viva voce* voting, and its example influenced Kentucky. The Illinois constitution of 1818 took its voting clause directly from Kentucky's, as did Missouri, which then was copied by Arkansas. And in drawing up its constitution, Oregon relied on Missouri and Kentucky. The geographical pattern of this diffusion also helps explain the ultimate extinction of *viva voce* voting. Virginia (and West Virginia), Arkansas, and Missouri all discontinued *viva voce* voting during the period of the Civil War and Reconstruction, as Radicals feared that traditional elites would be able to control the electorate— and especially the newly enfranchised freedmen—under open voting. Kentucky, which was unaffected by Reconstruction, retained *viva voce* voting until 1891, when it was reluctantly abandoned. Ironically, Oregon continued to employ *viva voce* voting during the Civil War period precisely to ensure loyalty to the Union and did not discontinue it until 1872, after Congress had mandated the use of ballots for all congressional elections.

The replacement of *viva voce* voting with the ballot, however, did not provide secrecy for the voter. Although it had often been assumed that voters would prepare their own individual ballots in the privacy of their homes, from the beginning local political organizations prepared uniform ballots prior to the election and distributed them to their followers at the polls. To restrict such a practice, several states required that ballots be written rather than printed. But party leaders promptly employed clerks to write out the many ballots necessary for distribution to their partisans. Eventually, states recognized that the rise of political parties had frustrated any expectations of an independent electorate and repealed such laws. And some states, beginning with Maine in 1831, began to enact laws defining the paper and ink to be used in preparing printed ballots.

But state ballot laws generally specified only that ballots be paper ones and otherwise made no provisions for their shape, size, or color or for their distribution at the polls. Certainly there were no legal provisions to ensure secrecy. Perhaps only the short-lived Massachusetts ballot law of 1851 attempted to secure this end. Enacted by a coalition of Democrats and Free Soilers, it required that ballots be cast in sealed envelopes; the Whigs repealed this measure in 1853. Otherwise, states adopted the ballot in place of *viva voce* voting, as James Bryce remarked in 1888, "not so much as a device for preventing bribery or intimidation, but rather as the quickest and easiest mode of taking the votes of a multitude. Secrecy has not been specially aimed at, and in point of fact is not generally secured."

In the absence of official machinery and legal regulations, the task of preparing and distributing ballots was assumed by political parties. The natural consequence was the party ticket, a strip of paper, usually headed by a party symbol, on which were printed the names of the candidates of only the party that issued it. Anxious to distinguish their followers and maintain their support, party managers differentiated their tickets from those of other parties by size, color, or other characteristics. As late as 1879 only two states had legislation specifying the size of the ballot, so that the tickets of different parties often varied widely in size, and the voter's use of a ballot easily identified his choice of party as well. Parties also made their tickets distinctive by printing them on variously colored paper. In Boston's elections in 1878 the Republicans issued a ticket with red stripes on it, while their opponents used tickets of different colors for each precinct. Even when some states finally specified that ballots be black and white, Connecticut Democrats in 1882 adopted black ballots with white ink in order to recognize those who voted their party ticket. Even tickets of similar shape, size, and color were differentiated by the application of sharp perfumes, a common Tammany practice in New York City. California made the most thorough effort to ensure uniformity in ballots, but even there party managers developed "the isinglass ticket," made of translucent paper to reveal the nature of the vote cast.

The distribution and use of such party tickets further prevented secrecy while facilitating voter intimidation and election fraud. The tickets were distributed or "peddled" to the party's supporters by party workers known variously as peddlers, hawkers, and bummers, who stationed themselves near the polls and pressed their tickets on prospective voters. Indeed, as one Indiana editor wrote in 1883, voters were "compelled to be piloted up to the polls by 'workers.' " These contending hawkers, each trying to force his ticket upon the voter, contributed greatly to the tumult and chaos surrounding the polls on election day. At times workers of one party completely thronged the polls and allowed only their own partisans to approach the ballot box, driving from the vicinity the hawkers of the other party and, with them, the possibility of votes for that party. Receiving the party tickets in such an atmosphere, the voter had little or no time to examine his ballot before being hustled to the ballot box, where he deposited it in view of all interested observers. Certainly he had little opportunity to alter the ballot and vote a split ticket by crossing out the name of an unacceptable candidate and substituting that of a more agreeable one in his place.

Partisan control of ballots also permitted the distribution of "bogus ballots," tickets headed with the insignia of one party but listing the candidates of another. Bogus ballots were regularly issued by both major parties; in the 1882 Kansas gubernatorial election the Democrats circulated five different bogus tickets to deceive Republican voters and help elect the state's first Democratic governor. All parties took elaborate precautions against the possibility of counterfeit tickets and constantly cautioned their partisans to "be careful of spurious tickets next Tuesday and don't be hoodwinked and deceived." Party organizations sometimes deceived their own followers by the practice of "knifing" or "trading"; this also reflected party control over the printing and distribution of ballots. As

Abram C. Bernheim observed of New York City's political wars in 1889, "If these organizations fail to print a candidate's name on the ballot, or substitute, in pursuance of a bargain, the name of his party opponent on the regular party ticket; or if, after having printed, they conclude not to distribute any or all of the ballots; or if in the distribution they replace, in the party bunch, one of the party tickets with the corresponding ballot of another organization—greater and more wide-reaching frauds are accomplished than can be attained by more directly corrupt practices."

Such arrangements naturally placed a heavy responsibility for honest elections on the election officials. These officials were generally partisan officeholders who assumed their election duties *ex officio* or were appointed by, and therefore represented, the party in local ascendancy. They had little incentive to carefully canvass the ballots of their own opponents, and, as a consequence, "some of the worst frauds are committed," as one federal official noted, "with the assistance or connivance of the officers of election." The Cook County Grand Jury, for instance, found that only 7 of 171 Chicago precincts did not have violations of the election law in 1884 and concluded that "fraud was attempted or committed at every step as the election progressed; fraud at the registration, fraud at the reception and counting of ballots, and fraud at the final canvass of returns." But election laws generally provided slight obstacles to such partisanship, authorizing each party to have challengers, witnesses, or windowmen at each polling place to protect their voters and their ballots; not until the mid-1880s, or even later in some states, were bipartisan election officials and poll supervisors generally required. As a consequence, all too often the number of votes reported from each precinct, as San Francisco boss Abraham Ruef admitted, was limited "only by the modesty of the election officials." And a compliment paid an official by a ward boss was that "he's a handy man behind the ballot box."

The Federal Elections Law

Against such pervasive fraud there developed demands for electoral reform. One important result was the passage of the Federal Elections Law in 1871. Though historians have traditionally assigned the law to Reconstruction legislation directed against southern suppression of black suffrage, it developed primarily in response to election fraud in New York City and was directed at northern cities. In effect for almost a quarter century, the law constituted the largest federal attempt to regulate elections. This singular federal intervention occurred because state and local laws were inadequate and poorly enforced. The lack of rigorous registration and ballot laws was aggravated by the mass immigration and high geographic mobility of the late nineteenth century, and the general absence of state provisions for bipartisan public election officials until the 1880s cast a cloud of uncertainty over the validity of the whole electoral process.

The Federal Elections Law was designed not to ensure the right of suffrage but to guarantee that only eligible voters exercised the franchise. It prohibited impersonation, repeating, intimidation, and bribery of voters in congressional elections or registrations therefor, and it authorized the appointment of federal officials to enforce such prohibitions. The responsibility for conducting elections remained with state officials, but they were required to perform their duties completely and equitably. This federal regulation applied originally only to cities of 20,000 or more inhabitants and could be invoked by petition of two citizens expressing a fear of pending election fraud. The federal circuit court then appointed two federal supervisors, of different parties, for each election district. These supervisors were empowered to challenge suspected persons at registration or voting, inspect the voting process, count the ballots, and issue election certificates. Moreover, the U.S. marshal was authorized to appoint as many deputy marshals as he believed necessary to assist the supervisors in their duties, maintain order at the polls, and prevent fraudulent voting or fraudulent conduct by state election officials. The marshal, himself a partisan appointment, was not required to select deputies from both political parties and rarely did so.

This partisan aspect provoked considerable opposition to the legislation generally. Indeed, Democratic congressmen viewed the Federal Elections Law as a scheme to guarantee Republican control of New York, "the very climax of Radical attempts to obtain complete control of the United States," according to one. Not surprisingly, passage of the Federal Elections Law in Congress was strictly on a partisan basis. The administration of the law did little to dispel the cloud of partisanship. One partisan use of the legislation was evident in the striking disparities in the use of deputies and supervisors. Anyone could request the appointment of supervisors, and usually it was the minority party locally that did so, in the hope that having bipartisan supervisors would result in fair elections. In most northern cities this meant the Republican party; but where local politics and police were under Republican control, as in Philadelphia, it was the Democratic party that petitioned for the appointment of federal supervisors. But it was always Republicans who petitioned for deputy marshals, for they were to be chosen by the U.S. marshal, who as a federal appointee of the usually Republican president was a Republican regardless of local political tendencies. Thus, in Democratic cities, there were far more deputies used than in Republican areas, suggesting to some that the presence of armed federal election officials was intended to intimidate Democratic voters, particularly in certain ethnic neighborhoods, while their absence was intended to permit traditional pressure tactics by Republicans in areas they controlled. In 1892, for instance, federal expenditures for deputies were nearly six times as much in Democratic New York City as in Republican Philadelphia.

The cost of national supervision of elections indicated the scope and importance of this singular effort. Between 1871 and 1894 the federal government spent nearly $5 million, with the annual cost constantly increasing so that expenditures for both 1890 and 1892 surpassed that spent for the country as a whole during Reconstruction. Indeed, more deputy marshals were regularly used in a number of northern cities than were ever used anywhere in the South during the entire Reconstruction period. In 1876, for instance, 2,300 deputy marshals guarded the polls in New York City, another 700 in Brooklyn, and 1,200 in Baltimore. In 1892 nearly 8,000 were used in New York City. By 1892 the Federal Elections Law was operative in twenty-nine states. Many cities used it—fourteen cities in Massachusetts alone regularly invoking the legislation—but its application was concentrated in eight major cities: New York, Brooklyn, Jersey City, Philadelphia, Baltimore, Boston, Chicago, and San Francisco.

Republicans could at least maintain that the Federal Elections Law limited fraud. In *Ex parte Siebold* (1880), for instance, in upholding the constitutionality of the Federal Elections Law the Supreme Court sustained the conviction of Baltimore election judges for resisting the authority of federal supervisors who tried to stop them from stuffing the ballot box. Moreover, Republicans believed that the mere presence of federal deputies often averted possible vote fraud. The U.S. marshal in Chicago in 1882, for example, reported that his deputies "kept thousands of repeaters and illegal voters from the polls" and had to arrest only ten persons for actually violating election laws.

Democrats, however, charged the Federal Elections Law with actually encouraging fraud. Indeed, deputies were usually chosen from lists supplied by Republican party officials, and they often served on election day as Republican party workers, distributing Republican tickets at the polls that they were supposed to police. Some marshals even aided Republican repeaters in illegal voting and impersonation. At times the Republican marshals arrested local election officials who were Democrats and controlled the polls in their absence; at least once they arrested the Democratic federal supervisor himself. An 1880 congressional investigating committee concluded that the Federal Elections Law was administered in such a partisan fashion that, rather than protecting the ballot, it simply served to promote Republican interests.

From the date of its enactment, Democrats began a long campaign to repeal the law. Except for minor modifications, however, the Federal Elections Law remained intact, for the Republicans always controlled at least either the presidency or the Senate and were able to block Democratic efforts. In 1890, the Republicans unsuccessfully attempted to extend the law's provisions to all of the nation's congressional districts in the more famous Lodge Force bill, designed to protect black voting rights in the South. After the Democratic victories in the 1892 election, the Federal Elections Law was finally repealed two years later on a strict party vote. Thus its repeal as much as its enactment was a partisan development.

Ballot Reform

In the meantime, however, there had been important developments in the establishment of election procedures at the state level. The most significant of these was the movement for ballot reform. Three groups, all standing outside the normal two-party political system but with quite different motivations, led in this agitation: patrician Mugwumps, labor organizations, and radical political parties. Mugwump elements demanding ballot reform certainly were interested not in democratizing the political system, but the reverse. The Boston Brahmin Francis Parkman, for instance, already regretted the political consequences of entrusting the suffrage to "masses of imported ignorance and hereditary ineptitude" rather than restricting it to those with "hereditary traditions of self-government." Nor were they motivated by a desire to end voter intimidation. Indeed some of these self-designated members of the better element defended bribery and voter intimidation by employers as necessary to ensure that the "best men" controlled society. Their complaint, while couched in denunciations of election fraud, was directed against the party and its function as a mobilizer of popular will, undermining their traditional influence.

Radical agrarian and labor representatives, on the other hand, had different ends in view in similarly attacking election fraud, machine rule, and the existing electoral system. Not surprisingly, labor organizations particularly attacked intimidation of workers' voting by their employers, but the *Journal of United Labor* viewed the electoral process in as sweeping terms as any Mugwump: "Between the bribery of voters, the intimidation by employers, and the use of fraudulent ballots by corrupt politicians, to say nothing of the opportunities under present methods for a stuffing of the ballot by dishonest inspectors, . . . the will of the people is oftener outraged than respected." Greenbackers, Socialists, the Union Labor party, and others all criticized the system of balloting because of the costs and other burdens it imposed on small parties, thereby restricting their possible success and influence. The printing and distributing of ballots was expensive, eliminating many poor farmers and workers from seeking nomination and influence over public policy; the system also required a uniform organization across all election districts—something that few third parties had—if every voter were to have an opportunity to vote his principles. Led particularly by active single-tax organizations in many states, these groups advocated ballot reform as a way to secure legitimate and responsive republican government.

Ballot reformers promoted the Australian ballot. First adopted in Australia in 1856 and in Europe and Canada by the 1880s, this new voting system differed completely from the "party-ticket" system. In particular, reformers were attracted by three features of the Australian system. First, it provided an "official" ballot, prepared and distributed by public authorities; it therefore stripped parties of one of their most influential organizational functions. Theoretically, this feature also made it easier for independent organizations and candidates by minimizing their election costs, while it removed the parties' rationale for assessing their nominees and thus eliminated a major source of corrupt funds. Electoral corruption was also to be eliminated by a second characteristic of the Australian ballot: it was secret and therefore presumably discouraged vote buying. Finally, it was a consolidated or "blanket" ballot, listing all candidates instead of the candidates of only one party. This provision permitted more independent and split-ticket voting than was possible under the party-ticket system.

The popular demand for such a voting system became irresistible after the flagrantly corrupt presidential election of 1888, and by the end of 1889 ten states had passed Australian ballot laws; by 1892 only ten states had not passed an Australian ballot law, and they would shortly fall into line. Although most such state ballot systems established the basic secret, official, and blanket features, there was considerable variation in related details. One major decision involved specifying the particular format of the ballot itself. One basic format, initially adopted by Massachusetts in 1888, listed candidates in blocs according to the office sought, requiring the voter to sort through the various candidates to find his choice. Though partisan affiliations were indicated, this "office-bloc" ballot minimized partisanship and encouraged split-ticket voting. The second general format, pioneered by Indiana in 1889, grouped candidates by parties in parallel columns. In some states the ballot laws even placed emblems at the head of the columns to enable the voter to distinguish more easily the separate parties. Finally, lawmakers frequently added a device that facilitated straight-ticket voting: a party circle, when marked, constituted a vote for the entire party ticket. These developments represented legislative efforts to retain some of the familiar partisan features of the old ballot system while providing the secret and official characteristics of the new.

Certainly it is inaccurate to conclude, as some political scientists have, that such electoral reform ended the previous practice of manipulating the electoral framework for partisan purposes. Even though the Single Taxers, labor reformers, and Mugwumps led the movement for ballot reform, the actual laws were drawn up and enacted by Republican and Democratic legislators who had very different interests and perhaps a better understanding of the electorate and the whole political system.

In enacting the Australian system, to assure secrecy and an official ballot, lawmakers necessarily had to consider other subjects, such as the structure of the ballot, the question of who could be listed, the rules for registering nominees, and other questions that had heretofore been left up to the parties. In establishing these procedures, politicians often responded to political conditions and manipulated the rules to achieve partisan ends. Perhaps most important, election legislation now had to specify the procedures by which candidates could gain a place on the ballot. Generally, the law provided that a political party securing a certain percentage of the total vote in the preceding election could have its nominees listed on the official ballot for the electorate's consideration. North Dakota's 1891 law, for example, authorized printing the names of, and limiting straight-ticket voting privileges to, those parties that had received at least 5 percent of the total vote in the preceding election. This rule obviously bestowed benefits on the major parties that were not immediately available to the frequent but evanescent third parties of the period and raised obstacles to the formation of new or independent parties, just one of many developments not anticipated by some of the original advocates of the Australian ballot. In North Dakota, for instance, a Republican newspaper enjoyed the irony in 1892 that agrarian reformers "now find that the Australia system of voting which they asked for . . . is something of an obstruction to the launching of the new people's party, as it is not entitled to a place in the heading of the ticket."

A second method by which candidates could secure a place on the ballot was by petition of interested citizens. The number of petitioners required varied, not only among the different states but also according to the office sought. Many of the original laws mandated fairly small numbers for a nomination by petition but then frequently raised that number in order to limit voters' options and protect the regular parties. In New York, for instance, the legislature doubled the required number in 1891 and again in 1896. New York also stipulated a geographical distribution of petitioners, at least fifty from each county, placing a premium on uniform and systematic organization—precisely what independent candidates did not have. In 1897, Kansas quintupled the number of signatures required to gain a ballot position in order to keep "small bodies of reformers out of politics." Other states established not a fixed number but a percentage of the total voters as the basis for determining the number of signatures necessary to nominate by petition. Nevada's 1893 law, for example, specified 10 percent of the electorate, a level so high as to virtually prohibit this form of nomination. And finally, four states simply refused to allow candidates to be nominated by petition. Not surprisingly, then, did the *Nation* attack ballot reform in 1891 by pointing out that "under the old system" parties had had to pay for printing and distributing their ballots and had been unable to prevent the distribution of independent tickets, but that under the new system "party politicians can have their own ballots printed and distributed at public expense, while all independent ballots are practically prohibited from getting into the polling places."

However—or if—candidates qualified for the ballot, they still had to follow detailed regulations for filing their nomination papers. Generally, candidates for state offices were required to file their certificates of nomination with the secretary of state, and local candidates with their county clerks or auditors. Such papers usually had to be filed well in advance of the election, frequently merely to reduce the chance that disgruntled bolters from the regular party nomination would secure a place on the ballot. Nomination papers usually had to provide a variety of personal and political information about the candidate, his supporters, the nature of the nominating process, and other details. These regulations often proved burdensome to parties lacking professional officials or regular legal counsel. In 1892, for example, the Prohibition party failed to adhere fully to such regulations imposed by South Dakota's ballot law, and Republican state officials accordingly refused to place the Prohibition ticket on the official ballot. Having prevented the Prohibitionists from voting for their own party, the Republicans confidently expected that the Prohibitionists would have to support the Republican ticket, guaranteeing its triumph in what had been viewed as a close election with the Democrats.

The obvious partisan use possible in the new ballot laws soon led to an important and enduring innovation in electoral legislation known as the antifusion law. This law became so widely adopted—and so useful politically to the dominant party in each state—that its provisions came to be seen as logically necessary and unexceptionable. But in the 1890s, the law was a source of great controversy, and its implementation fundamentally changed the existing political process—with serious implications for a democratic polity. It is a superb example of the dangers of viewing the electoral process or institutional framework as a given.

Fusion was the term applied to the common nineteenth-century practice by which two or more political parties attempted to combine the votes of their followers by nominating the same candidates. Fusion typically involved a third party cooperating with the weaker of the two major parties, in opposition to the stronger major party, in the hope of sharing political influence that would otherwise be denied to both when acting separately in an electoral system based on single-member districts and plurality victories. In an electorate of multiple parties, fusion helped to prevent plurality rule, promoted majority rule, and protected the minority's access to power. Fusion helped maintain a significant third-party tradition by guaranteeing that dissenters' votes could be more than symbolic protest, that their leaders could gain office, and that their demands might be heard. Most of the election victories normally attributed to the Grangers, Independents, or Greenbackers in the 1870s and 1880s were a result of fusion between those third-party groups and Democrats. That some politicians regarded fusion as a mechanism for proportional representation is not surprising. Fusion was particularly appropriate given the electoral equilibrium between the two major parties in the late nineteenth century and the important share of the vote regularly captured by minor parties. The strong partisan identifications of the time, however, made the tactic a tenuous one; for voters insisted on their own party's ticket, candidates, and principles and did not want to vote directly with another party, which often represented antagonistic groups and values. The use of separate party ballots had facilitated fusion by allowing partisans of fusing parties to cast their votes without explicitly acknowledging their shared behavior or its implications.

Beginning in 1893 Republican-dominated legislatures in the Midwest and West modified the new Australian ballot to take advantage of the partisan attitudes of the electorate by simply prohibiting a candidate's name from being listed more than once on the official ballot. This stipulation resulted either in splitting the potential fusion vote, by causing each party to nominate separate candidates, or in undermining the efficacy of any fusion that did occur; for in this time of intense partisanship many Democrats refused to vote for a fusion candidate designated "Populist," and many Populists were equally reluctant to vote for a "Democrat." Given the closely balanced elections of the late nineteenth century, the elimination of even a small faction of their political opponents in this fashion helped guarantee Republican ascendancy. This simple prohibition against double-listing became the basic feature of what the Nebraska supreme court described as a Republican effort to use the Australian ballot as a "scheme to put the voters in a straight jacket."

But other ballot adjustments increased the political effectiveness of this prohibition. Related regulations had the effect of restricting straight-ticket voting by fusionists and even of eliminating one of the fusing parties, thereby antagonizing its partisans and causing them either to oppose fusion or to drop out of the electorate altogether. Combined with the adoption of the party-column ballot format, for example, the prohibition against double listing meant that a candidate could be identified with only one party affiliation, and the second party to nominate a fusion candidate would appear on the ballot as having no nominee for that office at all. Those wishing to fuse thus lost the symbolic protection of voting for their own party and were forced to vote as members of another party. The ultimate consequence of fusion for the second party, moreover, was the sacrifice of its legal identity and existence, for by not having candidates on the ballot it was unable to poll the minimum percentage of the vote required for legal recognition as a political party and for a position on the ballot in subsequent elections.

In the 1896 presidential election, when Democrats, Populists, and Silver Republicans fused on the candidacy of William Jennings Bryan, the operation of these antifusion ballot provisions caused the legal dissolution of the minority parties in each fusion coalition. Stricken from their place on the ballot, these parties ceased to exist until their partisans successfully petitioned to secure ballot representation again. Even the Democratic party had no standing in those states, like Oregon and Washington, where it fell victim to antifusion regulations. But of course the smaller or poorer parties faced particular difficulties in regaining a place on the ballot. By preventing effective fusion, the antifusion law not only assured Republican electoral success but also ended the importance and even existence of significant third parties and discouraged voter turnout among their traditional constituencies. Unwilling either to vote as a member of the "corrupt" old parties or to cast a futile ballot for a symbolic third party, they were citizens legislated out of the effective electorate. Such use of the Australian ballot system convinced Populists that it had become, as one maintained, "a means for the repression instead of the expression of the will of the people," and they argued for its repeal. But ballot "reform" had diminished their political influence while providing the major parties with privileges and protection.

Nominations

The specification of procedures by which candidates were placed on the ballot, which figured so prominently in antifusion legislation, was only part of the establishment of formal regulations for nominating candidates necessitated by the introduction of an official blanket ballot. Previously, nominations were made in an elaborate pyramidal system of delegate conventions organized by the political parties. The basis of the entire delegate convention system was the local popular caucus or primary. Theoretically, this local primary was a meeting of all the members of a party in its particular ward or township. It nominated party candidates for the elective offices of its locality and also elected delegates to city and county conventions. These conventions, in turn, nominated candidates for elections conducted at their level of aggregation and also chose delegates to conventions at the district and state level. The state conventions then nominated candidates for state offices and selected delegates to the national nominating convention. At each level of this hierarchy of conventions, delegate representation was apportioned to the relevant lower districts on the basis of the party vote in each, and thus the delegate-convention system and its nominations were assumed to be representative of the party rank-and-file members.

In reality, primaries were generally controlled by party officials and frequently characterized by gross fraud and violence. The local party organization decided when and where the primaries would meet, named their presiding officers, determined the eligibility of prospective voters, and counted the ballots. Often the primaries were held in saloons or other places that the machine could pack with dependable subordinates. Indeed, only a small number of party members ever attempted to participate in primary elections. One observer described these primaries in New Jersey in 1861 as "so disgustingly corrupt that the mass of the people have long since come to regard them as an unmitigated nuisance. In most cases not three voters in a hundred attend these caucuses. As a general rule, two or three scheming managers have the whole matter arranged beforehand." Extra precautions were sometimes taken to ensure that control: one San Francisco primary was held on the third floor of a building accessible to the prospective voter only by climbing a thirty-foot ladder—held and shaken by thugs loyal to the party boss. Such tactics were possible because political parties had originated outside the law and were not responsible to public authority. Mentioned in no state constitutions, they were purely private associations. As V.O. Key, Jr. (1964) noted, "it was no more illegal to commit fraud in the party caucus or primary than it would be to do so in the election of officers of a drinking club."

There were two major phases in the attempt to reform this primary system. The first tried to secure open and honest proceedings in the conventions; the second sought to replace the convention system altogether with the direct primary. In 1866, following violent and fraudulent elections in the primaries of the Union party, California enacted the first law to regulate primaries. It required parties to issue a public call for a primary meeting, specifying the time, place, and mode of election, identifying the presiding officer, and detailing the qualifications of those who would be permitted to vote. It also prohibited illegal voting and fraudulent counting. Though this law was comprehensive, it was entirely optional and applied only to those parties that wanted to invoke it. And it provided that all expenses of the primary and the operation of the law be borne by the party and not by the government. In the same year New York passed a mandatory law, but it was not comprehensive, covering only matters of bribery and intimidation, and like California's it did not contemplate public control over party primaries.

These laws did not therefore grant political parties any special privileges or public status, but they did constitute an important first step toward government regulation of party procedures. Beginning in the 1870s, other states passed similar laws, again often optional and frequently directed at the larger cities, where machine domination and manipulation of party primaries appeared most flagrant. Missouri, for example, limited the application of its 1875 law to St. Louis. By 1890 half the states (most of them in the North and West) had some type of primary law.

In the 1890s there was a rapid extension of primary regulation. The adoption of the Australian ballot necessarily transformed state and local parties from private organizations into public agencies, and a corollary of its official recognition of parties on the ballot was state involvement in their nomination process. But at least initially, as John F. Reynolds and Richard L. McCormick have written, "governmental regulation amounted to little more than self-regulation: hardly an exorbitant price to pay in exchange for a permanent and privileged place on the ballot and in the electoral process." Several states, for example, provided protection for the regular party organizations by giving them effective authority to keep off the official ballot the nominations of dissident party factions—an advantage that they never enjoyed under the party-ticket system. In other states, public regulation of primaries often represented efforts to consolidate the power of the dominant party, indicating again that electoral "reform" was a matter of perspective. In South Dakota, for instance, the 1899 Republican legislature enacted a "pure caucus bill" forbidding voters to attend the caucus or convention of more than one party. Republicans described the measure as reform legislation to prevent fraudulent voting at primaries; but Populist Governor Andrew E. Lee vetoed the bill, which, he said, should have been titled "a bill to destroy political independence." Lee argued that it was designed to inhibit the necessary consultation between parties considering fusion as well as to "prevent men by force of law and under penalty from changing their political allegiance."

Ultimately the extension of state authority over party functions produced the direct primary, described by Austin Ranney as "the most radical of all the party reforms adopted in the whole course of American history." The making of party nominations by direct vote of party members rather than indirectly by delegate conventions had been initiated by local Democrats in Crawford County, Pennsylvania, in 1842. Thereafter, this "Crawford County System" had been voluntarily used in scattered localities, usually by such radical parties as the Populists, but the major parties generally ignored it. Beginning in the early twentieth century, however, states began to mandate direct primaries, requiring the parties to select their candidates in state-administered elections similar to general elections, often using the same polling places, equipment, procedures, and officials. Commonly, these state laws also specified the dates for such primary elections, established voter qualifications for participation, and provided that the states bear the expense for conducting these primaries.

In 1901, Florida, Oregon, and Minnesota enacted limited direct-primary laws, restricting their applicability to certain jurisdictions or offices, or leaving the responsibility and expense of conducting primaries to party officials. Under pressure from Governor Robert M. La Follette, the Wisconsin legislature passed the first mandatory and comprehensive direct-primary law in 1903. Oregon followed in 1904 with a similarly comprehensive measure, and virtually all states enacted direct-primary legislation in the next few years. By 1917, forty-four states had direct-primary laws, most of which provided for mandatory, comprehensive, and legally regulated direct primaries.

The primary laws of most southern states diverged from this general tendency. Alabama, Arkansas, Delaware, Georgia, and Virginia adopted only optional laws, and most southern states also failed to make the direct primary a legally regulated election. Instead, Arkansas, Georgia, Mississippi, South Carolina, and Texas permitted parties to establish their own rules for conducting primaries. The party still determined voter eligibility for participation (which led to the creation of the "white primary"), appointed judges, printed the ballots, counted the votes, and assumed the expense of the primary by assessing its candidates. Southern primary laws also frequently provided for second primaries, or runoff elections, if no candidate received a majority of votes; whereas northern states allowed plurality votes to be decisive.

Many of the advocates of a direct primary believed that it would end "boss rule"; but because state primary laws, like ballot laws, were enacted by partisan legislatures they often gave party decisions the force of law. For instance, the primary legislation that did specify voter eligibility established tests for party affiliation that reinforced party control over the electorate, even as the primary itself increased popular participation in party decisions. A number of states required of primary voters a promise to support the party's nominees in the general election; others required voters to swear that they had voted the party's ticket at the previous general election. Most states began to keep records of party affiliation to regulate participation in primaries. Some states further defended the regular party organization by modifying direct-primary laws to prohibit the candidacies in the general election of candidates defeated in the primaries. Kentucky, for example, made any candidate defeated in the primary ineligible for the same office during that year; Maryland, Oregon, and California prohibited such a candidate from becoming the candidate of any other party or from running as an independent; Indiana required that a candidate seeking to appear on the ballot as an independent file his papers before the primaries.

There were other ways in which the direct primary served party purposes. Its rapid adoption in the early twentieth century may have resulted from the political realignment of the 1890s that created conditions of one-party domination in large areas of the country, with the Democrats entrenched in the South and the Republicans in much of the North and West. In such areas without effective party competition, the direct primary replaced the general election as the focus of voter interest and the decisive struggle for political control. It thus reinforced single-party domination by taking from the other party its remaining role of controlling the political opposition. And by regularizing intraparty competition within the ruling party it minimized the possibility of a realignment of parties that would topple that party from power.

While the operation of the direct primary seriously weakened the minority party, it also ultimately had obvious effects on the majority party. V.O. Key, Jr. (1964) has best described the dynamics involved:

> The adoption of the direct primary opened the road for disruptive forces that gradually fractionalized the party organization. By permitting more effective direct appeals by individual politicians to the party membership, the primary system freed forces driving toward the disintegration of party organizations and facilitated the construction of factions and cliques attached to the ambitions of individual leaders. The convention system compelled leaders to treat, to deal, to allocate nominations; the primary permits individual aspirants by one means or another to build a wider following within the party. . . . Indeed, the fact that aspirants for nomination must cultivate the rank and file makes it difficult to maintain an organizational core dedicated to the party as such; instead leadership energies operate to construct activist clusters devoted to the interests of particular individuals.

The primary was much less readily applied to presidential elections than to state and local elections. The difficulty of devising an operative national-primary system, and the impossibility of inducing each state to adopt it, meant that the national nominating convention survived with little change. The 1912 campaign demonstrated these matters. Theodore Roosevelt based his unsuccessful challenge to William H. Taft for the Republican nomination on his greater popularity in primaries compared to Taft's control of the party machinery. By 1912, however, only twelve states had enacted presidential-primary legislation, with Florida (1904), Wisconsin (1905), and Pennsylvania (1906) introducing the direct election of national-convention delegates, and Oregon (1910) introducing the direct vote on presidential aspirants as well. Over half the states adopted presidential primaries by 1916; but then the movement declined, and eight states actually discontinued presidential primaries between 1917 and 1945.

Restrictive Electoral Procedures

A more pervasive change in electoral processes at this time occurred in voter-registration procedures at the state level. The earlier registration systems, as noted above, were typically weak ones, usually applying only to urban areas and providing for nonpersonal registration in which the responsibility for registering voters was often assumed by the political parties. The limited effectiveness of these weak registration systems soon led to the adoption of more stringent voter-registration systems in the 1890s and the Progressive period. These systems typically required personal registration, shifting the burden of demonstrating eligibility from the party or election official to the individual voter. Indeed, election officials, no longer partisans but civil servants, were often directed to make regular purges of the registration rolls by deleting the names of those who had not voted in the immediately preceding elections. Some states even compelled voters to periodically renew their registration by appearing in person before the registrar to prove their identity and eligibility. This change to personal, periodic registration had two apparent effects on voting: reducing fraudulent voting but reducing as well the turnout of many voters of marginal social and economic status and political interest, particularly blacks and poor whites in the South, and ethnic groups in the North. In fact, strong personal-registration statutes were often deliberately designed to minimize voting by such groups, an indication of the continuing partisan and class motivations underlying electoral "reform." Northern Republicans and Mugwumps could agree that lower-class ethnic groups that tended to vote Democratic were suitable objects of discriminatory reform, just as southern Democrats wanted to restrict the political role of blacks and poor whites, who constituted a real or potential electoral opposition. Indeed, it is these additional procedural barriers imposed by the system of personal registration that account for a significant portion of the lower voter turnout in the United States compared to that in European countries.

In addition to stringent registration laws, the southern states at this time adopted a variety of other restrictive electoral procedures. Most important were poll tax laws, introduced by Georgia as early as the 1870s and enacted by every southern state by 1904. These laws required voters to pay a tax, as much as a year before election day, and to present the receipt as proof of their eligibility at election time. Some states made these poll taxes retroactive and cumulative, and they came to constitute a major obstacle to political participation by blacks and poor whites. As J. Morgan Kousser has carefully concluded, "By lopping off the lower economic strata, the poll tax preserved southern institutions by creating a fairly homogeneous polity—white, middle-class, and Democratic." For similar racial, class, and partisan reasons, most southern states (beginning with Mississippi in 1890) adopted a literacy test as another procedural barrier to voting by blacks and poor whites. Administered discriminately, it too helped to reduce voter turnout and potential opposition to Democratic hegemony. Of course, the South was not alone in employing such devices at this time. Connecticut and Massachusetts had actually introduced the literacy test in the 1850s, and ten other northern states instituted this procedural requirement in the 1890s or early twentieth century. These instances of electoral reform, like the registration statutes, were generally directed against the political influence of immigrants and of political bosses who depended on their votes. Indeed, the Australian ballot was frequently championed—and in some states used—as a literacy test to disenfranchise immigrant Democrats.

Other important innovations in electoral procedures were introduced in the immensely creative Progressive Era. These include the establishment of woman suffrage, implemented first at the state level by fifteen different states and then nationally by the Nineteenth Amendment in 1920; the adoption of the initiative and referendum by twenty-two states from 1898 to 1918, enabling voters themselves to propose, enact, and veto legislation; the achievement of direct election of U.S. senators; and the development of corrupt-practices legislation to regulate campaign procedures.

The Seventeenth Amendment, providing for the direct election of senators, was the culmination of a long process to revise the original constitutional requirement that senators be elected by state legislatures. The initial conception of the Senate as a body representing the states rather than the people was attacked as early as the 1820s when the House of Representatives first considered an amendment providing for popular election. By the late nineteenth century, support began to build for such a change. Greenbackers, Populists, and labor organizations pressed for popular election as a democratic reform to make the government more responsive to their needs. A series of flagrantly corrupt senatorial elections alienated public opinion, while many other elections dragged on interminably, seriously interfering with normal legislative business. The House of Representatives passed direct-election amendments in 1893, 1894, 1898, 1900, and 1902, but the Senate consistently rejected the proposals. Some states began to implement procedures to circumvent legislative election. In some instances, party conventions endorsed nominees for the Senate. In 1890 Illinois Democrats nominated a senator at their primaries, a practice soon followed in other states, especially in the South. Oregon in 1901 instituted nonbinding popular elections of senators. Although the balloting had no legal force, it became effective in conjunction with popular pressure on candidates to pledge to support the winner of the popular vote. Six western states adopted the Oregon method, and by 1912 twenty-nine states had legally established senatorial primaries. A scandal over the corrupt election of William Lorimer by the 1911 Illinois legislature broke down the remaining Senate opposition to direct election. Congress approved the Seventeenth Amendment in 1912, and it was promptly ratified by the states in 1913.

Legislation limiting campaign expenditures effectively began in 1890 with New York's Corrupt Practices Act, which was modeled on the British Corrupt Practices Act of 1883. The New York law required candidates to file expense statements and prohibited certain types of campaign expenditures, but it was a weak law that prescribed no disclosure of campaign contributions and did not apply to campaign committees. Nevertheless, twenty states passed similar laws within the next few years, led by Colorado and Michigan in 1891. Massachusetts initiated a more comprehensive approach in 1892 by enacting legislation that applied to committees and private individuals as well as to candidates. Most important, it decreed that each political committee have a treasurer to keep detailed records and report promptly its receipts, expenses, and disbursements.

Congress passed the first national campaign-financing legislation in 1907, forbidding national banks and corporations from making campaign contributions. Beginning in 1910 Congress required the disclosure of campaign expenditures in congressional elections and then in primaries as well. In 1911 Congress first established general limits on candidates' campaign expenditures and, in 1918, tried to regulate the uses to which campaign funds were put. Congress codified all this legislation in 1925 in the Federal Corrupt Practices Act, which served as the basis of campaign finance regulation until the reforms of the 1970s. In 1940 Congress imposed limits on expenses by political committees and contributions by individuals, but by failing to limit the creation and number of committees the law made evasion easy. The most notorious example of such subversion of congressional intentions occurred later, in Richard Nixon's presidential reelection campaign of 1972. In 1947 the Republican Congress prohibited political contributions by labor unions, then the largest source of campaign financing for Democrats.

A new phase in congressional regulation of campaign finances began in 1971 with the passage of the Federal Election Campaign Act (FECA), which was extensively amended in 1974 after the abuses of the Nixon campaign and again in 1976 and 1979. The FECA provided for broad disclosure of campaign expenditures, enforceable ceilings on contributions and candidate expenditures, public financing of presidential primaries and elections, and the creation of an administrative agency, the Federal Election Commission, to enforce the act. While many of these reforms were obviously necessary, they often had troubling implications. Public financing of presidential elections discriminated in favor of the Republicans and Democrats and still further hampered third parties, which were subject to restraints upon their receipts without the compensation of public subsidies. But, as with the earlier adoption of the direct primary, such regulation simultaneously weakened the major parties as well. Because public funds were provided directly to the candidates, not to the parties themselves, at the same time that, indeed, parties were restricted in their financial role, candidates became increasingly independent of their nominal party organizations, and parties became less influential in the electoral process. Expenditure and contribution limits also seemed to favor incumbents, who had the political and publicity advantages provided by officeholding. Moreover, the net effect of simultaneously restricting contributions while permitting unlimited personal expenditures gave important advantages to candidates who were personally wealthy; and the electorate soon witnessed, especially in 1980 and 1982, the spectacle of fabulously wealthy individuals lavishly competing for a position of public trust, especially in the Senate. Finally, the FECA permitted the creation of political action committees, or PACs, the activities and expenditures of which (while subject to a variety of restraints) were not counted in computing a party's or candidates' expenditures and thus had the practical effect of negating the basic concepts of the regulatory legislation. Such PACs proliferated, particularly in the support of the 1980 presidential candidacy of Ronald Reagan, and seemed to reveal more than ever the influence of special interests in the electoral process.

Federal Regulation

Although the adoption of deliberately restrictive electoral procedures during the Progressive Era had reversed the historic trend toward increased political participation, subsequent electoral changes frequently modified or even nullified many of those earlier developments. Much of this stemmed from the increasing intervention of the federal government into the areas of electoral regulation traditionally reserved to the states. This not only encouraged a trend toward uniformity of electoral processes, as had been the case with earlier federal actions, but also produced an electoral system more in accord with national political and ideological considerations rather than with the particularistic concerns of the different states and their social and political systems.

This was perhaps first evident with respect to the white primary, a key part of the southern electoral system. Initially, in 1935, the Supreme Court upheld the white primary on the grounds that parties were private associations and thus entitled to establish their own rules for participation in their primaries. In 1941, however, the Court ruled that the federal government did have the right to regulate state primaries, for they were an essential element of the process for choosing candidates for public office. And in 1944, in *Smith v. Allwright,* the Court invalidated the white primary as a violation of the Fifteenth Amendment.

Other federal actions regulating the electoral process slowly followed. In 1962 Congress passed the Twenty-fourth Amendment, abolishing the poll tax in federal elections; it was promptly ratified in 1964. In 1966 the Supreme Court extended the prohibition on poll taxes for all elections, on the basis that the poll tax violated the equal-protection clause of the Fourteenth Amendment—over the dissent of conservative Justice John Marshall Harlan that the Court was simply responding to the "current egalitarian notion" of the moment. Literacy tests were substantially abolished by the Voting Rights Act of 1965, which provided for the assignment of federal examiners to register voters without regard to literacy tests or other devices used to discriminate against black voters in federal, state, local, and primary elections. Southern conservatives objected that the Constitution gave states the authority to regulate state and local elections, but the act was based on the Fifteenth Amendment, which gave Congress the right to enforce through legislation its prohibitions against racial discrimination in voting. The Supreme Court upheld this law in 1966, and Congress extended its terms in the 1970 Voting Rights Act by banning literacy tests, an action upheld by the Court the same year. Such developments were made possible not only by the effective pressure of the civil rights movement but also by the black migration to northern cities, which created an electorate of strategic importance to which the national Democratic party had to respond.

Another part of the electoral process where federal intervention had profound consequences involved apportionment. Historically, state governments controlled the apportionment of legislative representation. But for much of the twentieth century many legislatures had simply refused to reapportion their election districts, despite great population shifts and often despite requirements in their own constitutions to do so. The result, as Alfred Kelly and Winfred Harbison described it, was "a species of constitutional deformity that gravely imperiled the democratic political process." In California, for example, the population of legislative districts varied from 14,000 to six million. Efforts to challenge such discriminatory arrangements in federal courts were unsuccessful for many years because the courts simply refused to review state apportionment laws. But in *Baker v. Carr* (1962) the Supreme Court held that state legislative apportionments could be invalidated by federal courts under the equal-protection clause of the Fourteenth Amendment. In subsequent decisions the Court struck down numerous state apportionments based on unequal representation by population and even ruled that representation in both houses of state legislatures had to be proportional to population. The more conservative Burger Court began in the 1970s to accept wider variations in the populations of electoral districts than the Warren Court had allowed in the 1960s, but the principle of federal review remained intact.

In two final areas federal action in the 1970s significantly reshaped the electoral process. One involved the issue of the minimum voting age. Traditionally, the states had established the voting age at twenty-one, although Georgia (1943) and Kentucky (1955) had reduced it to eighteen, and Alaska and Hawaii had entered the Union with voting-age requirements of nineteen and twenty, respectively. In 1970, perhaps responding to the unpopularity of the war against Vietnam among young Americans, Congress enacted a law lowering the voting age for all elections to eighteen. The Supreme Court restricted the law's application to federal elections, and so Congress passed a constitutional amendment to establish the new age limit for state and local elections as well. This Twenty-sixth Amendment was promptly ratified in 1971.

The federal government also minimized the effect of durational residency requirements for voting. States and localities had routinely required persons to live in the community for periods ranging from ninety days to a year prior to permitting them to vote. But one provision of the Voting Rights Act of 1970 reduced the residency requirement for voting in presidential elections to thirty days everywhere in the nation. In *Dunn v. Blumstein* (1972) the Supreme Court invalidated all durational residence requirements for voting as unconstitutional, but it recognized a "clerical necessity" of closing registration before an election. In suggesting that such a date be not more than thirty days before an election, the Court established a short *de facto* residency requirement as well as implicitly mandating a liberal registration period. Indeed, in another 1972 decision federal courts ruled that local election officials must permit registration until thirty days before an election.

Although such actions had the effect of alleviating the restrictive procedural regulations adopted earlier, the history of American electoral processes does not suggest that such reforms would not be "reformed" again.

Bibliography

Herbert E. Alexander, *Financing Politics: Money, Elections, and Political Reform* (Washington, D.C., 1976), provides a detailed discussion of the extensive federal legislation of the 1970s on campaign financing. Peter H. Argersinger analyzes the partisan motivations and political consequences of the 1890s electoral-reform legislation in " 'A Place on the Ballot': Fusion Politics and Antifusion Laws," in *American Historical Review*, 85 (1980) and "Regulating Democracy: Election Laws and Dakota Politics, 1889–1902," in *Midwest Review*, 5 (1983), reprinted in this volume as chapters 6 and 7 respectively; Paul F. Bourke and Donald A. DeBats, "Identifiable Voting in Nineteenth-Century America: Toward a Comparison of Britain and the United States before the Secret Ballot," in *Perspectives in American History*, 11 (1978), emphasizes the behavioral importance of the legal forms of electoral practice and provides a useful analysis of *viva voce* voting. Walter Dean Burnham, *Critical Elections and the Mainsprings of American Politics* (New York, 1970), a provocative work, introduces the political context of the rules changes of the "System of 1896" and argues that they served to demobilize the electorate and protect the hegemony of corporate capitalism. James W. Ceaser, *Reforming the Reforms: A Critical Analysis of the Presidential Selection Process* (Cambridge, Mass., 1982), reviews the historical transformation of the nominating process from an original emphasis on representative decisions to an increasing stress on "direct democracy." This work is particularly useful for its analysis of the recent party reforms and for detailing the normative assumptions underlying reform proposals. James S. Chase, *Emergence of the Presidential Nominating Convention, 1789–1832* (Urbana, Ill., 1973), explains the development of the convention in terms of stages of party development.

Richard Claude, *The Supreme Court and the Electoral Process* (Baltimore, 1970), demonstrates the importance of the Supreme Court in the historical extension and standardization of election laws. Robert J. Dinkin provides a wide range of useful information on the origins of the American electoral system in *Voting in Provincial America: A Study of Elections in the Thirteen Colonies, 1689–1776* (Westport, Conn., 1977) and *Voting in Revolutionary America: A Study of Elections in the Original Thirteen States, 1776–1789* (Westport, Conn., 1982). Lionel E. Fredman, *The Australian Ballot: The Story of an American Reform* (East Lansing, Mich., 1968), is the most recent examination of the Australian ballot but weak on political aspects of the adoption, design, and administration of the new ballot system. Joseph P. Harris, *Registration of Voters in the United States* (Washington, D.C., 1929), and *Election Administration in the United States* (Washington, D.C., 1934), are standard but dated accounts of their subjects. Alfred H. Kelly and Winfred Harbison, *The American Constitution: Its Origins and Development* (New York, 1976), briefly surveys several aspects of the electoral system, including the apportionment revolution of the 1960s. Valdimer O. Key, Jr., *American State Politics: An Introduction*

(New York, 1956), and *Politics, Parties, and Pressure Groups,* 5th ed. (New York, 1964), are both classics and useful on many relevant issues, particularly on the effects of the direct primary on parties and party systems. Paul Kleppner, *Who Voted? The Dynamics of Electoral Turnout, 1870–1980* (New York, 1982), is an important analysis of the various factors, including procedural changes, that have historically influenced political participation. Emphasizing partisan, class, and racial motivations in electoral legislation, J. Morgan Kousser brilliantly analyzes the origins of twentieth-century southern politics in *The Shaping of Southern Politics: Suffrage Restriction and the Establishment of the One-Party South, 1880–1910* (New Haven, Conn., 1974).

Steven F. Lawson, *Black Ballots: Voting Rights in the South, 1944–1969* (New York, 1976), is a detailed examination of the variety of forces and processes that culminated in the Voting Rights Act of 1965. One of the foremost students of the history of the American electoral process is Richard P. McCormick; among his works two are especially useful: *The History of Voting in New Jersey: A Study of the Development of Election Machinery, 1664–1911* (New Brunswick, N.J., 1953), is an excellent and singular study of the historical operation of the electoral process in a single state. *The Presidential Game: The Origins of American Presidential Politics* (New York, 1982), carefully analyzes the interaction between the electoral structure and the development of political parties in the presidential election process. Charles E. Merriam and Louise Overacker, *Primary Elections* (Chicago, 1928), is still useful. On their way to advocating the direct popular election of the president, Neal R. Peirce and Lawrence D. Longley provide excellent coverage of the origins of the electoral college and of the efforts to reform it in *The People's President: The Electoral College in American History and the Direct Vote Alternative* (New Haven, Conn., 1981). Austin Ranney, *Curing the Mischiefs of Faction: Party Reform in America* (Berkeley, Calif., 1975), examines the theory and practice of efforts to alter the structure and behavior of political parties through the adoption of party rules and public laws. John F. Reynolds and Richard L. McCormick, "An Honest and a Straight Party Vote: Ballot Reform and Split-Ticket Voting in New Jersey and New York, 1880–1910," a paper presented at the Organization of American Historians Annual Meeting, Cincinnati, 1983, is an excellent analysis of early ballot reform that demonstrates that it often "had the reverse effect of that attributed to it both by its advocates . . . and historians and political scientists." Jerrold G. Rusk introduces the "institutionalist" interpretation, emphasizing the importance of rules changes in shaping political behavior in "The Effect of the Australian Ballot Reform on Split Ticket Voting: 1876–1908," in *American Political Science Review,* 64 (1970). Jerrold G. Rusk and John J. Stucker, "Legal-Institutional Factors in American Voting," in William Crotty, ed., *Political Participation and American Democracy* (Westport, Conn., forthcoming), is a useful summary of both substantive and procedural laws influencing voting practices. Elmer E. Schattschneider, *Party Government* (New York, 1942), is the classic exposition of the importance of single-member legislative districts in the maintenance of the two-party system. Earl R. Sikes, *State and Federal Corrupt-Practices Legislation* (Durham, N.C., 1928), is of great value on the historical origins of corrupt-practices legislation. Lucius Wilmerding, *The Electoral College* (New Brunswick, N.J., 1958), examines the possible alternative modes of presidential election and advocates direct election as what the Framers had in mind.

3

The Value of the Vote: Political Representation in the Gilded Age

"If a fair representation of the people be not secured, the injustice of the Govt. shall shake to its foundation," Edmund Randolph warned his fellow delegates at the Constitutional Convention in 1787. Indeed, issues of representation had already led Americans to question the legitimacy of existing governments in the Regulator movements, Shays's Rebellion, and the American Revolution itself. Representation was accordingly considered the most important question at the Constitutional Convention. The Constitution's resolution of the issue placed representation at the center of the republican experiment, and there it remained. More than a century later, for example, Benjamin Harrison expressed a widely held belief when he declared that the American people regarded "equal representation as the price of their allegiance to laws and civil magistrates." If the meaning of equitable representation had changed, the insistent concern for it had not.[1]

Yet historians of American politics have neglected the subject of representation. In the past two decades, historians have dramatically improved their understanding of the nature and operation of the American political system in the nineteenth century. They have examined and explained the socioeconomic bases of mass political behavior and of political party constituencies. They have investigated the determinants of legislative behavior among electoral elites at both the

From Peter H. Argersinger, "The Value of the Vote: Political Representation in the Gilded Age," *Journal of American History*, vol. 76 (June 1989), pp. 59–90. Reprinted with permission of the Organization of American Historians.

An earlier version of this essay was presented to the Soviet-American Committee on Quantitative History Conference on Political and Social History, New Orleans, December 18, 1986. The author is indebted to the commentator at that time, Allan G. Bogue, and to David P. Thelen and the referees of the *Journal of American History* for their helpful criticism and advice.

national and state levels. More recently, some historians have attempted to explain policy outputs. That research, as Richard L. McCormick has suggested, has nonetheless left the relationships among those basic political phenomena critically unclear. One major reason for the difficulty is historians' failure to analyze the intervening variable between electoral and legislative behavior: systems of representation and apportionment. Such neglect reflects assumptions about the operation of American politics held by most historians. By focusing on electoral and legislative behavior, historians have implicitly assumed the existence of a democratic system of representation in which the government reflects public opinion and changes in popular sentiment. But it is the system of representation that determines the relationship between public opinion and political influence.[2]

This failure to analyze representation systems is particularly striking in light of the extensive attention devoted to the subject both by Americans in the past and by contemporary scholars studying the political systems of other countries, but it is merely part of American historians' tendency to overlook the institutional framework of the electoral system. From a comparative perspective, it seems clear that modern representative democracy developed through reforms in suffrage, ballots and the voting process, distribution of constituencies, and representation.[3] But although American historians have traced the course of suffrage reform, they have only recently examined the voting process and have nearly altogether ignored the questions of constituency distribution and representation, which are arguably more important.[4]

Modes of representation are central to democratic institutional arrangements. They establish rules for the allocation of representatives within a political system; they specify procedures for the selection of presidential electors, legislators, and members of Congress; they decide which groups or individuals effectively participate in elections. Thus representation systems affect government stability by influencing turnover; shape legislative performance by facilitating or impeding the creation of effective legislative majorities; help determine the responsiveness of legislatures, executives, and other officials to public opinion; and affect the construction and implementation of public policy. That the representation system can at times have such consequences quite independently of changes in popular voting behavior simply emphasizes its influence in determining the possession, distribution, and exercise of political power. An awareness of the influence of particular modes of representation has led one political scientist, in a phrase that is scarcely hyperbole, to describe the legislative reapportionment beginning in the 1960s as "the most remarkable institutional transformation in twentieth century America."[5]

Modes of representation also have serious consequences for political parties. The Electoral College, for instance, virtually created the political parties its devisers hoped to discourage; third parties are regularly destroyed by the same mechanism.[6] Moreover, representation systems have determined the institutional, geographic, and population bases of political parties, affected party decisions from nominations to campaign tactics, and shaped party competition as well as electoral outcomes.

Representation has historically been the focus of struggles not only between competing political parties but also between conflicting social ideals, economic interests, cultural values, and ethnic and racial groups. In the nineteenth century, for example, ethnocultural animosities were expressed in debates over apportionment and alien suffrage as readily as in the much-studied arguments over liquor and school legislation. In the Progressive Era, municipal reform was essentially a controversy over systems of representation that permitted different socioeconomic groups and interests to dominate local government. In the 1920s, the clash of rural and urban visions of America had such resonance that Congress failed, for the only time, to enact mandatory reapportionment legislation. Today, legal contests over the effects of at-large elections on the relative representation of racial groups convulse jurisdictions.[7]

Analysis of representation systems can thus provide insight into the meaning of politics in American life. It can also establish a perspective for evaluating the performance of the political system, in national and comparative contexts. This essay will attempt to introduce the subject and its implications by examining the late nineteenth century, an era when conflicts over representation raged. Those conflicts are of interest for several reasons. They show how failures of representation undermined the legitimacy of existing government practices. They reveal perennial issues in American government. And they disclose a popular nineteenth-century concern about the very modes of representation that, in the absence of substantive reform, persisted for much of the twentieth century.

The variety of representation systems in the United States during the nineteenth century was surprisingly large. The national government had several different levels of representation as specified by the Constitution: the president, chosen by the Electoral College, in effect represented the electorates of the several states; the House of Representatives was elected by popular vote through congressional districts; and until 1913 the Senate's members were elected by state legislatures. The basis of representation at the state level varied according to the different state constitutions and election laws. States differed, for example, as to whether suffrage was restricted to males, taxpayers, or even citizens, and as to the basis for the allocation of legislative seats.

However, virtually all American representation systems shared two significant characteristics. First, they were spatially defined; that is, the unit of representation was a geographic district, which received legislative seats according to some formula, usually a function of its population. In the proportional representation systems more characteristic of European governments, the unit of representation is political: a party or interest receives seats according to its vote. Second, most American electoral systems employed the plurality method of voting, under which a candidate wins a seat by gaining a plurality of the district's votes. These two features operated almost inevitably to create serious forms of misrepresentation, including what nineteenth-century Americans called "practical" or "virtual disfranchisement."

Indeed, American ideals about political representation could not easily be implemented by the American electoral system. At the core of the theory of representative government as it had developed by the mid-nineteenth century, for example, were the beliefs that each voter should have equal influence and that political parties should win shares of seats in legislative bodies roughly proportional to their shares of the popular vote. Major figures in both parties asserted those ideals. Thus Benjamin Harrison believed that the representation system should produce "an equality of value in each ballot cast," New York Democratic leader David B. Hill maintained that each party should receive "only that representative strength to which it is numerically entitled," and the 1886 Indiana Republican platform demanded that "man for man, the votes of all parties shall be given equal force and effect" in securing representation. But this ideal of representative democracy, which Robert G. Dixon, Jr., has termed "the ideal of proportionate representation of parties (and the interests subsumed within them)," often conflicted with an electoral system established on geographic districts and the plurality vote.[8]

Representation on a geographic basis threatened the goal of equal constituencies. Although there was widespread acceptance of population as a standard for legislative districts and most states required both houses to be based largely on population, a variety of mechanisms allocated representation. Some states adopted the federal model by requiring political units to be equally represented in one house; others guaranteed each county a minimum representation; some prohibited the division of towns or counties in the creation of districts. As urbanization and immigration produced differential population movements, however, such requirements virtually assured significant disparities in district populations and some measure of malrepresentation. In Rhode Island, each town had one senator, which meant that by 1880 a voter in Jamestown (population 459) had 228 times as much representation as a voter in Providence (population 104,857).[9]

Even constituencies of equal population, however, did not assure voters equal political influence. Under a district system with a plurality formula, the electoral success of political parties is determined not just by the total vote cast for their candidates but also by the geographic distribution of their voting strength. In a system of single-member districts, partisan representation in the legislature proportionate to the popular vote distribution would occur only if the voting strength of all parties were concentrated perfectly by equal districts, as with all Republicans residing in districts 1, 2, and 3 and all Democrats in districts 4 and 5. In nearly all other cases, such an electoral system favors the dominant party, for it exaggerates that party's representation relative to its popular vote. If the vote of each party were, for instance, distributed uniformly throughout the state, the stronger party would win all the legislative seats, leaving the minority, however large, without any representation. In Kansas during the 1880s, for example, Democratic voters regularly cast from 32 percent to 40 percent of the popular vote for Congress, but they were never able to elect a single candidate. The Kansas Democratic voters, as one observer noted, "have no more hope of being represented in the Congress at Washington than if they had no vote at all; they have but the shadow of political liberty,—the substance being denied them as much as it is the Russian peasant or the Indian ryot."[10]

The practice of representing geographic districts, rather than political opinions, had consequences that troubled late nineteenth-century Americans, including some who profited from it. In 1870 Ohio Congressman James A. Garfield denounced the result as "the weak point in the theory of representative government, as now organized and administered." That system, he noted, made "a large portion of the voting people . . . permanently disfranchised. . . . There are about ten thousand Democratic voters in my district, and they have been voting there for the last forty years, without any more hope of having a Representative on this floor than of having one in the Commons of Great Britain." Such disparities between popular sentiment and political power constituted a severe challenge to the legitimacy of the political system. That representation system, one reformer pointed out, "acts as a practical disfranchisement of nearly half and sometimes of more than half the entire body of voters. All who are in the minority in any particular district are deprived of representation." Several congressmen warned that such systematic disfranchisement threatened to provoke a revolutionary uprising among Americans thus alienated from their government.[11]

Nor were the implications of such misrepresentation of partisan divisions limited simply to the practical matter of which party gained office or the ideological issue of virtual disfranchisement. Often partisan misrepresentation directly affected public policy. Political scientists have debated the connections between apportionment and public policy in recent years, but it seems clear that in the very different political universe of the nineteenth century—when partisan identifications were strongly anchored in the electorate, parties directed government policies, and partisan voting predominated in legislative bodies—the partisan bias of representation systems at times determined what legislation was enacted or not enacted.[12] For instance, the 1890 passage of the McKinley tariff, by strict party vote, was possible only because a biased representation system placed the Republicans in control of Congress despite their having gained a minority of the popular vote; a more equitable system would have enabled the Democrats to control Congress and establish a different tariff policy.[13] At the state level, the policy implications of partisan misrepresentation often appeared in the legislative fate of sumptuary laws, over which parties differed forcefully. In Connecticut, for example, the representation system permitted the minority Republicans to dominate the legislature and twice approve a constitutional amendment for prohibition. In a popular referendum, however, the amendment was soundly defeated by an electorate whose interests were neglected in the system of legislative representation. District representation, of course, effectively disfranchised other groups besides defeated political parties. Urban, labor, ethnic, and racial minorities all experienced the inequities of the system. "District lines," workers were told in 1886, "separate voters of like ideas and prevent them from cooperating." But the special importance of partisan factors warrants the evaluation of representation systems in terms of how they translate parties' popular votes into legislative seats.[14]

Besides exaggerating the representation of the winning party, the single-member district/plurality vote system of representation also has a bipolarizing effect on political parties. Since only one candidate can win in each district, this electoral form encourages coalitions and discourages multiple parties. It discriminates against smaller parties (unless their voting strength is geographically concentrated, as was that of some agrarian protest parties of the 1870s) to the point of virtually eliminating them. And by encouraging the tendency for the defeated major party to secure and retain a monopoly of the opposition, such an electoral mode guarantees that party's perpetuation even in defeat and thus establishes the two-party system, one of the most prominent and enduring features of American politics. Indeed, Maurice Duverger has described the necessary appearance of a two-party system under those institutional arrangements as nearly "a true sociological law."[15]

One practical response to the bipolarizing effects of the representation system was the widespread American political practice of fusion. Fusion constituted an attempt to maintain and promote minority parties and their distinctive political principles while temporarily creating a coalition that might secure representation in a plurality system. As one advocate explained, "Fusions must always be made with minorities, because the majorities do not have any occasion to make them." Though fusion was an imperfect and often divisive tactic for minority parties, it was their only realistic method of achieving fair representation. In practice, if not in theory, then, as accomplished fusionist Benjamin Butler noted in 1884, fusion was a mechanism for achieving proportional representation.[16]

A less successful, although often repeated, response to the disfranchising and bipolarizing effects of the representation system was agitation for a formal system of proportional representation. Many different groups campaigned for representation reform throughout the late nineteenth century, and some states and many municipalities adopted limited measures to improve representation, but most reform efforts failed for a simple political reason. With few exceptions, the reformers emerged from minority interests in their district or state and thus constituted a minority in the legislature or Congress that would decide the issue. The existing system, precisely because it did exaggerate the representation of the winning party relative to its popular vote, was generally supported by members of the dominant party in each district or state, whatever the party's identity or ostensible political philosophy. As one observer noted after a congressional debate over minority representation that pitted northern Republicans and southern

Democrats against northern Democrats and southern Republicans, no political party would voluntarily relinquish its unearned influence "for it is a law of party to obtain all the power possible."[17]

Critics also attributed a third major consequence to the prevailing electoral system: "temptations and opportunities" for election fraud and corruption. When the capture of 51 percent of a district's popular vote secured 100 percent of the district's representation, the incentive was great to manufacture or suppress a few votes or to intimidate or bribe a few voters to gain the margin of victory. Thus, corruption of electoral contests was related to the system of representation, and "legal disfranchisement" helped produce illegal disfranchisement. It was the competitive partisan balance in district-based elections determined by the plurality formula—not some alleged corrupt character inherent in politicians or voters—that led to the electoral corruption characteristic of the Gilded Age.[18]

A final consequence of the American system of representation was the periodic necessity for districting and apportionment. Because the "accident of sleeping place" is the decisive factor determining whether a party's supporters gain representation, even a minor change in the geographic distribution of the party vote in an election can produce great variations in electoral outcomes. Not surprisingly, then, the party in control regularly attempted to assure its own power by manipulating district lines to alter artificially the geographic distribution of partisan constituencies, thereby maximizing its own representation and minimizing that of its opponents. Such gerrymanders magnified the inequitable character of the district system and constituted, as one Indiana legislator explained, "usurpation under the forms of law." But as an important political process, apportionment revealed much about the electoral system.[19]

The "rules" for constructing a gerrymander were simple, as summarized by a political scientist of the time: "Make your district majorities as small as is safe; make your opponents' district majorities as large and as few as possible; throw away as few of your own votes and as many of your opponents' as you can." Concentrating voters of the minority party in several districts produces easy victories for a few representatives but at the expense of that party's ability to compete effectively in a greater number of districts. Its votes are "wasted" in building up huge district majorities that provide no more representation than would bare pluralities, while the dominant party magnifies its popular vote by creating many districts it can reliably but narrowly carry.[20]

Congressional redistricting in Ohio demonstrated the effect of that practice. In 1884, for example, under Democratic control the Ohio legislature gerrymandered the state's districts to enable Democrats to elect a majority of congressmen with a minority of the popular vote. The legislators arranged boundaries so that the average Democratic margin of victory was a modest 5.6 percent while the Republicans "wasted" their votes by carrying districts by twice as great a margin, 11.6 percent. In 1886 Republicans retaliated by redistricting the same electorate so that their winning margins averaged only 7.8 percent while the Democrats "wasted" their votes in a few landslide victories with average margins inflated to 24.2 percent. With but 3 percent more popular votes than the Democrats, the Republicans thereby captured 150 percent more congressional seats. Followed carefully, such rules could create an apportionment that, even in northern states with nearly balanced electorates, would give one party a massive advantage in representation. As one southern Democrat noted in 1881 of a Republican apportionment that virtually disfranchised almost half of Pennsylvania's electorate, "You can deny a free ballot just as effectively by so districting a county as to mass all the voters of one political opinion in certain districts as you can by a suffrage qualification; and that is the favorite mode now."[21]

Given the profound possible consequences of systems of representation, historians should analyze those systems thoroughly. Fortunately, statisticians, political scientists, and electoral geographers, especially in response to the reapportionment revolution initiated by the 1962 *Baker v. Carr* decision, have developed methods to evaluate the nature and performance of representation systems and apportionments. Those methods can be profitably applied to the large bodies of electoral data generated in the nineteenth century. Some of the measures focus on the degree of population equality in districts and the extent to which each voter had equal representation. The simplest such measure is the *index of inequality,* the ratio between the largest and smallest district populations. Constituencies in the 1885 Michigan senatorial apportionment, for instance, ranged from 84,600 to 31,617, producing an index of inequality of 2.7. A voter in the latter district had 2.7 times as much influence in the state senate as a voter in the former district. (See Table 3.1.) Although the index discloses extreme situations, it may not reveal much about variation in population among legislative districts generally. That variation can be suggested by calculating the degree to which the population of each legislative district deviates from the mean and averaging those figures for the entire legislative body. By this measure, the Michigan apportionment appears less inequitable, for the *average relative deviation* was 18.2 percent, not a particularly high figure for legislative bodies in the 1880s. (See Table 3.2.) However, districts represented by Republicans, who drew up the apportionment legislation, had an average population deviation of −12.3 percent while districts represented by their opponents had an average deviation of +12.8 percent: Republicans made more and smaller districts for themselves while wasting the Democrats' strength in larger but fewer districts. Perhaps more intuitively meaningful is a third measure of population inequalities in representation, the minimum percentage of the electorate that could elect a majority of the legislative body, a figure known as the *theoretical control index.* Under the 1885 Michigan apportionment, for example, 40.9 percent of the state's population could control the Senate. Although hardly satisfactory, such a figure pales beside the index for the grossly malrepresentative system in Vermont, 8 percent. (See Table 3.3.)[22]

Table 3.1

Index of Inequality for Selected Representative Bodies

Body	Year	Index
Illinois House and Senate	1893	1.5
Missouri Senate	1891	1.6
New York Senate	1879	1.8
Wisconsin Senate	1885	2.2
New York Assembly	1879	2.2
Michigan Senate	1885	2.7
Kansas Senate	1888	3.3
Michigan House	1885	3.7
Wisconsin Assembly	1885	5.0
Connecticut Senate	1881	5.3
United States House	1893	6.1
Connecticut Senate	1890	7.3
Montana Senate	1890	11.5
New Jersey Senate	1890	24.9
United States Senate	1875	104.4
Vermont House	1880	181.3
Rhode Island Senate	1890	186.9
Connecticut House	1890	199.6
Rhode Island Senate	1900	289.8

Sources: U.S. Census Office, *Compendium of the Tenth Census* (Washington, 1883), pt. I, 311–13; U.S. Census Office, *Twelfth Census of the United States. Population* (Washington, 1901), pt. I, 2, 19–20, 27–31, 89–90, 350; *Fifty-Third Congress, First Session, Official Congressional Directory* (Washington, 1893); *Chicago Daily News Almanac for 1894* (Chicago, 1894), 177–80; *New York Times*, April 5, 1879, p. 2; *ibid.*, April 24, 1879, p. 2; *Blue Book of the State of Wisconsin* (1891), 303–12; *Official Directory and Legislative Manual of the State of Michigan, 1891–92* (Lansing, 1891), 143–53, 630–32; *Register and Manual of the State of Connecticut, 1890* (Hartford, 1890), 407–8.

In assessing apportionments, historians should consider political as well as population questions. As Edward R. Tufte has observed, to be "minimally democratic" a representation system should be both responsive to changes in popular votes and "unbiased with respect to political party." The degree to which an electoral system is responsive and unbiased can be determined by examining the relationship between a party's share of popular votes cast and its share of legislative seats. While the majority party is usually disproportionately rewarded with legislative power relative to its popular support, electoral systems differ considerably both in their rate of conversion of votes into seats and in their deviation from partisan impartiality. Fortunately, regression analysis of voting and seat data from two-party systems provides two clear measures of these electoral characteristics, the *swing ratio* and the *bias*. The swing ratio (or slope of the regression line) indicates the responsiveness of the partisan composition of legislative bodies to shifts in the partisan division of the popular vote. The

Table 3.2

Average Relative Deviation for Selected Representative Bodies

Body	Year	Index
Illinois House and Senate	1893	9.1
Missouri Senate	1891	9.8
United States House	1893	11.0
Wisconsin Senate	1885	13.9
New Jersey Assembly	1890	15.9
Michigan House	1885	17.6
Michigan Senate	1885	18.2
Wisconsin Assembly	1885	20.6
New Jersey Assembly	1891	21.7
Kansas Senate	1888	22.6
Connecticut Senate	1890	37.1
Montana Senate	1890	60.4
New Jersey Senate	1890	64.0
New Jersey Senate	1900	71.2
Connecticut House	1890	80.7
Rhode Island Senate	1890	106.3
Rhode Island Senate	1900	111.2

Sources: U.S. Census Office, *Compendium of the Tenth Census* (Washington, 1883), pt. I, 311–13; U.S. Census Office, *Twelfth Census of the United States. Population* (Washington, 1901), pt. I, 2, 19–20, 27–31, 89–90, 350; *Fifty-Third Congress, First Session, Official Congressional Directory* (Washington, 1893); *Chicago Daily News Almanac for 1894* (Chicago, 1894), 177–80; *Blue Book of the State of Wisconsin* (1891), 303–12; *Official Directory and Legislative Manual of the State of Michigan, 1891–92* (Lansing, 1891), 143–53, 630–32; *Register and Manual of the State of Connecticut, 1890* (Hartford, 1890), 407–8.

smaller the swing ratio, the less responsive is the legislature. A swing ratio near zero would signify that the partisan distribution of legislative seats does not change as voters' preferences change. A high swing ratio, on the other hand, reflects a system with highly competitive districts in which minor shifts in the popular vote can easily reverse party domination in the legislature. Any apportionment with a high swing ratio thus increases the possibility of representative turnover, explaining at least partially why some gerrymanders failed to assure the districting party partisan supremacy for even a single election.[23]

The second figure, the bias, measures the advantage or disadvantage a particular party receives in the electoral system's translation of votes into seats. It is determined by calculating the difference between 50 percent and the percentage of votes the party needs to capture 50 percent of the seats.[24] The party bias derives from gerrymandered district lines, the inequality of district populations, and differential turnout rates by district electorates. The persistent pro-Republican bias in New England states in the late nineteenth century, for example, stemmed partly from the Republican control of the less populous rural districts. Thus Democratic seats represented more wasted votes than did Republican seats.

Table 3.3

Theoretical Control Index for Selected Representative Bodies

Body	Year	Index
Illinois Senate	1893	46.5
Missouri Senate	1891	45.7
United States House	1893	45.4
Electoral College	1892	44.5
Michigan House	1885	41.5
Michigan Senate	1885	40.9
Kansas Senate	1888	39.0
Connecticut Senate	1890	32.0
Montana Senate	1890	24.0
New Jersey Senate	1885	24.0
United States Senate	1875	20.8
New Jersey Senate	1900	19.9
Connecticut House	1890	14.5
Rhode Island Senate	1880	11.8
Vermont House	1880	8.0

Sources: U.S. Census Office, *Compendium of the Tenth Census* (Washington, 1883), pt. I, 311–13; U.S. Census Office, *Twelfth Census of the United States. Population* (Washington, 1901), pt. I, 2, 19–20, 27–31, 89–90, 350; *Fifty-Second Congress, Second Session, Official Congressional Directory* (Washington, 1893); *Fifty-Third Congress, First Session, Official Congressional Directory* (Washington, 1893); *Chicago Daily News Almanac for 1894* (Chicago, 1894), 177–80; *Blue Book of the State of Wisconsin* (1891), 303–12; *Official Directory and Legislative Manual of the State of Michigan, 1891–92* (Lansing, 1891), 143–53, 630–32; *Register and Manual of the State of Connecticut, 1890* (Hartford, 1890), 407–8.

Swing ratio and bias measure two different aspects of the performance of an electoral system. From 1876 to 1890, for instance, legislative elections in Connecticut and congressional elections in Ohio were both characterized by severe imbalances between parties' popular support and their share of elected representatives. But the causes and political consequences of the disparity differed significantly in the two states. In Connecticut, Republicans' inflated control of the lower house proceeded largely from districting arrangements that biased the electoral system in their favor by 3.2 percent. They needed only 46.8 percent of the vote to capture 50 percent of the house seats. Conversely, Democrats were systematically underrepresented. Despite periodically polling a majority of popular votes, they never gained control of the house. The imbalance between seats and votes in Ohio, on the other hand, stemmed not from a biased system (the bias was only 0.3 percent in favor of Republicans) but from an astonishingly high swing ratio of 9 percent. For each shift of 1 percent in a party's vote there was a change of 9 percent in its seats. Thus, although the division of popular votes between Republicans and Democrats changed relatively little from election to election, the party shares of congressional representation fluctuated almost violently, from 75 percent Republican in 1880, for instance, to 62 percent Democratic in 1882. Such switches of party control also encouraged constant redistricting, as the temporarily dominant party strove to protect its status. From 1876 through 1886, Ohio conducted six consecutive elections with six different districting plans. Obviously, the oft-noted fluctuations of party control and high turnover in the House of Representatives in the Gilded Age resulted not merely from the close partisan division of the electorate but also from the structural factor of apportionments with high swing ratios. As the dominant party in each state gerrymandered districts to maximize its seats by minimizing its vote margins, it created a situation where slight changes in the popular vote translated into large changes in representation.

Examinations of swing ratio and bias can clarify the operation of a representation system, reveal its complexity, and provide intelligible guidelines for its evaluation. An electoral system biased toward a specific party, for instance, is indefensible in a democratic polity. And a swing ratio near zero violates the democratic norm of electoral responsiveness. But what degree of responsiveness—how high a swing ratio—is desirable depends on other social and political goals and values. A Democratic legislator in Pennsylvania made a strong argument in 1883 for a high swing ratio when he demanded an apportionment "with as few certain and as many close and doubtful districts as . . . possible . . . so that the will of the people may have its full effect at all future elections . . . and all changes in public sentiment . . . may have due expression through the ballot box and full fruition in our halls of legislation." Such a system would obviously encourage the creation of legislative majorities with the power and the motivation to act promptly on issues of immediate political concern, but it could also disrupt electoral and policy continuity and give unwarranted influence to small groups of voters and to evanescent ideas. Pennsylvania Democrats, viewing the idea as a way to maximize the electoral opportunities of their minority party, unanimously supported the proposal in the legislature. Pennsylvania Republicans, confident of controlling the legislature without adopting a risky swing ratio, unanimously opposed the proposal.[25]

Other Americans opposed an electoral system with a high swing ratio, not on the basis of such partisan calculations, but because it denied fair representation as effectively as did a system with a partisan bias.[26] The Ohio congressional districts often constituted their point of reference. How could anyone defend a system, asked Garfield, where a change of a few thousand popular votes could change a state's congressional delegation from fourteen Democrats and five Republicans to seventeen Republicans and two Democrats? Disturbed by such disparities between parties' percentage of the popular vote and their percentage of the representation, Americans often calculated the number of votes each party polled per representative elected as a convenient measure of electoral distortion. Such figures are most dramatically presented in diagrams, as in Figure 3.1,

Figure 3.1. **Representation Disparities in Ohio Congressional Elections**

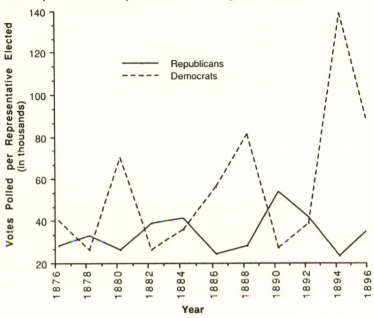

Sources: Congressional Directories (Washington, 1877–97).

which charts the fluctuating ratios for Ohio. (The sharp dips in the Democratic trend line correspond to short-lived redistrictings in 1878, 1882, and 1890 when Democrats temporarily controlled the Ohio legislature.) While some observers attributed the disparities to partisan gerrymanders, they actually reflected the high swing ratio in a relatively unbiased system.[27]

One final way to evaluate a representation system involves the concept of *vote distortion.*[28] Unlike the bias measure, which indicates the degree to which a particular districting plan is biased for or against one party or the other, vote distortion indicates the degree to which districting itself alters the practical influence of voting and favors or penalizes political parties, regardless of any particular apportionment. Positive figures signify that a party gains from vote distortion and measure the amount by which the electoral system overrepresents the party's popular vote. Negative figures demonstrate the degree to which a party is penalized by the representation system and fails to receive seats in proportion to its popular support. In Ohio's 1880 congressional elections, for instance, Republican vote distortion was + 45.3 percent while that of the Democrats was – 48.3 percent.

An examination of several states with differing electoral systems, using the measures of representativeness as well as the usual historical evidence, illustrates

This 1892 *New York World* cartoon satirized the inequities of Connecticut's system of legislative representation. Reproduced from Albert E. Van Dusen, *Connecticut* (New York, 1961).

many of the issues important in late nineteenth-century American politics and demonstrates how different representation systems affected political parties. A fixed allocation of representatives produced "constitutional disfranchisement" and governmental crisis in Connecticut. Periodic changes in both the basis and distribution of representative districts plunged New Jersey into a bitter politics of reapportionment and inequitable representation. A distinctive voting system provided Illinois with stable and equitable representation but also with disquieting consequences for voters and parties.

Like most other New England states, Connecticut had a representation system based largely on the town. For the lower house, each town incorporated before the Revolution was allocated two representatives, newer towns but one, an arrangement that with the passage of time produced very serious malapportionment. In 1874 a constitutional amendment provided a second representative to any of the latter towns if its population reached 5,000. The amendment was a clear recognition of population as a criterion for representation, combined with a political refusal to do much about it. New Haven, with a population in 1890 of 86,045, had the same representation in the house as rural Union, with but 431 people; the index of inequality was 199.6. A small fraction of the state's population (14.5 percent) could elect a majority of the House of Representatives, which, in turn, would decide public policy.

The Senate, by contrast, was designed to be the body of popular representation, reapportioned after each decennial census. For half a century, however, the

Table 3.4

Town Representation and Republican Strength in 1890 Connecticut House

Size of Town	% State Population	% Legislative Seats	% Republican
001–1,999	13.2	46.0	59.5
2,000–4,999	19.6	26.2	56.3
5,000–19,999	31.0	23.0	41.7
20,000+	36.2	4.8	8.3

Source: Register and Manual of the State of Connecticut, 1890 (Hartford, 1890).

senate districts remained as established after the 1830 census and therefore became progressively more inequitable. Finally, in 1881, over great opposition, the legislature passed a new senatorial apportionment, giving an additional senator to each of three heavily populated counties, and making the cities of Hartford, New Haven, and Bridgeport separate districts.

Although the reapportionment helped equalize districts within counties, it did little to correct the inequality of districts within the state (the index of inequality was 5.3), and it still permitted one-fifth of the state's population to elect a majority of senators. Democrats denounced the law vigorously but voted unanimously for it as a great improvement over the previous malapportionment.[29]

Such maldistribution of political representation guaranteed the supremacy of small towns and rural interests over those of the city, of Yankee Protestants over Catholic immigrants, and not incidentally, as suggested by the 1881 legislative fight, of Republicans over Democrats. Indeed, the basis of the Republican dominance in Connecticut was the system of representation. (See Table 3.4.) Throughout the 1870s and 1880s, Democrats often received a majority of Connecticut's votes, but after 1876, they never carried either house of the legislature, for the representation system was biased against them by 3.2 in the house and 2.1 in the Senate.

Nor was this biased representation system merely of local importance. Six times from 1879 through 1893, the malapportioned legislature elected a United States senator, each time a Republican. In four different congresses, Republicans controlled the Senate only by the vote of Connecticut Republicans representing a state in which a plurality of the voters were "constitutionally disfranchised" Democrats. Moreover, those Republican senators repeatedly provided the decisive votes on congressional roll calls over tariff, currency, pension, and other legislation. Not surprisingly, then, did southern Democrats resent the complaints of New England Republicans about elections in the South and attack the system of representation that made, as one Florida senator noted of Connecticut, "the ballot of a person living in one place five or perhaps ten times as powerful as in another place." Such a system, he contended, effectively denied the free ballot as much as did suffrage restrictions.[30]

Another feature of Connecticut's electoral system had political significance: the requirement that state officials be elected by a majority, rather than a plurality. Several nations have adopted majority systems of voting to preclude the possibility that a minority of voters can elect a candidate. France, for instance, requires a second ballot, and Australia employs the alternative-vote system. But Connecticut's rule virtually assured minority control, for, rather than allowing the electorate to decide the victor when no candidate initially achieved a majority, it simply assigned that task to the unrepresentative legislature. The rule placed a series of minority Republican candidates in the governor's office after 1885. The Democrats generally outpolled the Republicans in statewide elections, but the presence of minor third parties prevented the Democrats from achieving a majority and allowed elections to be determined by a legislature that, under the system of town representation, was invariably Republican. Democrats thus not only agitated for reform of the representation system but also demanded a constitutional amendment to establish plurality elections, regarding the majority system as "a Republican device for keeping the control of the State in Republican hands by making it possible for the legislature to choose for Governor and other officers candidates whom the voters of the State have declined to elect."[31]

The biased representation system and the majority election rule interacted in 1890 to produce what the *Hartford Post* modestly called "serious confusion, a wretched controversy, and a stoppage of public business." In that year's election, the Democratic state candidates again outpolled their Republican opponents, and Democrats even carried the state senate. The system of representation, however, produced a lower house of 133 Republicans from towns polling 42,019 votes and only 119 Democrats from towns polling 92,235 votes. The remaining question was whether the Democratic state candidates had a majority or again only a plurality of the popular vote. Compiling the returns, the state canvassing board calculated that in fact the Democratic candidates had received a majority of the vote, legally cast and accepted, and were entitled to office. The board then sent its figures to the General Assembly, which had the constitutional duty of declaring the election of state officials. The Democratic Senate accepted the returns and proclaimed the Democratic candidates elected. By strict party vote, however, the Republican-controlled house repudiated the board's findings, asserted its authority to go behind the returns, and contended that local election boards had improperly rejected ballots that, if counted, would so inflate the total vote that the Democratic majority would be only a plurality. The house therefore asked the Senate to meet in joint session to elect the state officials. With a majority of four on joint ballot, the Republicans would again be able to place in office their defeated candidates. The Senate countered that the legislature had no authority to go behind the returns but was required simply to declare the result from the official tabulations of the canvassing board. Having performed its function by declaring the election of the Democratic candidates, the Senate could lawfully take no further action.[32]

UNCLE SAM—Great Cæsar! Those wheels ARE badly blocked, but the Acting Governor seems to be quite comfortable.

An interested Uncle Sam observes Governor Bulkeley's exploitation of the 1891 deadlock created by Connecticut's electoral system. Reproduced from Albert E. Van Dusen, *Connecticut* (New York, 1961).

With the legislature deadlocked, controversy erupted over control of the state's executive offices, bringing into dispute the legitimacy of the government itself. The Democratic candidates took the oath of office, but the Republican incumbents refused to relinquish their offices. Thus Morgan Bulkeley, not even a candidate in 1890 and representing a party whose nominees had admittedly received only a minority of the vote, remained as governor. The Democratic Senate, however, refused to recognize his authority, accept his messages, vote on his nominations, or pass any legislation, including appropriation bills to keep the government functioning. The Republican house rejected compromise, for the continued stalemate allowed the Republican holdovers to retain power. To prevent action, in fact, Republican legislators, upon the advice of the party state committee, left Hartford, thereby precluding a quorum and forcing a suspension of the house. After thirteen months, Democratic house members finally seized upon an obscure parliamentary rule and staged what the press termed a "coup d'etat," forming a rump body with its own officers. This maneuver forced the Republicans to end their farce, return to the capital, and at last officially reject the senate resolution declaring the election of the Democratic candidates.[33]

By this action the house finally concluded its mandated role in the electoral process and made possible a Democratic appeal to the courts for relief. With Republicans continuing to stall, the subsequent case became (in the estimation of the *Nation*) "the longest, most vexatious, and most complex election trial ever held in this country." Finally, on the eve of the 1892 election, the Connecticut Supreme Court, by a strictly partisan vote of its justices, upheld the Republican position and nullified the Democratic claim to office. Democrats were enraged by the court's action, denouncing it as "another 'eight to seven' decision," a reference to the partisan vote by which the presidential election had been decided in behalf of the Republicans in 1877.[34]

But they recognized that the greater outrage, which had produced the original crisis of a deadlocked government and minority rule, was an electoral system that made the government of Connecticut, as the State Democratic Club declared, "more unrepublican than that of Spain, more undemocratic than that of Italy." As the major issue of their 1892 campaign, then, they called for a constitutional convention to establish plurality elections, a just system of representation, and "such additional reforms as will restore self-government to Connecticut." On that platform, the Democratic state candidates were elected by a clear majority, but Republicans retained a firm grip on the unrepresentative lower house where they blocked plans for a constitutional convention, which required legislative approval. Determined to protect their privileged position and to prevent popular rule, Republicans believed that electoral reform would allow "the masses of ignorant voters in a few cities" to control state politics. Blocked from calling a convention for systematic electoral revision, Democrats attempted to achieve the reforms by proposing individual constitutional amendments. In the political revolution of the 1890s, however, those proposals were also turned aside, becoming canonized (from the Democratic perspective) as "the lost amendments." In 1901 the constitution was amended to establish plurality elections, for no one wanted another governmental crisis, but the inequitable system of representation remained unchanged until a very different court intervened in the 1960s.[35]

New Jersey's system of representation, which shared some features with that of Connecticut, had other characteristics of particular analytical interest. In its evolution and operation, it is possible not only to recognize the limits of popular government but also to determine how different methods of representation influenced party behavior—and how partisan calculations, in turn, influenced the adoption and operation of such methods. This is especially obvious in the context of reapportionment, which scarcely figured in Connecticut but which often determined the functioning and success of New Jersey's political parties and affected the course of the state's public policy.

New Jersey's constitution established representation in the state Senate at one senator for each county, regardless of population. Reapportionment was thus not an issue with respect to the upper house. But the larger question of representation became critical when New Jersey, like Connecticut, experienced significant ur-

"PROGRESSIVE" CONSPIRACY.

A Democratic view of Republican efforts to secure power through illegitimate manipulation of the electoral framework, including "stealing" Connecticut through its system of representation. *Puck*, February 4, 1891. *Courtesy Enoch Pratt Free Library, Baltimore.*

banization and immigration in the late nineteenth century. In the 1880s, population expanded by three hundred thousand, with most of the growth occurring in three counties near New York City: Hudson, Essex, and Passaic. Some rural counties actually lost residents. Population indexes reveal the steady deterioration in the representativeness of the Senate as a consequence of the demographic changes. The index of inequality progressively grew until a voter in Cape May County had 24.9 times as much influence as a voter in Hudson County; average relative population deviations surpassed 60 percent by middecade; and the theoretical control index fell unceasingly until less than one-fourth of the state's population could elect a majority of the Senate.

Because partisan constituencies were not distributed evenly across New Jersey's counties, these population inequalities also affected party ability to secure senatorial representation. While the Democrats averaged over nineteen thousand votes in consistently carrying Hudson County in the 1880s, for instance, the Republicans achieved the same representation by polling less than a tenth of that figure in winning rural Ocean County. Thus the partisan distribution of Senate seats was very imperfectly related to the popular vote ($r^2 = .43$), and the electoral system for the Senates chosen from 1879 through 1887 had a pro-Republican bias of 3.4 percent. Vote distortion in senatorial elections was also significant. (See Table 3.5.) For six consecutive sessions, Democratic candidates gained more popular support than their Republican opponents, but the representation system continued to give control of the Senate to the GOP. Of course, the system penalized third parties most; they invariably suffered a −100 percent vote distortion. Democrats controlled the governorship from 1869 to 1896, but the unrepresentative character of the Senate kept it from reflecting statewide majority sentiments and frustrated Democratic efforts to govern.

Representation in the General Assembly corresponded somewhat better to the distribution of New Jersey's population and partisan sentiments. The constitution required that the house's sixty representatives be apportioned after each census among the counties on the basis of population, provided only that each county have at least one representative. In 1852, moreover, the legislature abolished the practice of holding at-large, countywide elections for assemblymen, a procedure that had usually enabled the majority party in each county to elect all the representatives to the exclusion of the other party. In its place, the legislature established a system of single-member districts within each county in order to effect, as Gov. George Fort declared, "a more direct responsibility of the representative to his constituents."[36]

Indeed, under the new system, the amount of vote distortion decreased considerably and the proportion of multimember county delegations that included representatives of more than one party increased from an average of 16 percent to an average of 57 percent. Election by district even facilitated representation of third parties, a virtual impossibility under the at-large system. In the decade from 1877 to 1886, for example, nine third-party candidates were elected to the assembly.[37]

But the district system also had drawbacks. Because it rested on geographic districts and the plurality vote formula, there remained a structural incentive for the two-party system and a tendency to reward the majority party disproportionately. Thus party strength in the assembly continued to be imperfectly related to the division of the state's party vote. Vote distortion averaged +17.7 percent for the majority party and −81.4 percent for third parties. Under the district system, moreover, the degree of inequality of representation increased. Growing inequality partially reflected constitutional restrictions that prevented apportionment legislation from fully recognizing the demographic changes of urbanization and immigration, but it also sprang from the failure to establish rules for districting after seats were apportioned to counties. And as the districting process was entrusted to those most immediately concerned—the legislators—the absence of rules encouraged gerrymandering, with districts varying widely in shape and population. Partisan efforts to control apportionment soon

Table 3.5

Vote Distortion in the New Jersey Senate

Legislative Session	Republican			Democratic			Third Party		
	% Vote	% Seats	Distortion	% Vote	% Seats	Distortion	% Vote	% Seats	Distortion
1883	48.7	57.1	17.2	49.3	42.9	−13.0	2.0	0	−100
1884	48.3	57.1	18.2	49.5	42.9	−13.3	2.2	0	−100
1885	47.6	52.4	10.1	49.9	47.6	−4.6	2.5	0	−100
1886	48.1	61.9	28.7	49.3	38.1	−22.7	2.6	0	−100
1887	46.9	57.1	21.7	48.8	42.9	−12.1	4.2	0	−100
1888	45.9	57.1	24.4	47.2	42.9	−9.1	6.9	0	−100

Sources: Annual Returns of the General Election (Trenton, 1882–1887).

dominated New Jersey politics as parties alternated in manipulating district lines, enacting ten different districting laws between 1861 and 1892. The frequent turnover of legislative control demonstrates that gerrymanders did not invariably guarantee partisan success, for in their effort to maximize the number of districts they could narrowly carry, party managers often overreached themselves by misestimating the margins voters would give their party. At times, moreover, the gerrymanders were so flagrant that the laws themselves became major campaign issues, and "an indignant and outraged people" ousted the offending party, only to have the other major party promptly commit an even greater violation of the right of representation. Each successive districting act established a new record of population inequality, as measured by average relative deviations, and vote distortion mounted steadily. The 1879 election, for instance, indicated the partisan advantage of district manipulation, for the Democrats outpolled the GOP but won scarcely a third of the assembly seats, a Democratic vote distortion of −24 percent.[38]

Politics became increasingly bitter, especially when arguments over representation incorporated the same cultural divisions expressed in the coincident political conflicts over liquor and other "moral" issues. Finding that the use of ward boundaries in Jersey City would not suffice to isolate the Democratic immigrant vote and minimize its political influence, Republican legislators resorted to defining districts by streets and even buildings in order to create the notorious Second, or Horseshoe, District, designed (as one Republican admitted) to place "all the political filth of Jersey City in one" district. They then constructed six small districts to elect six Republican representatives.[39] Legislative conflict grew more bitter as well; not only were apportionment laws always enacted by strict party votes, but protests from the minority party were expunged from the legislative journal. In 1881 Republican legislators enacted a vicious gerrymander by suspending normal rules of procedure and adopting a gag rule, thereby sacrificing, as one Democrat insisted, "not only the principle of true representative government, but their own sense of decency, in their efforts to make their power perpetual." Under this measure, New Jersey's electoral system during the 1880s had a solid Republican bias (1.6 percent), but a high swing ratio (4.3) combined with the Democrats' consistently greater popular support, the disruptive influence of third parties, and persisting demographic trends to make continued Republican success uncertain. In an effort to assure that control as well as to satisfy the cultural antagonisms of their disproportionately rural, native, Protestant constituents, Republicans used the legislative power provided by the biased representation system to enact a series of laws aimed at urban, ethnic groups: a local-option, high-license liquor law; a law, applicable only to Newark and Jersey City, requiring voters to register in person and answer detailed questions; and a "sunset law" restricting polling hours.[40]

When the Democrats finally regained power in the 1888 election, they immediately proceeded by party votes "to undo the principal legislative work" of their Republican predecessors. They not only repealed the liquor law, registration act, and sunset law, but they redistricted the assembly with a gerrymander that produced a small Democratic bias (0.9) and a record population inequality. They carefully amended that law in 1891 and 1892 to increase their representation even as their popular support declined (producing a vote distortion of 36.3 percent) and to depart still further from the principle of representative equality (the average relative deviation was 22.3 percent). Growing desperate, Republican officials appealed to the state Supreme Court to prevent the holding of district elections. In 1893, the court ruled districting unconstitutional and ordered a return to countywide elections.[41]

The court decision effectively ended the politics of gerrymandering, but not the problem of inequitable representation. Indeed, coinciding with a voter shift to the GOP in reaction to the depression beginning in 1893, the reestablishment of the county-unit system produced legislatures that reflected the state's political divisions far less accurately than had the district system. Whereas the latter had permitted legislative representation of the minority party in many counties, the county-unit system tended to submerge minority party votes and to produce county delegations entirely of one party. As a consequence, vote distortion increased dramatically, from an average of 17.7 percent in the eighteen years from 1876 to 1893 to an average of 36.3 percent in the eighteen years after the court's decision. The readoption of the county-unit system also curtailed representation of third parties. Although the average annual popular vote of third parties changed little between the two periods (averaging 5.2 percent before 1893 and 4.5 percent afterwards), third-party candidates elected declined from ten to two. Compared with the preceding Democratic gerrymander, the new system was less responsive to voter opinion (the swing ratio changed from 5.0 to 3.2) and more biased with respect to party (from 0.7 Democratic to 1.7 Republican). The result was consistently swollen legislative majorities for the GOP. Finally, reflecting the conflict between the constitutional requirements for apportionment and the accelerating demographic changes accompanying urbanization and immigration, population inequalities in representation, as measured by all three indexes, continued to increase in the years after 1893 as well.[42]

Although representation in New Jersey became less equitable after the abolition of the single-member district system, Illinois replaced its comparable system with a new electoral mode that significantly improved representation. Reacting to the "injustices and inequalities" associated with single-member district elections—vote distortion, inflated majority party strength in the legislature, gerrymandering, and, given the spatial distribution of partisans in Illinois, the effective disfranchisement of Democrats in northern Illinois and of Republicans in southern Illinois—the 1870 Illinois constitutional convention considered several proposals for representation reform. Influenced by contemporary developments in Europe, debates in Congress, and experiments in other states, the delegates devised a system of cumulative voting to choose members of the lower house of the legislature, the Illinois House of Representatives. This involved electing representatives in three-member districts, with each voter having three votes that could be cast for separate candidates or cumulated on one or two candidates. Although the district plan was retained, the assignment of three members to each district had advantages. Whereas a single-member district disfranchised the minority and a two-member district would either do the same or produce equal representation for both minority and majority, the three-member district maintained the principle of majority rule while securing representation to the minority party, provided it possessed at least 25 percent plus one of the participating electorate. The system was approved by popular referendum, and the *Springfield Illinois State Journal* proudly announced, "Our state will be the first to inaugurate a new system of government by which minorities, instead of being entirely disfranchised, will hereafter have a representation according to the strength which they are able to muster."[43]

Indeed, cumulative voting thereafter demonstrated its superiority over the standard system in securing representation more nearly congruent with popular sentiment. In 1872, for example, the first election held under the new system, only one of fifty-one house districts returned three representatives from the same party. Thirty-three districts elected two Republicans and one Democrat; seventeen districts elected two Democrats and one Republican. Southern Illinois elected twenty-three Republicans and northern Illinois thirty-six Democrats, enabling each party to represent more effectively the diverse interests of its constituents and its state. Party division in the house paralleled the popular vote distribution, with vote distortion for the majority party a minimal 2.4 percent. Those patterns persisted for the remainder of the century, reflecting an electoral system with virtually no partisan bias (0.1 Republican) and a responsible swing ratio (1.3). Figure 3.2 indicates the degree to which cumulative voting surpassed the single-member district system in making representation reflect voter divi-

Figure 3.2. **Republican Representation in the Illinois Legislature**

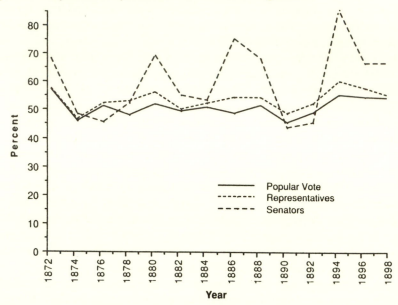

Sources: List of State Officers ... of the State of Illinois (Springfield, 1900); *Illinois Yearbook and Almanac for 1879* (Chicago, 1879); *Illinois Legislative Directory, 1881* (Springfield, 1881); *Chicago Daily News Almanac* (Chicago, 1885–1901).

Note: Graph lines reflect the aggregated legislative voting results from those districts simultaneously electing both a senator and representatives except for the years 1872, 1874, and 1878, when they indicate the state's popular vote for treasurer and the composition of the entire legislature.

sions. It compares the popular vote of Illinois Republicans to their representation in both house and Senate. House and Senate districts were coterminous: identical constituencies chose three house members by cumulative vote and one senator by plurality vote. Republican representation in the house parallels and nearly coincides with the party's changing share of the popular vote. Representation in the Senate, however, fluctuates and diverges from the popular vote distribution, with the party being disproportionately rewarded in most elections but being disproportionately penalized in the mid-1870s and early 1890s when Democrats and third-party agrarians successfully fused, thereby securing for themselves the inherent bias of the electoral system.

Cumulative voting had important effects on party organization and behavior. First, it did not seriously weaken the institutional incentives for a two-party system. Though third-party legislators were elected in every election from 1874 through 1890, third parties never secured representation proportionate to their popular support in Illinois. Third parties often had many votes statewide but rarely more votes than the weaker major party in any one district, a condition that promoted fusions. The cumulative method, then, provided for minority, but not proportional, representation; indeed, it actually strengthened the weaker major party by virtually guaranteeing success for its nominee. It was also obvious that the minority party in a district might be able to elect two of the three representatives if the voters of the majority party cumulated their votes too heavily on one candidate, or if the majority party either underestimated its strength and nominated only one candidate or overestimated its strength and nominated three candidates, "being foolish enough," noted the *Chicago Tribune,* "to believe they could elect them." That reality increased the structural incentive for strong party organization, both to control nominations and to direct voters. In practice, the dominant party in each district generally nominated only two candidates and the weaker major party one, essentially assuring the election of all nominees. Although the cumulative vote system established minority representation of parties, it thus often left voters with no real choice at the polls. That outcome finally prompted the state, in the twentieth century, to require that each party nominate at least two candidates in each district.[44]

Cumulative voting had other significant consequences for the political system. It minimized the politics and effects of gerrymandering, for the lesser party was almost certain to gain one member from each district and the majority party no more and no less than two. All three measures of population inequality for the 1893 Illinois apportionment, for instance, were among the lowest for any state in the period. (See Tables 3.1, 3.2, and 3.3.) There was still partisan conflict over apportionments, but it was relatively limited and restrained. Cumulative voting also had the effect of preventing massive and disruptive legislative turnovers as a consequence of political landslides. In the election of 1894, for instance, the single-member district system enabled the Republicans to carry 99 percent of Michigan's legislative representation, 83 percent of Indiana's, and 81 percent of Wisconsin's. But in Illinois they captured only 60 percent, a figure much more proportionate to the popular vote. Perhaps for that reason, cumulative voting, in combination with the strong party organization it required, may also have encouraged a relatively high degree of stability and experience among the house membership. A comparison of the ten sessions preceding and following the adoption of the voting system shows that the proportion of experienced legislators in the house rose from 11.2 percent to 17.5 percent, while in the Senate it declined from 14.8 percent to 12.9 percent. The policy implications of that differential in legislative experience obviously merit study. One consequence of the cumulative vote for public policy seems fairly clear. Because it did not establish proportional representation but instead promoted legislative stability and the two-party system, the method failed to enable Illinois to transcend significantly the limited range of policy initiatives that characterized other legislatures. As one disappointed citizen noted, "all reform issues are excluded as absolutely as elsewhere."[45]

Although the Illinois cumulative vote system was unique at the state level, the great variety of electoral systems in the United States, particularly at the local level, included other forms of minority representation, as well as far less democratic arrangements.[46] Rhode Island, for example, permitted universal male suffrage in mayoral elections after 1888 but imposed such a stringent property qualification for voting in city council elections and on local propositions to tax or spend money that nearly 60 percent of Providence's electorate was excluded. The result was an ineffectual polity with Irish Democratic mayors neutralized by Yankee Republican councils.[47] At the state level, moreover, important variations emerged even in similar electoral systems, as when some states assigned the task of reapportionment to agencies other than the legislature.

All levels of the national government also merit analysis in terms of representation. The United States Senate was a representative body in which each district—each state—received equal representation regardless of population. Thus a minority of the population could easily control that institution. Indeed, by 1875 one New York politician maintained that "the inequality of representation in the Senate" was so extreme that the United States no longer had a republican form of government. "It has in a great degree ceased to be a government of a majority and become the government of a minority." Quantitative analysis supports his concerns; the Senate's index of inequality at that time was 104.4, and its theoretical control index only 20.8 percent. The New Yorker rearranged the components of the latter index to create his own measure of misrepresentation: a majority of the national population resided in states with but 21.6 percent of the representation. "It is," he concluded, "the most absurd thing to call such a government a popular government." No better illustration of the political and policy effects of such inequities in the representation of population occurred than the ability of western senators to sustain the silver issue in congressional and national politics despite the opposition of senators representing a large majority of the American people. Applying the concept of vote distortion to sectional rather than partisan populations provides a precise measure of the West's overrepresentation in the Senate: +163.0 percent compared to −35.7 percent for the East. "We are punished," said one unhappy goldbug senator, "for making too easy the pathway of rotten boroughs into the Union."[48]

The Electoral College also constituted a system of representation that requires evaluation on its own terms. The election of minority presidents through the Electoral College in the late nineteenth century is well known, but not well understood. It derived from the common decision by state legislatures that electors should be elected on a general ticket by statewide vote. By producing a winner-take-all result, the general ticket transformed a state into the functional equivalent of a single-member district, maximizing the political influence of the dominant party in each state and effectively disfranchising voters in the minority. Both parties recognized that the general ticket biased the Electoral College in favor of the Republicans. When Michigan Democrats enacted a law for the district election of electors, Republicans challenged the law all the way to the United States Supreme Court, with President Benjamin Harrison's attorney general serving as counsel. Such inequities cast serious doubt on the very legitimacy of the government, particularly after the 1876 election. Even partisan Republicans conceded that the "dangerous" Electoral College "has never yet faithfully represented the people but has often misrepresented them."[49]

Apportionment in the House of Representatives also needs systematic analysis. It not only determined the power of different states in Congress but, because it allocated electors, directly affected the election of the president. Indeed, the peculiar apportionment of 1872, adopted in violation of the prevailing law mandating the method of allocating seats, was directly responsible for the 1876 election of Rutherford B. Hayes with a popular vote minority. Had the apportionment been equitable, even the Electoral Commission would have been unable to place Hayes in the White House. In congressional debates over apportionment, members expressed concern for virtual disfranchisement, proposed schemes of minority representation like that in Illinois, argued over the partisan consequences of mathematical principles, and exhibited such intense feelings that the House often became, as one horrified observer reported in 1882, "a mob" and "disorder became disgraceful."[50]

Nineteenth-century Americans were interested in representation and its implications for democracy. When historians begin to share some of that interest in the structure, operation, and consequences of systems of representation, they will better understand the performance of the American political system and the meaning of political participation. That the electoral system did not respond consistently or impartially to changes in aggregate voter preferences challenges many historians' implicit assumptions about the American political process; it also indicates the need to devote more attention to the institutional framework established by representation systems. Historians must examine the reasons for and the consequences of the electoral system's differential responses as well as the many related issues of representation.

Indeed, the study of representation systems in the American past raises a new set of questions for historians. First, and most basically, what were the various systems of representation in American politics? Why were they established? How did they operate? What difference did it make, for instance, that the two houses of legislative bodies often represented different constituencies? That executives generally represented a broader electorate and legislators particularistic constituencies? To what extent did such competing constituencies shape or limit public policy?

Second, what was the value of the vote? Which groups suffered and which groups benefited from inequities in representation and to what extent? In states such as Connecticut, Rhode Island, New Jersey, and New York urban residents, immigrants, and Democrats were disadvantaged and their oppositions advantaged. But what were the patterns elsewhere? Everywhere, districting as a system disadvantaged socialists, Populists, single taxers; in the South it also impeded black representation while reducing the incentive for northern Republicans to protect blacks' right to vote.

Third, how were political parties affected by the structural context established by the system of representation? Did they, as in Connecticut, model their internal committees and nominating conventions on the external representation system and thereby not only reflect but reinforce a biased polity and minimize the likelihood of responding effectively to changing socioeconomic conditions? To what extent did parties make nominating and campaigning decisions on the basis of the representation system? The Electoral College system was primarily responsible for the Democratic practice of nominating presidential candidates from New York, however much historians have stressed the presumed individual characteristics of Grover Cleveland, but how else did parties respond to their structural context? Did they fail, as in New Jersey, even to contest elections in seriously malapportioned districts, thereby rendering aggregate voting results misleading as indicators of voter interest or popular opinion? How did the representation system affect party decisions in government? Did the Democrats' unusual opportunity to reapportion northern legislative and congressional districts and fashion high swing ratios after their election victories in the census year of 1890 ironically contribute to the subsequent massive Republican seat gains in 1894 and thereby help establish the realignment of the 1890s? Under what circumstances did parties seek to change apportionments and entire systems of representation? To what extent did the representation systems frustrate attempts at political reform by preventing the effective mobilization of a discontented majority? As one critic observed, "in this country one citizen voting yea may on occasions nullify the votes of two citizens, or even more, who say nay."[51]

Fourth, what issues were addressed and, equally important, not addressed because of the method of representation? Researchers should examine not only issues with partisan connotations, such as tariff, sumptuary, and electoral legislation, but also the full range of public policy questions. How much of the difference in public policy response to similar socioeconomic changes in the neighboring states of Connecticut and Massachusetts may be attributed to their differing systems of legislative representation? While Connecticut's urban workers went underrepresented in their state legislature, Massachusetts based representation essentially on districts of comparable population, and its legislature—although as persistently Republican in the late nineteenth century as that of Connecticut—pioneered in business regulatory and protective labor legislation.[52]

If the study of systems of representation poses important new questions for historical analysis, it simultaneously provides a major framework for integrating diverse aspects of political history: constituencies, parties, campaigns, elections, and governance. Thoughtful application of quantitative techniques to the examination of varying systems of representation offers the possibility of illuminating many issues, ranging from party development and political participation to legislative behavior and the relationship between electoral realignment and policy. Rather than regarding the electoral structure as given and impartial, historians must analyze its role in shaping American politics. Otherwise, their explanations of American political history will remain incomplete and flawed.

Notes

1. For Edmund Randolph's remarks, see Michael Balinski and H. Peyton Young, *Fair Representation: Meeting the Ideal of One Man, One Vote* (New Haven, 1982), 6; for Benjamin Harrison's, *New York Times,* Dec. 10, 1891, p. 10. On the centrality of representation issues in the early republic and the "virtual hegemony" of representation based on population in America by 1850, see Rosemarie Zagarri, *The Politics of Size: Representation in the United States, 1776–1850* (Ithaca, 1987), esp. 148.

2. For a survey of voting behavior studies, see Peter H. Argersinger and John W. Jeffries, "American Electoral History: Party Systems and Voting Behavior," in *Research in Micropolitics: Voting Behavior,* ed. Samuel Long (2 vols., Greenwich, 1986), I, 1–33, reprinted in this volume as chapter 1. On legislative behavior, see Joel H. Silbey, " 'Delegates Fresh from the People': American Congressional and Legislative Behavior," *Journal of Interdisciplinary History,* 13 (Spring 1983), 603–27. One historian who has emphasized institutional factors, if not representation systems, in shaping policy outcomes is J. Morgan Kousser. See, for example, J. Morgan Kousser, "Restoring Politics to Political History," *ibid.,* 12 (Spring 1982), 569–95. For Richard L. McCormick's observation and his imaginative attempt to explain the relationship between voting and policy, see Richard L. McCormick, "The Party Period and Public Policy: An Exploratory Hypothesis," *Journal of American History,* 66 (Sept. 1979), 279–98.

The failure of quantitative historians to investigate representation is suggestive. The availability of massive relevant numerical data and the mathematical complexity of some aspects of the subject, which might have deterred some historians, should have attracted them. Moreover, the judicial revolution requiring representative systems based on the democratic principle of one voter, one vote occurred in the 1960s at the very time that quantitative historical analysis was rapidly developing. Those judicial decisions should have prompted American historians to consider the issues of constituency size, apportionment, and representation reform as a way to assess the historical performance of the political system. That they did not do so indicates the pervasive supposition of a democratic and impartial electoral system.

3. G. Gudgin and P.J. Taylor, *Seats, Votes, and the Spatial Organization of Elections* (London, 1979), 1–3.

4. For critical studies of suffrage and voting process, see J. Morgan Kousser, *The Shaping of Southern Politics: Suffrage Restriction and the Establishment of the One-Party South, 1880–1910* (New Haven, 1974); Peter H. Argersinger, " 'A Place on the Ballot': Fusion Politics and Antifusion Laws," *American Historical Review,* 85 (April 1980), 287–306, reprinted in this volume as chapter 6; and John F. Reynolds and Richard L. McCormick, "Outlawing 'Treachery': Split Tickets and Ballot Laws in New York and New Jersey, 1880–1910," *Journal of American History,* 72 (March 1986), 835–58.

5. Gordon E. Baker, "Threading the Political Thicket by Tracing the Steps of the Late Robert G. Dixon, Jr.: An Appraisal and Appreciation," in *Representation and Redistricting Issues,* ed. Bernard Grofman et al. (Lexington, Mass., 1982), 21–34, esp. 21.

6. See Richard P. McCormick, *The Presidential Game: The Origins of American Presidential Politics* (New York, 1982), esp. 11–12.

7. Historians have scarcely begun to address such issues, but see Ronald P. Formisano, *The Birth of Mass Political Parties: Michigan, 1827–1861* (Princeton, 1971), 81–101; Samuel P. Hays, "The Politics of Reform in Municipal Government in the Progressive Era," *Pacific Northwest Quarterly*, 55 (Oct. 1964), 157–69; Charles W. Eagles, "Democracy Delayed: Reapportionment and Urban-Rural Conflict in the 1920s," paper presented at the annual meeting of the American Historical Association, Dec. 28, 1987 (in Peter H. Argersinger's possession); and Abigail M. Thernstrom, *Whose Votes Count? Affirmative Action and Minority Voting Rights* (Cambridge, Mass., 1987).

8. *New York Times*, Dec. 10, 1891, p. 10; *ibid.*, Oct. 4, 1877, p. 1; *Appleton's Annual Cyclopedia, 1886* (New York, 1887), 442; Robert G. Dixon, Jr., "Fair Criteria and Procedures for Establishing Legislative Districts," in *Representation and Redistricting Issues,* ed. Grofman et al., 7–19, esp. 9.

9. On apportionment of representation in the states, see Robert B. McKay, *Reapportionment: The Law and Politics of Equal Representation* (New York, 1965), 275–475. On the Rhode Island towns, see U.S. Census Office, *Compendium of the Tenth Census* (Washington, 1883), Part I, 281.

10. "Legal Disfranchisement," *Atlantic Monthly*, 69 (April 1892), 545.

11. *Congressional Globe*, 41 Cong., 2 sess., June 23, 1870, pp. 4737–38; William Dudley Foulke, "Proportional Representation as a Remedy for Present Political Evils," *Proportional Representation Review*, 1 (Dec. 1893), 37–49, esp. 38.

12. For a useful survey of the political science literature, see David Saffell, "Reapportionment and Public Policy: State Legislators' Perspectives," in *Representation and Redistricting Issues,* ed. Grofman et al., 203–19. For the classic statement of the "political universe," see Walter Dean Burnham, "The Changing Shape of the American Political Universe," *American Political Science Review*, 59 (March 1965), 7–28. On partisan voting in legislatures, see William G. Shade et al., "Partisanship in the United States Senate: 1869–1901," *Journal of Interdisciplinary History*, 4 (Autumn 1973), 185–205; Jerome M. Clubb and Santa A. Traugott, "Partisan Cleavage and Cohesion in the House of Representatives, 1861–1974," *ibid.*, 7 (Winter 1977), 375–401; and Peter H. Argersinger, "Populists in Power: Public Policy and Legislative Behavior," *ibid.*, 18 (Summer 1987), 81–105.

13. *Vote distortion*, a measure of the imbalance between popular votes and representation, was +8.6% for Republicans in the House of the Fifty-first Congress and −2.1% for Democrats. Nor did the bias derive, as Republicans might have argued and historians expected, from the suppression of Republican votes in the South. Excluding the Confederate and border states from the calculation widens the divergence, the Republican figure becoming +15.5% and the Democratic −10.6%.

14. Gerald McFarland, "The Breakdown of Deadlock: The Cleveland Democracy in Connecticut, 1884–1894," *Historian*, 31 (May 1969), 381–97, esp. 392; *Journal of United Labor*, April 25, 1886.

15. Maurice Duverger, *Political Parties: Their Organization and Activity in the Modern State*, trans. Barbara North and Robert North (New York, 1963), 217. See also Douglas W. Rae, *The Political Consequences of Election Laws* (New Haven, 1971), 91–96.

16. Benjamin Butler to S.H. Pearsol, Aug. 19, 1884, Benjamin Butler Papers (Library of Congress); *Chicago Tribune*, Sept. 2, 1884, p. 1; Argersinger, "'A Place on the Ballot.'" See also Howard Scarrow, "Duverger's Law, Fusion, and the Decline of American 'Third' Parties," *Western Political Quarterly*, 39 (Dec. 1986), 634–47.

17. *Congressional Globe*, 40 Cong., 3 sess., March 2, 1869, appendix, 274.

18. Peter H. Argersinger, "New Perspectives on Election Fraud in the Gilded Age," *Political Science Quarterly*, 100 (Winter 1985/86), 669–87, reprinted in this volume as

chapter 4; David Dudley Field, "Representation of Minorities," *Journal of Social Science,* 3 (1871), 133–47, esp. 140.

19. Robert Luce, *Legislative Principles* (Boston, 1930), 393; Robert G. Dixon, Jr., *Democratic Representation: Reapportionment in Law and Politics* (New York, 1968), 459–63; William Dudley Foulke, *A Hoosier Autobiography* (New York, 1922), 90.

20. James A. Woodburn, *American Politics: Political Parties and Party Problems in the United States* (New York, 1906), 275. See also Bruce E. Cain, *The Reapportionment Puzzle* (Berkeley, 1984).

21. *Congressional Record,* 47 Cong., sp. sess., April 11, 1881, p. 250.

22. See Gordon E. Baker, "Quantitative and Descriptive Guidelines to Minimize Gerrymandering," in *Democratic Representation and Apportionment: Quantitative Methods, Measures, and Criteria,* ed. L. Papayanopoulos, *Annals of the New York Academy of Sciences,* 219 (1973), 200–208. For other methods of evaluating apportionments in relation to population and useful discussions of the limitations of the *index of inequality, average relative deviation,* and *theoretical control index,* see Glendon Schubert and Charles Press, "Measuring Malapportionment," *American Political Science Review,* 58 (June 1964), 302–27. The apparent discrepancy between the average relative deviation for Michigan and its two partisan components results from the exclusion from the second calculation of four districts whose boundaries were so rearranged that parts of each were represented by both Republicans and Democrats in the 1885 legislature.

23. Edward R. Tufte, "The Relationship between Seats and Votes in Two-Party Systems," *American Political Science Review,* 67 (June 1973), 540–54, esp. 553. The discussion of the calculation and analysis of swing ratio and bias is derived from this article; the exchange of correspondence between Walter Dean Burnham and Edward R. Tufte, "Communications," *ibid.,* 68 (March 1974), 207–13; and Edward R. Tufte, "Determinants of the Outcomes of Midterm Congressional Elections," *ibid.,* 69 (Sept. 1975), 812–26.

24. Solving the regression equation with the percentage of seats set at 50% provides the percentage of votes a party typically needs to carry the legislature. Subtracting that figure from 50% then provides a measure of the degree to which the party is advantaged or disadvantaged in gaining seats proportionate to its popular vote. This definition differs from the common measure of bias as the difference between the percentage of the popular vote and the percentage of seats won. All systems of district election disproportionately reward the dominant party, and the simpler measure fails to indicate whether the system favors one particular party or whether the other party would be equally advantaged with the same popular vote. For example, in the 1890 Connecticut state senate election, the Democrats captured 70.8% of the seats while polling but 51.8% of the popular votes. But rather than the system being biased *for* them by 19 points, it was actually biased *against* them; had the Republicans captured 51.8% of the votes they would have received 87.4% of the seats. Howard A. Scarrow has demonstrated the desirability of emphasizing the difference between each party's projected seat/vote ratios at the same vote percentage, but his use of partially reciprocal rather than completely identical vote percentages to calculate the measure introduces a distortion that, with the large swing ratios of the nineteenth century—before the recent "bipartisan gerrymanders" designed to protect the seats of incumbents regardless of party—would be inappropriate for this historical study. Moreover, the mathematical ease of his calculations is offset by their failure to produce a single figure useful for comparative purposes. By using the regression line suggested in this essay, however, such a figure can be achieved simply by solving the regression equation for the percentage of seats with the popular vote set at 50% and doubling the difference between that number and 50. (The same figure can also be derived from doubling the product of the swing ratio and the bias as calculated in the text.) Therefore even a small

party bias as measured in this essay would appear more dramatic using Scarrow's definition and would quickly become politically effective. A bias of 3%, combined with a moderate swing ratio of 2.5, would produce a differential between the two parties of 15 percent at any level of popular vote they each achieved. In this instance, the advantaged party would receive 57.5% of the seats with 50% of the vote, while the other party would receive but 42.5% of the seats with the same popular vote. The regression-derived measures of bias and swing ratio are sensitive to the number of possible outcomes projected, which should be limited to the region of the actual election result. Finally, the assumption underlying the construction of a projected seats-vote curve that vote swings are uniform across districts has proved troubling to some analysts evaluating national elections but seems somewhat more reasonable for state elections in the late nineteenth century. See Howard A. Scarrow, "The Impact of Reapportionment on Party Representation in the State of New York," in *Representation and Redistricting Issues*, ed. Grofman et al., 223–36.

25. *New York Times*, Aug. 17, 1883, p. 1; Tufte, "Relationship between Seats and Votes in Two-Party Systems," 544. In all states, apportionment bills consistently generated more partisan legislative voting alignments than bills on any other subject.

26. Neither the Ohio nor the Connecticut series of elections showed important relationships between votes polled and seats won (r^2 of .39 and .47 respectively).

27. *Congressional Globe*, 41 Cong., 2 sess., June 23, 1870, p. 4737; Walter C. Hamm, "The Art of Gerrymandering," *Forum*, 9 (July 1890), 543–44.

28. Vote distortion is calculated by expressing the difference between a party's share of legislative seats won and its share of the popular vote as a percentage of the latter.

29. *New York Times*, April 12, 1881, p. 1; *ibid.*, April 13, 1881, p. 1; *Appleton's Annual Cyclopedia, 1881* (New York, 1882), 198.

30. "This Week," *Nation*, Jan. 29, 1891, p. 81; *Congressional Record*, 47 Cong., sp. sess., April 11, 1881, p. 250; Edward McPherson, *A Handbook of Politics for 1884* (Washington, 1884), 57; Edward McPherson, *A Handbook of Politics for 1886* (Washington, 1886), 231; Edward McPherson, *A Handbook of Politics for 1888* (Washington, 1888), 175; Edward McPherson, *A Handbook of Politics for 1890* (Washington, 1890), 187; Samuel T. McSeveney, *The Politics of Depression: Political Behavior in the Northeast, 1893–1896* (New York, 1972), 10–11.

31. "This Week," *Nation*, Oct. 6, 1892, p. 250; *New Haven Evening Register*, Sept. 17, 1890; McSeveney, *Politics of Depression*, 8.

32. *Hartford Post* quoted in *Journal of the Knights of Labor*, April 13, 1893; *Appleton's Annual Cyclopedia, 1891* (New York, 1892), 234–36.

33. *New Haven Evening Register*, Feb. 2, 1892, Jan. 14, Feb. 26, 1891; *Appleton's Annual Cyclopedia, 1891*, 236–37.

34. "Connecticut's Ballot Lesson," *Nation*, Aug. 4, 1892, p. 80; *New York Times*, Sept. 28, 1892, p. 5; *New Haven Evening Register*, Sept. 28, 1892.

35. *Hartford Daily Courant*, May 8, 1891; *New York Times*, Sept. 14, 1892, p. 5. Representation reform was effectively prevented by the system itself, for it required the approval of either the unrepresentative legislature or an even more biased constitutional convention in which each town would have equal influence.

36. *Annual Message of Governor George F. Fort to the Legislature of the State of New Jersey* (Trenton, 1852), 19; Alan Shank and Ernest C. Reock, Jr., *New Jersey's Experience with General Assembly Districts, 1852–1893: Preliminary Draft* (New Brunswick, 1966), 7, 16. The adoption of single-member districts followed the recent precedent established by Congress and was part of Fort's program of electoral reform to bring "the exercise of political power nearer the source whence it is derived." Popular election of the governor had begun only in 1845, and Fort now proposed popular election of all other

state and county officers. He also urged the reapportionment of congressional districts according to equal populations. *Annual Message of Governor George F. Fort*, 18–19.

37. Shank and Reock, *New Jersey's Experience*, 11–14, 88–94.

38. Because of irregular data availability, vote distortion figures cover the elections from 1876, when the secretary of state began publishing some election statistics, through 1893 for the majority party and from 1881 through 1888 for third parties. *Trenton State Gazette*, April 5, 1878; *New York Times*, Feb. 7, 1879, p. 5; Shank and Reock, *New Jersey's Experience*, 73–74, 36, 41–45, 93–100; Richard P. McCormick, *The History of Voting in New Jersey* (New Brunswick, 1953), 140, 168; Stanley H. Friedelbaum, "Apportionment Legislation in New Jersey," *Proceedings of the New Jersey Historical Society*, 70 (Oct. 1952), 262–77.

39. Shank and Reock, *New Jersey's Experience*, 51–62; McCormick, *History of Voting in New Jersey*, 141.

40. *Trenton True American*, March 11, 1881; *New York Times*, Feb. 12, 1879, p. 2; *Newark Daily Advertiser*, Feb. 11, 13, 1879; *Appleton's Annual Cyclopedia, 1889* (New York, 1890), 591. William E. Sackett, *Modern Battles of Trenton* (Trenton, 1895), 286–87.

41. *Appleton's Annual Cyclopedia, 1889*, 591; Sackett, *Modern Battles of Trenton*, 290–93; Shank and Reock, *New Jersey's Experience*, 72–85; *State v. Wrightson*, 56 N.J.L. 126 (1893).

42. Shank and Reock, *New Jersey's Experience*, 88–92; Ernest C. Reock, Jr., *Population Inequality among Counties in the New Jersey Legislature, 1791–1962* (New Brunswick, 1963).

43. *Chicago Tribune*, Feb. 11, 1870, p. 1; *Springfield Illinois State Journal*, July 6, 1870, p. 2; *ibid.*, May 10, 1870, p. 2; Blaine F. Moore, *The History of Cumulative Voting and Minority Representation in Illinois, 1870–1919* (Urbana, 1920), 14–15, 26–27; George S. Blair, "The Adoption of Cumulative Voting in Illinois," *Journal of the Illinois State Historical Society*, 47 (Winter 1954), 373–84.

44. *Chicago Tribune*, Nov. 6, 1874, p. 1; *ibid.*, May 14, 1870, p. 2; Moore, *History of Cumulative Voting*, 14, 28–40. In the 765 district elections from 1872 through 1900, the minority party elected two of the three representatives 20 times. Only 3 times did the majority party elect all three representatives.

45. Catherine Spence, "The Transferable Vote," *Proportional Representation Review*, 1 (June 1894), 108–15, esp. 115; Moore, *History of Cumulative Voting*, 22; Charles S. Hyneman and Julian D. Morgan, "Cumulative Voting in Illinois," *Illinois Law Review*, 32 (May 1937), 27–29. For valuable excerpts from a contemporary survey of public opinion on the operation and effects of the cumulative vote in Illinois, see Matthias N. Forney, *Political Reform by the Representation of Minorities* (New York, 1894), esp. 43–47, 53–64, 65–87.

46. Pennsylvania adopted the cumulative vote in the 1870s for some judicial and local offices, and several cities did so for their councils. The 1872 Republican New York State legislature passed a bill establishing the system for New York City in an effort to weaken Tammany's control of the city, but Democratic Governor John Hoffman vetoed the measure. See *New York Times*, May 1, 1872, p. 5. Michigan's 1889 Republican legislature enacted a cumulative voting law for multimember urban districts only in a partisan attempt to gain some Republican representatives from Democratic cities without risking losses elsewhere. The state supreme court invalidated the law. *Maynard v. Board of Canvassers*, 84 Mich. 238 (1890). Both Ohio and South Dakota rejected statewide cumulative vote systems in popular referenda. Obviously politicians and voters evaluated representation systems in terms of their political consequences, and it was accordingly virtually impossible to replace a system biased toward the majority with a more balanced one,

regardless of popular dissatisfaction. Indeed, as the Michigan example suggests, the likelihood of change was toward a more biased system.

47. John D. Buenker, "The Politics of Resistance: The Rural-Based Yankee Republican Machines of Connecticut and Rhode Island," *New England Quarterly,* 47 (June 1974), 212–37, esp. 223. Many local representation systems included woman suffrage and constitute remarkably neglected opportunities for research in that important subject.

48. *Congressional Record,* 43 Cong., 1 sess., March 21, 1874, pp. 4133, 4138; John Spooner to Jeremiah Rusk, Jan. 27, 1891, John C. Spooner Papers (Library of Congress). Distortion figures are for the Fifty-second Congress.

49. Oliver P. Morton, "The American Constitution," *North American Review,* 124 (May–June 1877), 345–46; *New York Times,* Oct. 18, 1892, p. 1.

50. *New York Times,* Feb. 17, 1882, p. 1; *Congressional Record,* 41 Cong., 2 sess., June 23, 1870, p. 4735; *ibid.,* 46 Cong., 3 sess., Jan. 5. 1881, pp. 350–53; Balinski and Young, *Fair Representation,* 37.

51. J.W. Sullivan, "Our King-President," *American Federationist,* 1 (Oct. 1894), 173.

52. For Massachusetts's progressive position, see Richard Abrams, *Conservatism in a Progressive Era: Massachusetts Politics, 1900–1912* (Cambridge, Mass., 1964), 1–24; on Connecticut, see McFarland, "Breakdown of Deadlock," 392; and Buenker, "Politics of Resistance." That the Massachusetts legislature was more responsive to urban workers did not mean that they were satisfied with the representation system. The *Worcester Workingman's Advocate,* for instance, actively campaigned for proportional representation, using the state's senatorial elections to illustrate the inequities and inefficiencies of the prevailing method of representation. Its plan was to use the mechanism of the transferable vote to create voluntary constituencies based on shared political interests rather than mandatory constituencies based on residential location. See "Workingmen and Minority Representation," *Nation,* Sept. 16, 1886, p. 229.

4

New Perspectives on Election Fraud in the Gilded Age

The Gilded Age has been popularly linked with political corruption ever since it acquired its name, redolent of fraud and artifice, from the title of the 1873 novel by Mark Twain and Charles Dudley Warner. Subsequent scholars have generally followed Twain's lead and, in particular, have described the elections of the Gilded Age as being characterized by fraud and corruption. The highly competitive political system of the late nineteenth century, as Samuel T. McSeveney has written, "led to repeated charges, countercharges, and denials of corruption, coercion, bribery, and fraud—allegations that have been echoed by subsequent political biographers and historians. Taken at face value, these outcries would lead one to believe that the two parties alternated in cheating their opponents out of deserved victories." McSeveney could have easily added political scientists to the list of those who repeated the contemporary allegations of fraud. Philip E. Converse, in fact, has based a theory to explain the decline in voter turnout statistics in the early twentieth century on the elimination of massive electoral fraud he assumed to be characteristic of the earlier period. Rarely, however, have scholars carefully analyzed or documented the claims of widespread election fraud, and even Converse described the accounts of such fraud as "everywhere anecdotal."[1]

Recently, many of the practitioners of the "new political history" have sought to minimize the existence of election fraud in the Gilded Age, at least in the nonsouthern states. In contrast to Converse, they have argued that the recorded high rates of voter turnout reflected the voters' genuine attachments to the political parties and the values they represented. Emphasizing such concepts as party systems and secular realignment and seeking to explain the social basis of mass political behavior, these scholars have either ignored altogether the

From Peter H. Argersinger, "New Perspectives on Election Fraud in the Gilded Age," *Political Science Quarterly*, vol. 100 (Winter 1985–86), pp. 669–687. Reprinted with permission of *Political Science Quarterly*.

election corruption emphasized in traditional accounts or minimized its importance as highly colored but isolated incidents of relative insignificance compared
to the larger processes that capture their attention.[2] In his study of late nineteenth-century politics, for instance, Richard Jensen claims to have examined
"every known major case of significant election fraud, bribery, and coercion in
the Midwest for the period together with a few cases that were never publicly
known." His conclusion is that midwestern elections were quiet and honest with
little evidence of "massive irregularities."[3] Building on Jensen's work, Walter
Dean Burnham rejects the possibility of "pervasive vote frauds and overcounts"
in the rural areas of Pennsylvania and New York as well as in such midwestern
states as Iowa and Wisconsin.[4] Paul Kleppner and Stephen C. Baker also discount the charges of widespread electoral corruption, pointing out that "the
evidentiary base underpinning these broad claims is quite thin" and consists
mostly of secondary accounts.[5]

Howard W. Allen and Kay Warren Allen have undertaken the most extensive
analysis of "the published literature" on "fraudulent election practices." Their
conclusion is resolute: "The evidence to demonstrate the existence of election
fraud in the [contemporary] literature is not only anecdotal, it is unsystematic,
impressionistic, and by and large inconclusive. Almost all contemporary allegations of vote fraud were based primarily upon sweeping, generalized, often
highly emotional charges substantiated in most cases by only the most fragile
evidence, if supported at all."[6] The Allens and Kleppner and Baker also significantly clarify the issue by examining those who made the charges of election
fraud and asking what Kleppner and Baker term "the *relevant* questions: Who
were these people socially? What were their objectives?" Conceding that this
evidence is also "fragmentary and uneven," these scholars insist that those who
made these allegations came from the upper levels of society, were reacting
against the conditions of urbanizing, industrializing America, with its vast immigrant population, and hoped to weaken political parties and universal suffrage.
Such "Mugwumps" thus assumed the existence of what they described, believing that corruption inevitably followed from universal suffrage and democracy.
Their claims were thus more "deductive" from their perception of the political
system than documented from reality.[7]

The Setting and Significance of Election Fraud

The new political historians seem to have a motive of their own in attempting to
discount election fraud. This concern is most evident in the linked title of the
Allens' work, "Vote Fraud and Data Validity." As the Allens write, "if elections were universally fraudulent, then the results of those elections are distor-
tions of popular attitudes and of dubious validity. If election data are invalid,
then the study of mass voting behavior is an exercise in futility." Election fraud,
in short, would dramatically undermine the value of a number of recent and

impressive political studies based on analysis of election data. Richard Jensen agrees: if fraud and bribery determined elections, "then elaborate analysis of campaigns and voting patterns is an exercise in cynicism and futility."[8]

To some extent, this concern is something of a misperception of the problem. Persistent electoral fraud poses a more serious obstacle to the traditional political historians whose analysis of election returns is limited to the simple dichotomy of victory or defeat. Their attempts to understand popular attitudes through such election analyses can carry little weight for the late nineteenth century anyway, for the period was characterized by high levels of partisanship and electoral competitiveness, and slight shifts in voting or turnout could turn whole elections. Democratic presidential candidate Winfield Hancock carried California in 1880 by 22 votes; at the same time Republican James Garfield carried the entire nation by only 8,000 votes. The quantitative analysis characteristic of the more sophisticated recent political studies, on the other hand, is based not on a dichotomous approach but on the use of descriptive statistics to analyze numerical data in terms of central tendencies, variances, and relationships among interval variables. And while "massive fraud" injects distortion into any analysis, the reality of election fraud in the Gilded Age was its strategic, not massive, nature. Only in those areas where relatively minor changes in the recorded popular vote would result in a different electoral outcome was there any incentive for fraudulent activity. As Senator George Edmunds remarked in 1889, "divisions of parties in several of the States have been so close that the purchase of a comparatively small number of votes could easily turn the scale . . . and it can be assumed to be an undisputed fact that such temptation has been yielded to by the active managing agents of both the great political parties."[9] Moreover, as a politician of a later period liked to note about his supportive father, Joseph P. Kennedy, he was willing to buy as many votes as necessary to win, but he was damned if he would buy a single extra one.

Second to the highly competitive nature of the political system in encouraging or permitting fraud was the structure of the election process. For most of the period there was no secret ballot. Instead voters used party tickets, printed by the different parties, containing the names of only their own candidates, and often varying widely in size and color. Distributed at the polls by partisan "hawkers" or "ticket peddlers," these party tickets made the voter's choice of party a public act and rendered voters susceptible to various forms of intimidation and influence while facilitating vote buying. Most states did not have meaningful (or even any) registration laws, making it exceedingly difficult to determine voter eligibility, and the absence even of local residence requirements in such pivotal states as Indiana made possible the election-eve "colonization" of voters. Finally, election officials were generally partisan, rather than nonpartisan or even bipartisan, and mobs of excited party workers surrounded the polls.

A third but more diffuse factor which made election fraud possible was the existence among many segments of the electorate of a political culture that apparently accepted or tolerated electoral corruption. Such a political culture, with what it implies about citizens' expectations for politics and government, also obviously calls into question the interpretation of the Gilded Age electoral universe prevalent among the new political historians. Their view holds that voting was an act that expressed deeply felt cultural and religious values that were represented and implemented by the major parties, and that the party system satisfied the electorate. But widespread election fraud suggests that many voters did not regard their parties as essential vehicles of cultural expression nor their votes as especially important in either a symbolic or instrumental sense. Such a conflict may help explain the determination of these historians to minimize the existence of electoral corruption, though few have explicitly discussed it. Paul Kleppner, however, forcefully argues against the notion of pervasive election fraud precisely on the grounds that it would have been incompatible with the political culture described by the ethnocultural historians.[10] The subject of election fraud thus not only represents a challenge to the methodology of the new political history in terms of raising the problem of data validity, but also raises questions of deeper significance concerning the portrayal of political culture and the party system.

It is within this setting of electoral competitiveness, partisan or weak institutional arrangements, and an "indulgent" political culture that the issue of election fraud should be carefully evaluated. And to determine the nature and meaning of election fraud the scholar should consider not only the familiar sources already examined by recent scholars but alternative sources of information heretofore little utilized. The effort that follows is more suggestive than exhaustive.

Defining the Problem

First, of course, there is the problem of defining fraud. Scholars have often been careless in their use of the word "fraud," sometimes applying it in a nonspecific fashion, as did such disappointed partisans in the Gilded Age who simply attributed their defeat to "flagrant crimes against the ballot box."[11] Such scholars as Converse have assumed, on the other hand, that election fraud always had the effect of increasing the vote polled and thereby inflating apparent turnout rates. Howard Allen and Kay Warren Allen have sensibly considered the problem by attempting to differentiate between types of fraud and evaluating each. They emphasize the serious importance of fraud that violated the voters' "rational will," such as "falsification of the vote count by election officials," voter intimidation, and "repeating" or the casting of multiple ballots by one voter. Presumably this category would also include registration fraud, ballot-box stuffing, violence at the polls, impersonation, altering ballots to invalidate them or change their meaning, and altering returns. The Allens' other major category for vote fraud includes those techniques that ostensibly did not violate the voter's "rational will'' and, therefore, should not be regarded as seriously. In this classification they place ''heavy-handed political campaigning,'' such as employers warning their workers of possible unemployment in the event of a particular election outcome, and bribery, which they describe as a voter's ''willing'' acceptance of something in exchange for his ballot.[12]

It was, however, precisely the latter type of ''corruption'' that was most frequently alleged in the late nineteenth century, and so to define it away reduces the incidence of ''vote fraud'' while doing nothing to disprove the existence of an illegal activity viewed as troubling at the time. There is increasing evidence, moreover, that bribery and vote-buying were widely prevalent in Gilded Age elections. Genevieve Gist, for instance, has discovered massive vote-buying in rural Ohio, with up to 90 percent of the voters in Adams County selling their votes in the 1890s. As late as 1910, nearly 1,700 voters in that county, more than a fourth of its electorate, were convicted of vote-selling.[13] More recently, John Reynolds has estimated that in New Jersey in the Gilded Age and the Progressive Era ''perhaps as much as one third of the electorate commonly accepted money for their votes.'' Such vote-buying was so widespread as to be virtually ''socially acceptable'' among some groups and openly observed. A Newark newspaper noted in 1907 that ''the reproach of the purchased ballot is usually aimed at the cities and the lodging houses therein, but the evil exists to a much greater extent in many rural sections, where even well-to-do farmers expect to be paid well for the loss of time in going to the polls for themselves and their laborers.'' Thus, ''what was most often being 'purchased,' '' notes Reynolds, ''was not the voter's support for a given party or candidate, only his registering that choice on election day.'' In that sense, vote-buying would clearly correspond to the Allens' category of not violating the voter's rational will. But it was not simply patrician Mugwumps who denounced this practice. Governor David B. Hill told the New York legislature that such money spent to get out the vote was distributed under a ''transparent excuse for bribery and corruption,'' for its ''real design or effect is to influence the man whose teams or services are nominally employed.'' But Reynolds insists that vote-buying in this period ''flourished not because voters or politicians were more corrupt, but because it was well suited to the party system'' and to the highly competitive electoral system. Reynolds believes vote-buying did promote high turnout levels but, unlike Converse, believes it performed ''a genuine public service.''[14]

The more serious and disruptive forms of election fraud, however, remain to be studied carefully. As Reynolds observes, the widespread acceptance of vote-buying means ''more is known about bribery at the polls than [is known about] the clandestine acts of a few election officials.'' Other scholars agree as to the difficulty of the task. ''Successful dirty politics, by definition,'' concludes Jensen, ''is never discovered.'' Burnham believes it a ''virtual impossibility'' to specify vote fraud. And the Allens note, ''The very nature of the subject matter, of course, like other illegal, immoral, or irregular activities, makes it unlikely that conclusive documentary evidence of fraud will be found. Few individuals were likely to have recorded for posterity their involvement in such acts.''[15]

Part of the difficulty, however, lies in the limited nature of the historical evidence so far examined. As Kleppner and Baker remark, analyses of nineteenth-century electoral corruption have been invariably based on such contemporary journals as *Century, Forum, The Nation,* and *North American Review.* ''What we know, or think we know, of the operation of the electoral process in the nineteenth century derives largely from this corpus of contemporary materials.''[16] And, together with Howard Allen and Kay Warren Allen, they have clearly demonstrated the undocumented and biased character of such literature. It should be noted, however, that that was the nature of the type of literature they were examining—undocumented essays in generalist journals directed to the literate and respectable public.[17] It need not follow that the substance was inaccurate because the style was suspect and the motive self-seeking.

New Evidence of Fraud

There is, in fact, a wide array of other types of contemporary literature alleging the existence of election fraud, the authors of which differ in almost every imaginable way from the elitist Mugwumps exposed by the Allens and Kleppner. These sources include books, correspondence, and newspapers written by members of groups prominent among the democratic elements of the electorate. Spokesmen of the frequent third parties of the time continually complained of various kinds of election fraud. In an autobiography, a Pennsylvania Greenbacker of the 1870s described the counting out of his party by local election judges who simply credited Democratic candidates with enough votes to carry the district.[18] In his autobiography, a Detroit Socialist recalled false counts and ballot box stuffing against his party and an investigation that revealed ballot box tampering in an unsuccessful effort to cheat an elected Socialist out of his seat.[19] Agrarian parties of the western states similarly attacked election officials for illegal behavior. In private correspondence, one member of the Minnesota Farmers' Alliance lamented, ''The rotten Democratic returning board of Morrison County have counted me out'' by one vote, returned after all judges went to bed except one who was himself a candidate. The Democratic officials, the Allianceman concluded, were a ''gang of unscrupulous ballot box manipulators.'' Other members of agrarian third parties complained privately of ''repeaters'' and of ''the colonizing of voters'' used against their candidates.[20] In more public actions, Kansas Populists in 1893 contested eighteen legislative elections awarded to Republican candidates by the Republican-controlled State Board of Canvassers. One Republican candidate had been awarded the election certificate because of the transposition of voting totals with his Populist opponent, a maneuver of the Republican county clerk that the State Board acknowledged but refused to correct. Other Republicans declared elected included ineligible postmasters and nonresidents, and the Populists challenged still others on the basis of illegal votes, bribery, and miscount of ballots. Third party newspapers regularly reported instances of election fraud. In 1878, for instance, an Indianapolis Greenback paper charged Republicans with practicing repeating, bribery, and fraudulent vote counting as flagrantly in Indiana as Democrats did in the South. An Iowa Populist newspaper in the 1890s had an all-inclusive indictment of its Republican opponents, accusing them of "fraud, intimidation, coercion, bribery, false promises, illegal voting, and ballot box stuffing."[21]

Labor organizations and representatives were even more vociferous and frequent in their complaints of various kinds of election fraud. Not surprisingly, much of the chorus was directed against intimidation of workers by their employers. The worker's political desires, the *Journal of United Labor* declared, were "smothered by the decree of his employer, who dictates what ticket he must vote." Knights of Labor leader Terence Powderly attacked, on the other hand, "the system by which votes are counted" as "so flagrantly corrupt that it is the easiest thing in the world to purchase venal election officials." Labor candidates Benjamin Butler in 1884 and Henry George in 1886 both complained that ballots cast for them in New York City were counted for their Democratic opponents.[22] One labor editor viewed the voting system in as sweeping terms as any Mugwump: "Between the bribery of the voters, the intimidation by employers, and the use of fraudulent ballots by corrupt politicians, to say nothing of the opportunities under present methods for a stuffing of the ballot by dishonest inspectors, . . . the will of the people is oftener outraged than respected."[23]

But if agrarian and labor representatives agreed with the Mugwumps as to the existence of election fraud, their motives and concerns were different. Conceding that immigrants were often the bribed voters, one Knights of Labor editor insisted, "Yet it is not they who should be damned; but the system which makes such a state of affairs possible and the men who uphold it." In attacking that electoral system, laborites, Single Taxers, Populists, Greenbackers, Nationalists, and Socialists demanded reforms to liberate the voter and promote democracy, including the abolition of poll taxes, the adoption of women's suffrage, and the establishment of direct elections. Mugwumps, on the other hand, proposed not to expand but to restrict democracy, championing suffrage limitations by education, property, and nativity and the appointment, rather than the election, of public officials. While all critics sought to curtail election fraud by advocating the Australian ballot system, with its provisions for a secret ballot instead of party tickets and for public rather than partisan control of the election process, Mugwumps viewed the reform as a way to weaken the political parties that functioned to mobilize the mass electorate. Populists, Greenbackers, laborites, and related groups saw the reform as a vehicle to end intimidation of voters and increase popular influence in the political system.[24]

Finally, despite the common belief in the primacy of the Mugwump element in the spread of the Australian ballot reform, caused at least in part again by scholars relying on a restricted body of historical evidence, Greenbackers, laborites, and Single Taxers were often more influential in pressing for reform of the ballot system, however perverted those "reforms" sometimes became in practice. The first Australian ballot bill introduced in a state legislature, for instance, was written by George Walthew, a Greenbacker in the 1885 Michigan legislature, and two years later Judson Grenell, a socialist Knight of Labor legislator, revised the bill and secured its passage in the Michigan assembly. But even they had predecessors, such as Ohio Greenback legislator John Seitz. Seitz's campaign to enact a bill "to preserve the purity of elections" succeeded in 1879 when he was able to take advantage of the public outrage produced by startling revelations of fraud in Ohio's congressional elections.[25]

Thus, there were many observers besides the elitist and antidemocratic elements who complained of election fraud and mobilized to restrict it, and the literature of these other groups is readily available and should no longer be overlooked.

There are, moreover, other sources besides the secondary accounts cited by the Allens that provide ample documentation of the common existence of various kinds of election fraud. It is not necessary to rely on reformers' allegations, for legal records, official investigations, and politicians' own statements (public and private) all lend support. Whether such frauds were systemic or destructive of the validity of election statistics is perhaps difficult to determine, but their existence is certain. Their putative unimportance follows only if those reported represent most of those that occurred, a possibility already discounted above.

Howard W. Allen and Kay Warren Allen note that "rarely have politicians admitted to having committed vote fraud."[26] But given its illegal nature, it is instead surprising how many such confessions are readily available. Some examples appear in political correspondence that went astray and received great contemporary publicity. Perhaps the most notorious of these was the letter written by the Republican campaign official in 1888 instructing Indiana party workers to "Divide the floaters into blocks of five and put a trusted man with the necessary funds in charge of these five and make him responsible that none get away and that all vote our ticket." The New York Times accurately called this letter "a direct incitement to criminal acts. It is an election day handbook for the official vote buyers and bribery corps of the Republicans in Indiana."[27] Other confessions are contained in correspondence that retained its private character at the time, only to be exposed by subsequent scholars. Thus, 1880 Democratic National Chairman William H. Barnum, anticipating Republican fraudulent activity, instructed his party workers "to organize some plan to keep even with them."[28] The private correspondence of Horace Congar, a member of New Jersey's Republican executive committee, reveals that party officials regarded vote-buying as a standard feature of their campaign effort because of what one called "a large purchasable element among the voters." The party leaders were concerned about the prompt distribution of money to purchase such votes because "our workers *will not* make the necessary promises and arrangements unless the funds are *in hand* to meet them."[29] Republican Governor Francis Warren of Wyoming Territory enlisted employer intimidation from railroads and other large employers, writing one hotel operator, "I hope you will see your way clear to persuade all the voters at the Pacific Hotels in Wyoming to agree with us."[30] The cryptic phrasing required in such letters was also evident in the correspondence of James Garfield and W.W. Dudley to encourage John D. Rockefeller to cooperate with a Standard Oil supervisor who "would like to bring all his men into line" for the Republicans. Garfield was warned that it was "risky writing" of such plans for corporate intimidation of employees.[31]

Another type of political confession involves reminiscences or later testimony by party leaders. San Francisco boss Abraham Ruef, for example, admitted that the number of votes reported from his precincts was limited "only by the modesty of the election officials." The notorious William M. Tweed himself admitted upon interrogation substantially the same for New York: "The ballots made no result; the counters made the result."[32] Such actions were sometimes so flagrant as to outrage even members of the offending party, and their anguished disclosures of that corrupt conduct constitute evidence of election fraud more persuasive than the accusations of opponents. In New Jersey in the 1890s, for instance, a number of Democratic politicians formed an association to protest their own party's use of "all sorts of trickery, bribery, deception, fraud, ballot box stuffing, false registering, perjured Election Officers, etc."[33]

At times, personal animosities led to confessions of election fraud. For instance, one small-time Baltimore politico implicated himself in bribery, repeating, intimidation, and colonization when he exposed an operation because someone else was getting the credit for his own success in arranging vote fraud. John Dugan confessed that he had taken nine hoodlums from the Baltimore jail to the nearby village of Clarksville, where he lined them up, "and we filed past the poll. Each dropped in his ballot. Then we kept going around in a circle, each of us putting a ballot in every time round, until we had polled several hundred votes. We voted until we had voted all the names on the register, and we could not do more than that, could we?"[34]

Although the postelection grumbles of the losers can be discounted, there were other ways in which political leaders revealed the existence and dimensions of election fraud. Partisan newspapers all conceded the prevalence of vote buying. As the *Watertown* (N.Y.) *Times* noted in 1888, "Both parties were into it by mutual consent, and feeling secure from this cause there has been no secrecy in it. Men openly boast of buying and voters boast of the price they were able to get." An Indiana Democratic newspaper exulted that in the struggle to buy the "floating vote," "although the Republicans had lots of 'boodle,' the Democrats got a good share of them."[35] The equanimity with which some forms of political corruption were accepted was weakened only by their cost to party treasuries. In some instances, political leaders even agreed across party lines to standardize bribery practices and prices. Actions ostensibly taken to end vote bribery were frequently more protective than destructive, indicating again the practical acceptance of such tactics despite the often outraged rhetoric. After massive election bribery was exposed in New Jersey in 1883, for example, the legislature passed a new antibribery law, the actual purpose of which was to void the indictments for bribery then pending under earlier laws. Similarly in Maryland in 1887, a score of Baltimore election judges awaiting trial for election fraud escaped prosecution when the legislature repealed the law under which they had been indicted and then reenacted it without providing for pending prosecutions.[36]

Legal Sources

Despite these subterfuges, legal records do constitute another source of information concerning election fraud. The Allens argue that if election fraud were extensive, court cases should have been cited in the literature.[37] But the absence of such citations reflects more the nature of the popular literature surveyed than the absence of election fraud. There are, however, peculiarities about the judicial decisions recorded in the *Reporter* series that serve to limit the indications of such crimes. The cases recorded include only those appealed to a higher court on a point of law rather than the more typical routine violations and convictions. Nevertheless, even this publishing practice provides suggestive hints of election tactics across a wide spectrum, as even a cursory examination of decisions reveals: Maine politicians admitted bribing voters but argued that it was not illegal; an Indiana politician admitted bribing voters and the illegality of that act but argued that the prohibitory law was unconstitutional; a St. Louis politician admitted registry fraud but argued that there was no proof that the names he copied into the registry were of real people and, therefore, no crime had been committed; New York politicians also admitted falsifying registration lists but argued that a technicality in the law's language exempted them from prosecution in a particular jurisdiction; a Vermonter charged with repeating argued that his first vote was illegal and should not have been accepted, making his second vote acceptable; Pennsylvania election officials convicted for conspiracy to defraud by making false returns argued that the state had to prove they entered into such conspiracy before becoming election officers rather than merely as they falsified the returns; an Ohio politician convicted of adding fraudulent ballots to the ballot box during the count argued that the law prohibited only election officials, not bystanders, from such behavior.[38] Even without resulting in convictions of specific culprits, other cases provided incontrovertible evidence of impersonation, ballot box tampering, ballot falsification, and other acts of election fraud as courts spelled out procedural rules for conducting elections.[39] For the still larger bulk of legal evidence of election fraud, scholars will simply have to examine the local contemporary newspapers and unpublished court records. Only that painstaking work will reveal the common arrests and convictions for ballot box stuffing, repeating, miscounting, and false registration.[40]

Other aspects of the availability of legal evidence are also relevant to understanding and examining election fraud. State courts consistently ruled that ballots could not be released for use as evidence in investigations and trials of election officials charged with criminal behavior such as ballot box stuffing. The California supreme court, for instance, conceded in 1892 that such ballots constituted "the best means of proving" frauds by election officers but noted that state legislatures invariably passed laws prohibiting their use for "the enforcement of the . . . penalties for frauds of election officers." In 1895 the Missouri supreme court ruled similarly, with a statement suggestive of the political culture in which such frauds were practiced: "The tyranny of giant corporations and concentrated wealth on the one hand, and the combinations of laborers and workingmen on the other, to say nothing of the influence of parties, make it exceedingly difficult for any save a bold and courageous man to vote an open ticket, and the courts should be exceedingly careful, therefore, in discrediting the secret ballot" by permitting its use as trial evidence.[41] Thus many potential court cases never materialized because the "best" evidence was excluded from consideration.

Finally, the relative lack of legal citations for widespread election fraud might also reflect the failure of partisan grand juries to indict or juries to convict obviously guilty officials. Such failures, in turn, indicate the tolerant attitudes that large segments of the political community held toward electoral corruption. In 1880, in Philadelphia, for instance, nearly three dozen Republican election officers were arrested for election frauds that one newspaper described as "protean in shape, from the destruction and changing of ballots to the altering of returns after the votes had been counted." But the grand jury refused to indict the officials, and the district attorney had to postpone action on political offenses until a new grand jury convened. "Clearly the remedies against frauds at the ballot box were in the hands of a political Grand Jury," one newspaper concluded. Protected by such political influence, partisan election officers "had become comparatively indifferent regarding the concealment of their methods and practices."[42] In Indianapolis in 1886 a grand jury failed to indict anyone for election frauds despite overwhelming evidence. The presiding judge was astonished and sharply censured the jury for its apparent partisan motivation. In another midwestern city, an all-Democratic jury refused to return indictments against Democratic election officials despite voluminous evidence of repeaters, colonized voters, and other fraudulent acts. Local Greenbackers charged that the grand jury was "run as a partisan machine" and "manipulated by politicians to defeat justice and shield criminals because they are Democrats." Indeed, they concluded, "the machinery of justice in this county is so securely held by the Democratic party that fraudulent voting cannot now be punished."[43] Such partisan behavior by juries should not be surprising given the recognized partisan nature of other governmental bodies at the time, including election officials as well as police, legislatures, and civil bureaucracies.

Official investigations by state and federal governments constitute another source of evidence for election fraud. In 1885, for instance, Secretary of the Navy William C. Whitney summarized an investigation of electoral intimidation in the government's own navy yard: "the vote of the yard was practically coerced and controlled by the foremen. . . . The men were obliged to take their ballots in a folded form from a table presided over by one or more of the foremen, hold the ballot in sight while walking to the polls, 100 feet distant, between men stationed for the purpose of preventing any change of ballots on their part, and the ballot deposited without the voter having had the opportunity to see or know its contents or to exercise any choice for whom he should cast his ballot."[44]

Though congressional investigations were often partisan themselves and must be used judiciously, they often provide indisputable proof of election fraud, as when the minority report concedes such behavior or when witnesses confessed to their own illegal activities. To a congressional committee investigating intimidation and fraud in Massachusetts, for instance, a Republican party official admitted urging employers to pressure their workers to vote for the GOP, while the Republican state chairman admitted bribing voters in Boston. In an investigation of widespread violations of election law by Republican election officials in Cincinnati in 1884, one Democratic election supervisor casually testified that Democrats regularly and severely beat with wagon spokes any blacks who attempted to vote and drove them away from the polls.[45]

Evidence taken before congressional committees hearing contested election cases sometimes demonstrated intimidation, bribery, colonization, and other fraudulent practices. Certainly the relatively small proportion of congressional elections contested on such grounds does not accurately reflect the incidence of such practices. As Speaker of the House Thomas B. Reed conceded, never was Congress more completely partisan than in determining such contests. It made little sense to go to the expense and trouble of contesting elections, regardless of the grounds, unless one's own party already controlled the chamber. Even then other factors often proved decisive. The effort made by Ignatius Donnelly to contest his defeat in an 1878 Minnesota congressional election, documented with bribery, voter intimidation, and other illegal election practices, is illustrative. The Republican defense against such charges was that such practices were followed by all parties and, therefore, not of particular relevance.[46]

Indeed, the widespread acceptance of election fraud as appropriate and omnipresent sometimes actually militated against complaints about it. As one Indiana newspaper declared in reflecting this general attitude, "in the race for place and power, it is every man for himself and the devil take the hindmost. The man who gains a seat in Congress through a contest is looked upon as occupying a place he is not entitled to." In urging Democrats not to contest their defeats, this Democratic newspaper noted that "There was undoubtedly bulldozing and buying of votes, in a moderate and quiet way, on both sides, and means used to secure votes not in accordance with even political honesty and fair dealing," but "as elections are now conducted, we are of the opinion that . . . [the Republican candidates were] fairly elected."[47]

Perhaps of more use in evaluating the presence of election fraud, although subject to many of the same limitations, are the contested cases argued at the level of the state legislatures. Though more difficult to investigate than congressional cases, these data indicate the prevalence of various kinds of election fraud. A few examples are suggestive. The Kansas Populists contested eighteen legislative seats in 1893 on grounds of violation of election laws. An 1889 investigation by the Committee on Elections of the Rhode Island General Assembly uncovered widespread vote-buying and election corruption "almost beyond belief." In Montana in 1889 partisan actions of election officials (characterized by the *New York Times* as equivalent to those of "Southern returning boards") resulted in five contested election cases. These provided fascinating testimony explaining the monetary limits of vote-buying per voter and, ultimately, led to the organization of two legislatures and the election of four different United States senators. This type of election fraud perhaps reached its apogee in the celebrated 1891 "steal of the senate" in New York when Democrats gained control of that body by the partisan disposition of contested election cases.[48] Another legislative investigation, in New Jersey in 1890, found evidence of "extensive frauds . . . covering so many precincts and so connected in method and purpose as to demonstrate a common conspiracy." The Senate elections committee took 2,800 pages of testimony documenting false registrations, widespread repeating, colonizing, intimidation, miscounting, and illegal ballots. Ultimately, sixty-six men were sent to prison for their involvement in these practices.[49] Another form of election fraud revealed by a study of legislative sources is illustrated by the 1897 Indiana legislature's voting on partisan lines to unseat Populists who, all reports conceded, had received the majority of popular votes cast in their districts.[50]

Deflationary Fraud

Finally, while it is not the intention in this article to enter the controversy between Converse and others as to the precise level of voting fraud, it is incorrect to assume that fraud always inflated turnout statistics, as Converse believes.[51] Much substantiated election fraud involved manipulations, miscounting, or discarding of actual ballots by corrupt election officials rather than repeating or ballot box stuffing.[52] Violence and intimidation at the polls, which caused many voters *not* to vote, was another type of "deflationary" fraud. Indeed, violence was a common characteristic of Gilded Age elections and not at all limited to the South. The United States Marshal for Philadelphia admitted in 1881 that fraudulent voting and violence were so endemic in that city that "Never an election goes by without a riot" and in some wards "scarcely an election goes by without somebody being killed." A Cincinnati newspaper reported as a quiet election one in which only eight people were killed. In many cities riots were often orchestrated to drive people away from the polls, with protection provided for those carrying the "right" party ticket. A midwest newspaper noted in 1884 that nearly everywhere in America voting was "an arduous task attended by . . . personal danger. Every peaceable man and every household dread the approach of election day."[53] Such turmoil at the polls was so characteristic that the Kansas supreme court ruled in 1887 that election violence, including fights between rival party challengers, threats of physical retaliation, and "boisterous conduct," constituted only "a slight disturbance and casual fray, such as frequently occurs at elections" and would not "vitiate an election, or justify voters in abandoning the polls."[54] One New York City election inspector reported: "I think it next to impossible for any man to go down and get a square vote at that precinct unless he had a regiment of soldiers with fixed bayonets. . . . The crowd got around me and threatened my life, so that I was advised I had better leave, and did so, as I did not want to be killed." Richard Croker, eventually to become Tammany boss, got his political start as a bully to intimidate possible Republican voters and as a repeater, voting seventeen times in one election. In 1874 he was arrested for murdering one opponent at the polls.[55]

Other forms of election fraud that reduced, rather than increased, turnout included repeated verbal challenges, sometimes "unduly prolonged by the connivance of the [election] judges," by which legal voters were "unable to reach the [voting] window and actually tender their ballots." In some cities, turnout was reduced by the partisan use of law officers to arrest voters of the opposing party to keep them from the polls. The Cincinnati police, controlled by the Democratic city administration, in 1884 made a sweep through an area of heavy black population and arbitrarily arrested 113 black males on election eve and sequestered them in a basement under the jail until the polls closed the next day, whereupon they were released without charges ever being pressed.[56] In St. Louis 1,028 deputy marshals, appointed by Republican federal officials, arrested hundreds of Democrats to prevent their voting, and then released them without charges.[57]

The combination of violence at the polls and the role of law officers suggests one last source of information on election practices virtually ignored by historians and political scientists. This involves the records of the Department of Justice generated by the implementation of the Federal Elections Law.[58] Although usually incorrectly regarded as part of Reconstruction legislation, the Federal Elections Law, passed in 1871 and not repealed until 1894, applied to elections in the North and represented the federal government's only effort to regulate elections until the second half of the twentieth century. This law was passed in response to election fraud in the North and was designed to end impersonation, repeating, intimidation, and bribery in congressional elections or voting registrations. It authorized the appointment of federal supervisors of elections and of deputy marshals to assist the supervisors and maintain order.

Northern Democrats charged the Federal Elections Law with actually encouraging election fraud. As the deputies were federal appointees, they were invariably Republican. Indeed, deputies were usually chosen from lists supplied by local Republican party officials. Democrats maintained that such deputies intimidated potential Democratic voters, particularly immigrants. The number of deputies was often quite large, as in New York in 1892 when 8,000 deputies were appointed. At times such deputies served on election day as Republican party workers, distributing Republican tickets at the polls they were supposed to police. Some marshals even aided Republican repeaters in illegal voting and impersonation. In a revealing indication of partisan emotions and election day practices, Delaware's Democratic legislature in 1881 passed a resolution authorizing the state to defend all persons indicted for assaulting U.S. marshals or voting illegally. An Ohio Democratic newspaper demonstrated the same sentiments and the common reality of election violence when it denied the legitimacy of federal deputies in elections and maintained that "They can all be kicked and cuffed about like ordinary citizens, and will be compelled to take their chances with common people on election day."[59]

Republicans, of course, countered that the Federal Elections Law limited election fraud. Court decisions based on the application of the law demonstrated the validity of this assertion, at least in some instances. In 1880, for example, the Supreme Court upheld the conviction of Baltimore judges for resisting the authority of federal supervisors who tried to stop them from stuffing the ballot box. Moreover, Republicans believed that the mere presence of federal deputies often averted possible vote fraud. The U.S. marshal in Chicago in 1882, for example, reported that his deputies "kept thousands of repeaters and illegal voters from the polls" and had to arrest only ten persons for actually violating election laws.[60] On the other hand, an 1880 congressional investigating committee concluded that the Federal Elections Law was administered in such a partisan fashion that, rather than protecting the ballot, it simply served as a tool to promote Republican interests.[61] In any event, the records of the supervisors and marshals contain considerable information on election practices and election fraud that must be examined.

Conclusions

Scholars must recognize that election fraud, whatever its precise level or influence, was a common characteristic of Gilded Age elections. Arduous work remains to be done, but by consulting these new sources of information the full parameters of the subject will become clear. Obviously, allegations of voting fraud did not come solely from elitist Mugwumps or always signify an underlying determination to restrict the democratic aspects of the political system, whatever the final outcome of electoral "reform" might have been. But just as obviously, election fraud was rooted in the political system. The interaction among the institutional framework, the competitive partisan balance of the party system, and an indulgent political culture encouraged and made possible election fraud in the Gilded Age. Any changes in those interrelated factors would affect the incidence of election fraud.[62] And as even one Mugwump reformer in New York City noted, election abuses were more "directly attributable to the insufficiency of our election laws" than to "any inherent tendency to corruption."[63] Scholars must recognize that legal and political determinants of the actual conduct of elections often shaped electoral outcomes as much as did issues, candidates, or the social bases of mass political behavior.

Notes

1. Samuel T. McSeveney, *The Politics of Depression: Political Behavior in the Northeast, 1893–1896* (New York: Oxford University Press, 1972), 7; Philip E. Converse, "Change in the American Electorate," in Angus Campbell and Philip E. Converse, *The Human Meaning of Social Change* (New York: Russell Sage, 1972), 263–337, quote on 282.

2. Converse finds "remarkable" the extent to which "modern scholars working on nineteenth-century voting data" have ignored accounts of election fraud. Converse, "Change in the American Electorate," 282. John Reynolds believes that the different attention devoted to vote fraud "stands as one salient issue distinguishing the 'new' from the 'old' political histories." John Reynolds, " 'The Silent Dollar': Vote Buying in New Jersey," *New Jersey History* 98 (Fall–Winter 1980): 191–211, quote on 194.

3. Richard Jensen, *The Winning of the Midwest: Social and Political Conflict, 1888–1896* (Chicago: University of Chicago Press, 1971), 35–36.

4. Walter Dean Burnham, "Theory and Voting Research: Some Reflections on Converse's 'Change in the American Electorate,' " *American Political Science Review* 68 (September 1974): 1018.

5. Paul Kleppner and Stephen C. Baker, "The Impact of Voter Registration Requirements on Electoral Turnout, 1900–16," paper presented at the 1979 Annual Meeting of the American Political Science Association, Washington, D.C., 31 August–3 September 1979, 38. A revised version of this paper appears in *Journal of Political and Military Sociology* 8 (Fall 1980): 205–26. Citations in the present essay are to the more detailed APSA version.

6. Howard W. Allen and Kay Warren Allen, "Vote Fraud and Data Validity," in Jerome M. Clubb, William H. Flanigan, and Nancy H. Zingale, eds., *Analyzing Electoral History: A Guide to the Study of American Voting Behavior* (Beverly Hills, Calif.: Sage Publications, 1981), 155, 167, 179. Much of the work of the Allens and Kleppner and Baker is in explicit reaction to Converse's claims of "gross and endemic fraud."

7. Kleppner and Baker, "The Impact of Voter Registration," 42–44; Allen and Allen, "Vote Fraud," 181–83. See also Paul Kleppner, *Who Voted? The Dynamics of Electoral Turnout* (New York: Praeger, 1982), 58–60.

8. Allen and Allen, "Vote Fraud," 154; Jensen, *Winning of the Midwest*, 34.

9. George F. Edmunds, "Corrupt Political Methods," *Forum* 7 (June 1889): 350–51.

10. Kleppner and Baker, "The Impact of Voter Registration," 45; also see Jensen, *Winning of the Midwest*, 36.

11. Quoted in Jensen, *Winning of the Midwest*, 34.

12. Allen and Allen, "Vote Fraud," 156–57.

13. Genevieve Gist, "Progressive Reform in a Rural Community: The Adams County Vote-Fraud Case," *Mississippi Valley Historical Review* 48 (June 1961): 60–78.

14. Reynolds, "Vote Buying in New Jersey," 194, 196, 201, 204, 209; Harold F.

Gosnell, *Boss Platt and His New York Machine* (New York: Russell and Russell, 1924), 146. These instances of rural fraud suggest the necessary modification of the still popular view equating election fraud with urban areas. Certainly other observers agreed with the Newark editor. The Cincinnati *Times-Star*, a Republican newspaper, claimed that Ohio's small towns and rural areas held fraudulent elections and that rural politicians could give "pointers" to city bosses on election fraud. The mugwumpish *Nation* agreed that the same was true for "the country districts" of New York and New England. *Nation*, 5 May 1892, 333.

15. Reynolds, "Vote Buying in New Jersey," 194; Jensen, *Winning of the Midwest*, 35; Burnham, "Theory and Voting Research," 1017; Allen and Allen, "Vote Fraud," 155–56.

16. Kleppner and Baker, "The Impact of Voter Registration," 39.

17. See, for example, William M. Armstrong, "Godkin's *Nation* as a Source of Gilded Age History: How Valuable?" *South Atlantic Quarterly* 72 (Autumn 1973): 476–93.

18. *The Path I Trod: The Autobiography of Terence V. Powderly* (New York: Columbia University Press, 1940), 68–71.

19. Richard Oestreicher, "Socialism and the Knights of Labor in Detroit, 1877–1886," *Labor History* 22 (Winter 1981): 11–12.

20. R.C. Dunn to Ignatius Donnelly, 27 November 1890; C.P. Carpenter to Donnelly, 28 October 1890, Ignatius Donnelly Papers, Minnesota Historical Society, St. Paul, Minn.

21. Peter H. Argersinger, *Populism and Politics: William Alfred Peffer and the People's Party* (Lexington: University Press of Kentucky, 1974), 153; Indianapolis *Daily Sun*, 9, 10, 18 October 1878; Des Moines *Farmers Tribune*, 11 November 1896.

22. *Journal of United Labor* (Philadelphia), 8 August 1889, 10 September 1886; *Butler's Book: Autobiography and Personal Reminiscences of Major-General Benjamin F. Butler* (Boston: Thayer, 1892), 983–84; Charles A. Barker, *Henry George* (New York: Oxford University Press, 1955), 474, 479, 481.

23. *Journal of United Labor*, 14 February 1889.

24. Ibid.; Henry George, "Money in Elections," *North American Review* 136 (1883): 201–211.

25. L.E. Fredman, *The Australian Ballot* (East Lansing: Michigan State University Press, 1968), 35; Allen Myers, *Bosses and Boodle in Ohio Politics* (Cincinnati: Lyceum, 1895), 142–43.

26. Allen and Allen, "Vote Fraud," 192n.

27. *New York Times*, 2 November 1888.

28. William H. Barnum to William H. English, 10 and 17 August 1880, William H. English Papers, Indiana Historical Society, Indianapolis, Ind.

29. Reynolds, "Vote Buying in New Jersey," 197–98.

30. Lewis L. Gould, *Wyoming: A Political History, 1868–1896* (New Haven: Yale University Press, 1968), 102, 117–18.

31. Herbert J. Clancy, *The Presidential Election of 1880* (Chicago: Loyola University Press, 1958), 194n; Robert D. Marcus, *Grand Old Party: Political Structure in the Gilded Age* (New York: Oxford University Press, 1971), 55.

32. Alexander Callow, Jr., "San Francisco's Blind Boss," *Pacific Historical Review* 25 (August 1956): 265; M.R. Werner, *Tammany Hall* (Garden City, N.Y.: Doubleday, 1928), 130, 134.

33. Thomas Weldon to W.H.H. Miller, 1 May 1891, Justice Department: Letters Received, Box 258, Record Group 60, National Archives, Washington, D.C.

34. *New York Times*, 7 May 1880.

35. *Watertown* (N.Y.) *Times*, quoted in ibid., 19 November 1888; Marcus, *Grand Old Party*, 145.

36. Richard P. McCormick, *The History of Voting in New Jersey: A Study of the Development of Election Machinery, 1664–1911* (New Brunswick, N.J.: Rutgers University Press, 1953), 150–51, 167; Charles J. Bonaparte, "Political Corruption in Maryland," *Forum* 13 (March 1892): 16.

37. Allen and Allen, "Vote Fraud," 176.

38. *State v. Jackson*, 73 Me. 91, 40 Am. Rep. 342 (1881); *State v. Schoonover*, 135 Ind. 526, 35 N.E. Rep. 119 (1893); *United States v. O'Connor*, 31 Fed. Rep. 449 (1887); *New York Times*, 21 November 1888; *State v. Perkins*, 42 Vt. 399 (1869); *Commonwealth v. Shaub*, 5 Lanc. Law Rev. 121; *United States v. Fisher*, (C.C.) 8 Fed. 414 (1881).

39. For examples, see respectively *United States v. Chamberlain*, (D.C.) 32 Fed. 777 (1887); *United States v. Hayden*, Fed. Cas. No. 15,333; *Conway v. Carpenter*, (Pa. 1881), 11 Wkly. Notes Cas. 169; *Russell v. State*, 11 Kan. 308 (1873). An example of the incompletely developed institutional structure facilitating election fraud occurred in Rhode Island when it was determined that impersonation was *not* illegal if the voter did not also vote under his own name, which would have rendered him guilty of the crime of repeating. *State v. McClarnon*, 15 R.I. 462, 8 Atl. Rep. 688 (1887).

40. For instance, see Cincinnati *Commercial Gazette*, 8 October 1884, for a description of the Cincinnati election which resulted in the conviction of twenty-three men for violating election laws with sentences of up to thirteen months in prison.

41. *Ex parte Brown*, 97 Cal. 83, 31 Pac. Rep. 840 (1892); *Ex Parte Arnold*, 128 Mo. 256, 30 S.W. Rep. 768 (1895).

42. *New York Times*, 15 April 1880.

43. Indianapolis *Sun*, 9 July 1878; Princeton (Ind.) *Clarion*, 9 December 1886.

44. Detroit *Free Press*, 23 April 1885.

45. U.S. Congress, Senate Select Committee to Inquire into Frauds in the Late Elections, *Intimidation and Fraud in Massachusetts*, Report No. 497, 46th Cong., 2d Sess., 1880, 89, 90, 105, 108; U.S. Congress, House of Representatives, *Lot Wright, U.S. Marshal*, Report No. 2681, 48th Cong., 2d Sess., 1885, xviii–xix, 459–61, 465, 474.

46. Thomas B. Reed, "Contested Elections," *North American Review* 151 (July 1890): 112–20; Martin Ridge, *Ignatius Donnelly: The Portrait of a Politician* (Chicago: University of Chicago Press, 1962), 187–95.

47. Plymouth (Ind.) *Democrat*, quoted in Princeton (Ind.) *Clarion*, 7 December 1882.

48. William E. Parrish, "The Great Kansas Legislative Imbroglio of 1893," *Journal of the West* 7 (October 1968): 471–90; *New York Times*, 1 June 1889; James Hamilton, *From Wilderness to Statehood: A History of Montana* (Portland, Oregon: Binfords and Mort, 1957), 558–65; Arthur Wallace Dunn, *From Harrison to Harding: A Personal Narrative*, vol. I (New York: G.P. Putnam, 1922), 50–51; Matthew Hale, "How the New York Senate Was Captured," *Forum* 13 (April 1892): 179–92.

49. *Journal of the Forty-sixth Senate of the State of New Jersey* (Trenton, N.J.: Sharp Printing Co., 1890), 720–51, quote on 721; McCormick, *History of Voting in New Jersey*, 171–73.

50. *Journal of the Indiana House of Representatives, 1897* (Indianapolis, 1897), 360–65.

51. For a recent and imaginative demonstration of the existence and importance of "deflationary fraud" achieved by paying voters to stay away from the polls, see Gary W. Cox and J. Morgan Kousser, "Turnout and Rural Corruption: New York as a Test Case," *American Journal of Political Science* 25 (November 1981): 646–63. For another view of turnout statistics that is relevant to this controversy, see Ray M. Shortridge, "Estimating Voter Participation," in Clubb, Flanigan, and Zingale, *Analyzing Electoral History*, 137–52.

52. In addition to previous citations, see particularly D.W. Lusk, *Eighty Years of*

Illinois: Politics and Politicians (Springfield, Ill.: Rokker, 1889), 481; *Philadelphia Inquirer,* 14 April 1880.

53. U.S., Congress, Senate, *Alleged Frauds in the Late Elections,* Report No. 916, 46th Cong., 3d Sess., 1880, 22; Cincinnati *Enquirer,* 15 October 1884; George W. McCrary, "Our Election Laws," *North American Review* 128 (May 1879): 451; Princeton (Ind.) *Clarion,* 20 November 1884.

54. *Tarbox v. Sughrue,* 12 Pac. Rep. 935 (1887). The court also ruled that illegal voting or fraud would not necessarily invalidate an election; there had to be sufficient demonstrated illegal ballots to change the result.

55. Werner, *Tammany Hall,* 150; Lothrop Stoddard, *Master of Manhattan: The Life of Richard Croker* (New York: Longmans, Green, 1931), 46, 56.

56. George W. McCrary, *A Treatise on the American Law of Elections* (Chicago: Callaghan, 1897), 130n; Cincinnati *Commercial Gazette,* 15 October 1884; U.S. Congress, *Lot Wright,* xx. Those who promised to vote the Democratic ticket (at 60¢ each) were released in time to do so.

57. U.S., *Congressional Record,* 53d Cong., 1st Sess., vol. 25, pt. 2, p. 2046.

58. In Record Group (RG) 60, Department of Justice, National Archives (NA), Washington, D.C., these papers contain a wealth of information, but apparently only Albie Burke has used them for any published work, and that was for a quite different purpose. See Albie Burke, "Federal Regulation of Congressional Elections in Northern Cities, 1871–1894," *American Journal of Legal History* 14 (January 1970): 17–34.

59. Cincinnati *Enquirer,* 21 September, 7 October 1878; A.M. Jones to Benjamin H. Brewster, 5 December 1882, Justice Department, RG 60, NA; Albie Burke, "Federal Regulation of Congressional Elections in Northern Cities, 1871–1894" (Ph.D. dissertation, University of Chicago, 1968), ii–iii, 169–71; U.S. Congress, *Alleged Frauds,* 1880, xi; *New York Times,* 28 January 1881.

60. *Ex parte Siebold,* 100 U.S. 371 (1880); Jones to Brewster, 5 December 1882, Justice Department, RG 60, NA.

61. U.S. Congress, *Alleged Frauds,* 1880, iv, xi–xii. For other evidence of partisanship in election administration and of "riot and bloodshed" at the polls, see A.M. Jones to Charles Devens, 27 October 1880, Lot Wright to Benjamin Brewster, 25 September 1884, and Channing Richards to Benjamin Brewster, 27 October 1884, Justice Department, RG 60, NA.

62. See, for example, Reynolds, "Vote Buying in New Jersey," 204–209. Of course the turn-of-the-century political transformation involving these factors had other important results as well. For suggestive comments with respect to matters of governance and forms of political participation, see Richard L. McCormick, *From Realignment to Reform: Political Change in New York State, 1893–1910* (Ithaca, N.Y.: Cornell University Press, 1981).

63. William Ivins, *Machine Politics and Money in Elections in New York City* (New York: Harper & Brothers, 1887), 30.

5

From Party Tickets to Secret Ballots: The Evolution of the Electoral Process in Maryland during the Gilded Age

In recent years, historians have significantly altered our understanding of Gilded Age politics. They have shifted the focus from party elites and national platforms to the mass constituencies of political parties and the social issues that animated them. They have carefully specified typologies of elections and subtly explored the creation of partisan cultures.[1] But the reexamination of the period's politics is incomplete without an analysis of the role of the electoral process itself. This subject involves a number of apparently mundane matters, such as selecting election officials, managing the polls, identifying qualified voters, overseeing the mode of voting, counting the ballots, and reporting the returns. But historians must not regard election machinery and electoral rules merely as givens. As politicians and their opponents recognized, the electoral structure both reflected and shaped politics and had significant practical consequences for voters, parties, and public policy. The evolution of the electoral process in Maryland during the Gilded Age demonstrates this important reality.

During the 1870s and 1880s the electoral process in Maryland was dominated by the political parties, operating within a loose legal framework that facilitated electoral abuses and controversy. In the first place, the election officials designated to oversee the polls—three judges and two clerks at each voting precinct—were appointed by partisan politicians who had a vested interest in the conduct of elections. In Maryland's counties the elected county commissioners selected

From Peter H. Argersinger, "From Party Tickets to Secret Ballots: The Evolution of the Electoral Process in Maryland during the Gilded Age," *Maryland Historical Magazine,* vol. 82 (Fall 1987), pp. 214–239. Reprinted with permission of the Maryland Historical Society.

such officials; in Baltimore, the responsibility was assigned to a board of elections supervisors appointed by the governor. Fairness was supposedly guaranteed by mandating that the party affiliation of one judge differ from that of his two colleagues, but this requirement was sometimes blatantly ignored or, more often, subtly subverted. Partisan Democratic supervisors, for example, frequently appointed as the putative Republican judge representing the minority party "Democrats in Republican disguise," Republicans hostile to the ticket of their own party, or persons dependent on the goodwill of the Democratic officials for their occupation or liquor. As one Democratic elections supervisor admitted in 1885, his procedure was simply to appoint as judges "the two sharpest Democrats and the weakest Republican" he could find in each precinct. One Labor candidate for the Baltimore City Council in 1886 observed that many people thought the Board of Supervisors should be tarred and feathered for their choice of election judges. And a Republican candidate in the 16th ward withdrew on election eve because "The character of the judges appointed by the Board of Supervisors is such that it would be a waste of time and money . . . to remain in the field." He noted that in five precincts the Republican minority was represented by "notorious Democrats." Indeed, an investigation of the election judges in Baltimore in 1886 revealed so many with criminal records that one critic concluded that possession of such a record was a "qualification for the position of judge." These officials were required impartially to judge the qualifications of voters, maintain order at the polls, receive and count the ballots, and prepare the election certificates, but frequently their partisanship influenced their actions. The behavior of such officials was a constant source of controversy, particularly their refusal to prevent illegal voting by members of their own party.[2]

Their determination of an individual's right to vote on election day was supposedly guided by the voter registry completed weeks before by another official appointed in each district by the governor. As the governor during this period was invariably a Democrat, so were the voting registrars. Sitting in session in local communities several times a year, registrars recorded the names of voters who presented themselves as meeting the state's sex, age, and residency requirements for suffrage and supposedly struck from the books the names of those who had died or moved from the district since the last election. But the registrars were partisan officials, and as one of the main functions of the political party was to maximize the enrollment of its potential constituents, registrars not infrequently approached their work with a zealous partisanship. In 1885, for example, in nearly a third of Baltimore's 180 precincts, registrars recorded on the books more voters than a simultaneous police census found living in the precinct.[3]

The use determined party workers could make of such padded registry rolls is revealed in an incident during the 1879 election which also demonstrated the failure of partisan judges to conduct elections fairly. A small-time Baltimore politico took nine hoodlums from the Baltimore jail to the nearby village of Clarksville in Howard County. There he lined them up, he later recalled, "and we filed past the poll. Each dropped in his ballot. Then we kept going around in a circle, each of us putting a ballot in every time round, until we had polled several hundred votes. We voted until we had voted all the names on the register, and we could not do more than that, could we?"[4]

Not only could registrars thus provide opportunity for illegal repeat voting by members of their own party, they also could (and did) deflate the potential vote of their party's opponents, simply by illegally removing from the registry the names of qualified voters. Judicial investigations, usually undertaken too late to have practical consequence for the election, frequently revealed such activities, particularly directed against black voters, who were assumed to be Republicans. Other voters found, to their dismay, that they had been stricken from the registry only when they attempted to vote or that, although still registered, someone else had already voted under their name. Not surprisingly, Republicans, Independent Democrats, and members of third parties like the Greenbackers all denounced Maryland's registration laws. "The registration laws of the State," declared the 1879 platform of the Independent Democrats, "instead of affording a protection against fraud, have been, by the criminal neglect of duty of many of the officers, used to perpetrate the greatest outrages against the purity of the ballot."[5]

One of the most important electoral processes, and the one that perhaps enabled political parties to exercise the most influence in shaping politics and political culture, involved the actual mode of voting. Although Maryland had long ago replaced *viva voce* voting with the use of ballots, the act of voting was still largely an open, not secret, one. There were no legal provisions to ensure secrecy and little practical attempt to provide it. Maryland's voters were required to carry their own ticket to a voting window, behind which sat the election officials. Standing in the street or on the steps or porch of the building housing the polls, in full view of all interested observers, the voter had to announce his name for the clerk to find on the registry and record on the poll list, and then hand his ballot through the window to the officials who were to deposit it in the unseen ballot box. The ballots were not provided by the election officials, and unlike other states Maryland had virtually no regulations specifying the format of the ballot to be used. In the absence of official machinery and legal regulations, the task of preparing and distributing ballots was assumed by the political parties. The natural consequence was the party ticket, a strip of paper usually headed by a party symbol, on which appeared the names of the candidates of only the party that issued it. Anxious to distinguish their followers and mobilize their support, party managers often differentiated their tickets from those of other parties by size, color, or other characteristics. Thus the voter's use of a ballot easily identified his choice of party as well.[6]

Partisan control of ballots also led to the appearance of "bogus ballots," tickets headed with the insignia of one party but listing the candidates of another. Bogus ballots were regularly issued by both major parties or factions thereof. All parties had to take elaborate precautions against the possibility of counterfeit

Figure 5.1. **1876 Democratic Party Ticket. (Collection of the Maryland Historical Society.)**

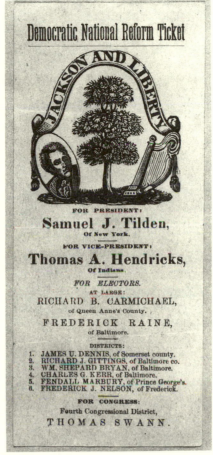

tickets and constantly cautioned their partisans to scrutinize their tickets care-fully before turning them in at the polls in order to avoid deception. The Wash-ington County Republican Central Committee, for instance, warned party members in 1886 that "a large number of ballots" with a Republican heading but listing Democratic candidates "have been circulated with the intent to de-ceive voters." Conversely, in Allegany County, tickets purporting to be Demo-cratic were issued with Republican candidates' names. "Examine your tickets carefully," the *Cumberland Times* urged its Democratic readers. "Beware of fraudulent tickets." In Baltimore, a favorite Democratic tactic was to circulate tickets among black voters listing Democratic nominees under a portrait of Abra-ham Lincoln or U.S. Grant. Local party organizations also sometimes deceived their own followers by the practice of "knifing" or "trading." This involved replacing a regular nominee with the favorite of another faction or even with the candidate of another party, sometimes out of spite or jealousy, sometimes for monetary reward. In the 1879 election in Anne Arundel County, for instance, the Democrats in charge of printing the party's tickets substituted the name of the Republican candidate for county commissioner for the Democratic nominee, reflecting and continuing a factional feud within the party.[7]

The unregulated private preparation of tickets also produced the famous "pudding tickets." These were tickets much shorter and narrower than usual and printed on tissue paper, which were folded inside a regular ticket to permit multiple voting. The skilled voter could even crimp his ticket with accordion folds, as a fan, with a pudding ticket concealed in each fold; the skilled election judge, in depositing the ticket in the ballot box, could fan it out and cause the different pudding tickets to fall out and mix with other tickets already cast. In Baltimore's 1875 election, these tissue pudding tickets accounted for the discrepancy in one precinct between the 542 voters recorded on the poll list and the 819 ballots counted out of the box.[8]

The distribution and use of party tickets further prevented secrecy while facilitating voter intimidation and election fraud. The tickets were distributed or "peddled" to the party's supporters by paid party workers known as peddlers, hawkers, holders, or bummers, who stationed themselves near the polls and pressed their tickets on prospective voters. These contending hawkers, each trying to force his ticket upon the voter, contributed greatly to the tumult and chaos surrounding the polls on election day. At times workers of one party completely thronged the polls and allowed only their own partisans to approach the ticket window, driving from the vicinity the hawkers of the other party and, with them, the possibility of votes for that party. Although the widespread and often fatal violence that characterized Baltimore's elections during the Know-Nothing period was not repeated, election day riots and disorder remained common as competing gangs attacked (and sometimes still murdered) voters, assaulted election officials, and even stormed the voting window to stuff the ballot box, a tactic known as "rushing" or "crowding" votes. Such "rushing" in Baltimore's 1875 election, for instance, placed in some ballot boxes large rolls of tickets that had never been separated and distributed but that "appeared in shape as they came from the printing press." What the *Frederick Citizen* called "radical bulldozing" of voters was commonplace, as voters were forced to reveal their tickets before being allowed to reach the voting window. Receiving party tickets in such an atmosphere, the voter often had little or no time to examine his ballot before being hustled to the window. Certainly he rarely had an opportunity to alter the ballot received and vote a split ticket by crossing out the name of an unacceptable candidate and substituting that of a more agreeable one in his place.[9]

One other way that party leaders mobilized a full vote for their party under these conditions involved vote-buying. The use of party tickets and the lack of secrecy insured that a purchased vote was delivered, and the buyer might also

Figure 5.2. **A "bogus ballot" to deceive illiterate voters: an 1876 Democratic ticket headed by a portrait of Republican hero U.S. Grant. (Collection of the Maryland Historical Society.)**

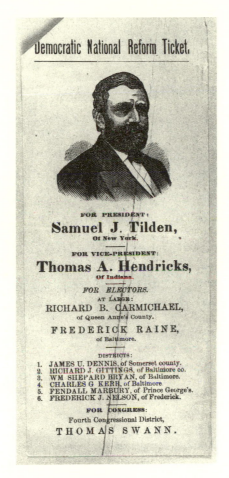

accompany the seller to the voting window to observe him submit the ticket. Party officials regarded vote-buying as a routine and necessary campaign tactic. One observer noted the interaction of party tickets, hawkers, vote-buying, and election day violence in describing the typical election day scenes in Washington County:

> What we see in Hagerstown is a ward worker off at some distance negotiating with a rounder. A group of men, or maybe one or two standing off and refusing to vote until they have been "seen." Then comes a politician to the window holding a floater by the arm and making him vote the ticket he has just given him. Or it may be that a politician on the other side claims this

Figure 5.3. A ticket of the Workingmen's Party in Baltimore. (Collection of the Maryland Historical Society.)

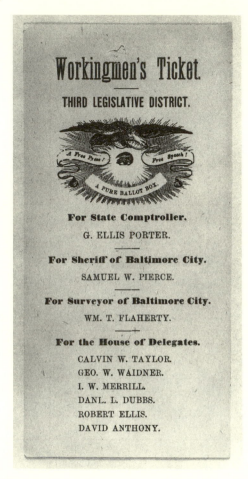

particular floater and grabs him by the other arm and thrusts a different ticket into his hands and then a struggle ensues, in which frequently the whole crowd becomes involved, and it becomes a question of physical strength which party shall receive this free and enlightened vote. It may be that the floater is a negro, in the hands of a Democrat, and then there is sure to be a riot. The unfortunate voter is in that case set upon by those of his own color.

The scene varied little ''in the country districts'' around Hagerstown, only in that the vote sellers stood ''a little nearer to the voting window'' and that ''the men who are holding off, waiting to be 'fixed,' make less 'bones' about it.''[10]

One final feature of Maryland's electoral process involved the Federal Elec-

Figure 5.4. A ticket of the Workingmen's Party with regular comptroller nominee G. Ellis Porter "knifed" and replaced by Democratic nominee Thomas Keating. (Collection of the Maryland Historical Society.)

tions Law. Although usually incorrectly regarded as part of Reconstruction legislation, this statute—enacted in 1871 and not repealed until 1894—responded to election fraud in the North and was designed to end impersonation, repeating, intimidation, and bribery in congressional elections. It authorized the appointment of federal supervisors and of deputy marshals to assist the supervisors and maintain order. Of course, federal supervision was limited only to congressional elections and did not cover mayoral, legislative, or state elections held in odd-numbered years, and its effects were controversial. Maryland Republicans contended that the federal law limited election fraud. And, indeed, the U.S. Supreme Court decision that upheld the constitutionality of the act involved the conviction of Baltimore judges for resisting the authority of federal supervisors who tried to stop them from stuffing the ballot box.[11]

Maryland Democrats, on the other hand, charged that the federal law actually encouraged fraud. As the deputies were federal appointees, they were nearly invariably Republican. Indeed, deputies were usually chosen from lists supplied by local Republican party officials. Democrats maintained that such deputies intimidated potential Democratic voters, particularly immigrants. The number of deputies was often quite large, as in Baltimore in 1876, when more than one thousand two hundred deputies were appointed. At times such deputies served on election day virtually as Republican party workers. As the *Hagerstown Mail* declared, ''We all know that Federal Election Supervisors are merely Republican hustlers.'' In session after session, Maryland's Democratic-controlled legislature appropriated money to defend state election officials charged with violating the federal election law or with obstructing federal election officials.[12]

These public and partisan aspects of Maryland's electoral process helped to shape the state's political culture during this period, with its strong partisan commitments and identifications among the electorate, high levels of voter mobilization and participation, straight-ticket voting, and dramatic campaign techniques. The giant rallies, uniformed marches, and other features of ''army-style'' campaigns were designed to motivate an electorate that necessarily had to regard voting as a public act involving the affirmation of group solidarity. To print and distribute tickets and organize voters for participation, parties had to develop the ''machines'' that constituted such a major feature of the period's political culture.[13]

The evolution of Maryland's electoral process during the Gilded Age was fitful and contentious. Most people could and did agree publicly upon the necessity for controlling violence and disorder during elections, and so it was with little difficulty, if surprisingly gradually, that the General Assembly passed laws disarming the electorate by prohibiting the carrying of guns, dirks, razors, billies, and bludgeons on election days: in Kent, Montgomery, and Queen Anne's counties in 1874, in Prince George's County in 1884, in Calvert County in 1886.[14] In most other respects, however, the subject of election ''reform'' was a highly charged one, for the objectives and implications of procedural change were controversial and momentous. A variety of groups, all critical of the election machinery but with quite different motivations, led in the agitation for election reform: Republicans, patrician mugwumps, labor organizers, third-party radicals, and conservative businessmen.

The Republican interest, at least, was obvious: Republicans were convinced that without election reform and effective bipartisan administration of the election machinery they would never be able to oust the entrenched Democratic party. Denouncing elections in Maryland under Democratic control of the election machinery as ''a burlesque upon republican institutions,'' Republican platforms repeatedly demanded the enactment of laws to ''secure an honest registry, a free vote, and a fair count." State Chairman H.C. Naill bitterly declared in 1886, "if the election system is rendered insecure by corrupting and polluting the ballot-box by fraud, the will of the people is circumvented, and the ballot-box, instead of reflecting the will of the people, becomes an instrumentality by which their will is absolutely silenced."[15]

Nominally nonpartisan and professedly disinterested, Maryland's small contingent of mugwumps constituted a second group that persistently demanded election reform. Their complaint, however, while couched in denunciations of election fraud, was actually directed against the political party and its function as a mobilizer of the popular will, undermining the public influence they felt they deserved. Thus in demanding electoral reform, they were interested not in democratizing the political system but the reverse. A self-conscious and elitist minority, sharing inherited social status, established economic position, and educational and professional interests, the mugwumps valued order, deference, and stability. Holding elitist views of the mass electorate as ignorant, venal, and incompetent, mugwumps were appalled by the ascendancy of mass political parties. The positive functions such parties fulfilled—mobilizing voters, recruiting candidates, and representing group values—they regarded as loathsome and dangerous. Party control of election machinery, they believed, stimulated political organization, developed politicians and party workers into a distinct class, and reinforced the electorate's partisan loyalties. The mugwumps' typical reform objectives, grandly styled as "good government," were accordingly restrictive, designed primarily to weaken the political influence of the masses and of the political party that functioned to mobilize the popular will. In particular they condemned the party-ticket system. By permitting parties to print and distribute their own tickets at the polls, it required parties to collect large sums of money and create large and disciplined organizations or "machines." The money needed to prepare ballots and hire ticket peddlers in every election district provided parties with the excuse for the assessment of candidates, which in turn led the unscrupulous partisan, once elected, to use his public office to recoup his political expenses at the cost of the taxpayer, a process the mugwumps termed "the cycle of corruption."[16]

Maryland's mugwumps, led by the "peacock of Park Avenue," Charles J. Bonaparte, organized themselves into two major and overlapping groups, the Civil Service Association of Maryland and the Baltimore Reform League, virtually a who's who of the city's social register. Because of the Democratic dominance of state and city politics, they directed their energies at attacking the Democratic party organization, personified by state "boss" Senator Arthur P. Gorman and Baltimore City "boss" I. Freeman Rasin. They prided themselves that their attacks on electoral corruption produced among these Democratic politicians "rancorous and unremitting hostility, varied by occasional exhibitions of abject terror." The persistent class animus of such reformers was always obvious, as when they condemned the appointment as election officials of "drivers of hacks, peanut vendors"—people "whose very occupations . . . rendered their appointment a simple outrage." They demanded instead the appointment of election supervisors only "from the business community, who have neither the ambitions nor the temptations" of politicians.[17]

Not surprisingly, the mugwumps often found common cause with the Independent Democrats, a group of conservative Democrats based in the Baltimore business community, led most prominently by John K. Cowen of the Baltimore & Ohio Railroad. Their program resembled that of the mugwumps in condemning "machine politics" and "corrupt elections" and in advocating election reform and civil service. Their objectives, if different, were no more disinterested. Such reforms, they believed, would weaken the regular party organization by restricting its patronage, its control over nominations and thus public policy, and its capacity to mobilize Maryland's farmers and workers at the polls. Their ultimate motive was revealed in a public address they issued in 1887: "It is by power wielded through these fraudulent elections," they asserted, that the regular Democrats established public policy and levied taxes for "jobs and corrupt expenditures." What the Independents wanted was to reduce their existing taxes and prevent the adoption of any additional tax legislation. Indeed, the Independents' periodic crusades against "ring rule" paralleled the regular Democrats' periodic attempts to achieve tax reform in response to the complaints of farmers and workers. The Independents' opposition to tax reform reflected their determination to maintain the tax exemptions for corporations for which Maryland was notorious—"Cowenism," declared one regular Democrat, stood for the "aggrandizement of corporate influence in the state and nation"—and to preserve the immunity from taxation of other forms of business property. It took the form of an argument to restrict the functions of government, which they believed had been unnecessarily inflated by a party machine too responsive to the lower classes in its determination to win elections. R.E. Wright, a prominent Baltimore merchant, for instance, complained of the city's "rapidly enlarging and dangerous proletariat" which, because it was mobilized for elections by the regular party organization, required appeasement by the subsequent adoption of extravagant public expenditures and by representation on the public payroll. "Our complaint," declared Wright to the Landlords Mutual Protective Association,"*is* that there is a party."[18]

Such conservative Democrats wanted to replace party-based government with a government run "like a business," with appointed officials motivated by "efficiency." "Our offices must no longer be scrambled for at every election, nor handed about as bribes," declared Cowen. A limited, efficient, and nonpartisan government would require less taxation and minimize the need for the more equitable tax laws that would reach their exempt intangible properties such as rents and mortgages. A report by Johns Hopkins University economist Richard Ely to the 1888 Maryland Tax Commission, recommending that the state shift to corporate and income taxes and the city to taxes levied on realty and business

rents, particularly prompted business groups to invoke the issue of election reform to cover their objective of preserving their vested economic interests. Not
surprisingly, the Landlords Mutual Protective Association was a major advocate
of election reform. If revenue were needed, Cowen told an enthusiastic meeting
of the Landlords Association, it should come not from taxation on businesses but
from high license fees on saloons, a tactic that would force the city's lower
classes to fund the government expenditures their presence demanded as well as
weaken the regular party organization that depended upon saloons as organizing
bases. "But to obtain these or other reforms," Cowen told the businessmen, "we
should direct our efforts primarily to the enactment" of new election laws.[19]

In similarly attacking election fraud, machine rule, and the existing electoral
system, third parties and labor organizations had still different objectives. Not
surprisingly, labor organizations particularly condemned the intimidation of
workers' voting by their employers under the system of open voting. Some labor
leaders complained of intimidation by the workers' other "master, the political
boss, . . . the ward-heeler." Improved conditions for the working class, it was
argued, required the emancipation of the worker from the domination of either
master. Greenbackers, Industrials, Prohibitionists, and other third-party groups
all criticized the party-ticket system because of the hardships it imposed on small
parties, thereby limiting their possible influence. The printing and distributing of
ballots were expensive, excluding poor citizens from nomination and influence
over public policy; the system also required a uniform organization across all
election districts—something few third parties had—if every voter was to have
an opportunity to vote his principles. Paying for the printing of tickets and their
distribution at every polling place by hawkers was effectively beyond the reach
of small third parties. Each major party spent $7,000–8,000 per election on
printing and distributing ballots and paying challengers in Baltimore's 180 precincts, but the total campaign funds collected by the Industrial Party for the
city's 1886 election was only $196.30. As a consequence, third parties often had
no one in some precincts to distribute their tickets, which limited the possibility
of their attracting votes. Labor parties and Prohibitionists sometimes took out
advertisements in the newspapers directing their prospective voters to homes and
offices where their tickets would be available, a necessary tactic that increased
the "costs" of voting for their followers.[20]

Third parties also complained about partisan control of election machinery. In
1877, for instance, candidates and supporters of the Workingmen's Party maintained that Democratic election judges in Baltimore cheated them out of victories
in thirteen wards through ballot-box stuffing, intimidation of voters, and excluding their representatives from the windows and from witnessing the count. "We
are called defeated," said one, "not defeated but defrauded." In the 1886 election, the Industrial Party, based on the Knights of Labor, similarly charged the
election officials with miscounting, ballot-box stuffing, interference with voting
and with witnessing the count, and destruction of the Industrial tickets, distinc-

tive by their hickory tree symbol. Moreover, in working-class wards Democratic election officials tried to minimize the potential vote for the Industrials by placing the voting windows out of reach of the voters. In one precinct of the third ward, for example, the Industrials had to build a platform so that their supporters could reach the voting window; in another precinct, voters had to climb a ladder to reach the window nine feet above the street. Other third parties, including the Prohibitionists, also regularly complained that election officials did not count their votes as cast. Greenback-Laborites reflected a common third-party interest, then, in their 1879 platform demand for election laws giving all parties, not just the two major ones, a judge and clerk at each poll and requiring party approval of their appointment in order to prevent the selection of bogus or renegade representatives.[21]

In advocating election reform, then, workers and political radicals, whether organized as interest groups or separate political parties, sought to democratize the electoral process and secure both equal political participation and legitimate and responsive republican government.

Despite their varying objectives, Republicans, mugwumps, conservative businessmen, labor organizations, and third parties all agreed on the necessity of electoral reform and agitated constantly for it. Frequently, they engaged in joint political activity and even, at times, campaigns, recognizing fusion as the only practical method of defeating the dominant Democratic organization. Independent Democrats and Republicans fused in 1875, for instance. In 1886 Republicans endorsed Industrial candidates in some wards and Independent Democrats in others. Some labor unions (like the Cigarmakers Union) endorsed the Independent Democrats. Mugwump lawyers from the Baltimore Reform League provided legal guidance to labor parties on the subject of election laws, and labor leaders encouraged the League's investigations of election officials for fraud. "Keep it up!" declared the Baltimore *Critic,* the leading labor newspaper. "We must have square men in the polling-places to secure square voting."[22]

Popular anger over election practices reached a new height as a consequence of blatant fraud in the 1886 elections, which left the Democrats still in power but in a critical situation. The Reform League obtained the prosecution and conviction of numerous Democratic election judges for fraud in a series of trials holding public attention for months. The Knights of Labor, complaining bitterly of illegal Democratic manipulation of the labor vote, seemed ready to challenge the party's traditional hold over Baltimore's working class. Conservative Democrats, led by Cowen, again seized the emotional issue of election fraud as an attractive cover for their demand for a party reorganization on the basis of opposition to tax reform and business regulation. And Republicans, seeking to capitalize on public sentiment and attract the Independents' support, campaigned in 1887 on "fair elections" as "the paramount issue before the people of this State," demanding the enactment of a sweeping election bill prepared by the Reform League and avoiding any mention of tax reassessment.[23]

The Democratic organization responded to this challenge by making accommodations in an effort to retain its electoral coalition. Earlier it had appealed to its critical agrarian/labor wing by enacting tax and labor reform laws and by accepting minor modifications in election laws. Now, although again promising economic reforms, it shifted its emphasis to the elections issue and proposed major changes to head off the popular outcry. The party's 1887 state convention conceded that existing election laws were "ineffectual to accomplish . . . fair elections" and pledged the 1888 legislature to reform registry and election laws, appointing a committee to prepare such legislation immediately.[24]

With election reform "almost the sole issue" in the 1887 campaign, Democrats narrowly defeated the fusion of Republicans and Independent Democrats and entered the 1888 legislature with both clear pledges to fulfill and a conviction that party interests dictated limits to electoral reform. They modified the registry law for Baltimore to provide bipartisan registrars and biennial registration, at the precinct rather than the ward level, but they rejected the Reform League demand for annual registration because of the expense and effort it would have imposed on the party. They also altered the election laws to require minority representation among Baltimore's Elections Supervisors and not merely among the election judges and clerks the supervisors appointed. In order to prevent the two supervisors representing the Democratic majority from imposing bogus or renegade Republican election officials on the supervisor representing the minority Republican party, the law gave each supervisor a veto over the appointment of such precinct officials. Election judges and clerks were finally required to be able to read and write English and to be "skilled" in arithmetic, the lack of which qualifications had often produced misunderstandings and errors which appeared to patrician critics to be as fraudulent as the deliberate falsification of ballots and counting. New laws also required glass ballot boxes in order to prevent ballot-box stuffing and authorized each party to have a representative in the polling room to watch the casting and count of the vote.[25]

The Baltimore Reform League praised Democrats for these laws but remained unsatisfied, demanding voter registration annually in the city and quadrennially in the counties and the abolition of "the unhappy practice of voting through a window," which prevented strict surveillance of election officials. The failure to adopt these changes, declared the *Civil Service Reformer*, was "precisely in the direction in which the professional ballot box stuffer or false counter of votes would desire to remain unhampered by prohibitory or restrictive enactments." Moreover, the League was outraged that the new registry law repealed the 1882 provision that had permitted interested citizens to appeal to the courts against the registration of other voters. The League had repeatedly used that power to challenge the actions of registrars and to remove illegally registered names from the rolls. Mugwump anger increased upon discovery that a score of election judges

Figure 5.5. **1887 party tickets reflecting fusion: Republicans and Independent Democrats of Baltimore nominated the same candidates under their own separate headings. (Collection of the Maryland Historical Society.)**

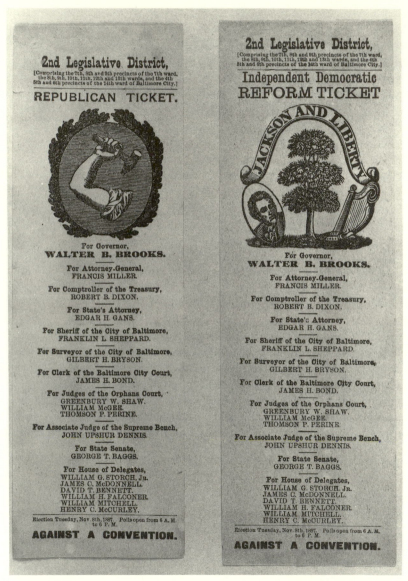

awaiting trial for fraud had escaped prosecution when the legislature repealed the law under which they had been indicted and then re-enacted it without providing for pending prosecutions. When Democratic Governor Elihu Jackson pardoned other election judges and clerks convicted earlier for fraud, mugwumps were convinced that the Democratic party remained under boss control. Moreover, workers still sought assurance of their ability to wield political influence without interference, Independent Democrats remained hostile to the regular organization, and Republicans still sought victory at the polls.[26]

After the 1888 legislative session, all such electoral reformers focused their activities on ballot reform and the achievement of the Australian ballot. An examination of the process by which Maryland secured this law demonstrates the interaction between political conditions and electoral change, the continued partisan features of electoral legislation, and the growing role of the state in the electoral process. First adopted in Australia in 1856, this new voting system differed completely from the party-ticket system. In particular, reformers were attracted by three features of the Australian system. First, it provided an "official" ballot, prepared and distributed by public authorities; it therefore stripped parties of one of their most influential organizational functions and promised dramatically to alter campaign practices by abolishing the disruptive ticket peddlers. Theoretically this feature also made it easier for independent organizations and candidates by minimizing their election costs and reducing their dependence on party organizations for nominations, while it removed the parties' rationale for assessing their nominees and thus eliminated a major source of corrupt funds. Electoral corruption was also to be eliminated by a second characteristic of the Australian ballot: it was secret and therefore presumably discouraged vote-buying while providing workers with "an escape from the dictation and prying eyes of employers and overseers." Finally, it was a consolidated or "blanket" ballot, listing all candidates instead of only those of one party. This provision permitted more independent and split-ticket voting than was possible under the party-ticket system and seemed likely to weaken party control over the electorate, a prime objective of most reformers.[27]

Election reformers eagerly championed this new system. Labor organizations were the most active in promoting its popular acceptance. The Maryland Labor Conference raised the subject in its 1888 meeting and encouraged public discussion. The Knights of Labor, in particular, agitated for legislative action, drawing up a model ballot law for the next legislature to consider.[28] In 1889, the mugwumps of the Reform League also drafted an election bill, although rather than requiring a blanket ballot it provided for separate party ballots from which the voter would select in secret. This adaptation reflected the mugwump conviction that the Australian ballot would effectively disfranchise illiterate voters. Whereas mugwumps in other states, particularly those with large immigrant populations, praised the Australian system precisely for its possible disfranchising effect on illiterates, in Maryland a substantial portion of the illiterate population consisted of blacks whose votes, mugwumps realized, were essential to any possible election victory of a fusion coalition. Both Republicans and Independent Democrats reached the same conclusion and accordingly euphemistically endorsed those aspects of the Australian system which were "appropriate" for Maryland.[29]

Even many partisan Democrats joined in the demand for ballot reform. Among them was a new group, the Democratic Business Men's Association of Baltimore, which although opposed to the party machine refused to desert the party and join in the fusion of Independent Democrats and Republicans. They did, however, appoint a committee to draw up an Australian bill and to lobby for its enactment. Still another ballot bill was prepared by Kent County Democratic legislator J.A. Pearce. He feared that election reform might permit Republicans to gain more power but declared, "I cannot fail to perceive the terrible and growing evil of fraudulent registration, voting, and election returns; nor the inevitable certainty with which it is converting the Democratic majority of Maryland into a minority . . . we must correct this evil at any cost, . . . the ultimate permanence of our party can only be secured in this way."[30]

In 1889, as in 1887, the issue of election reform dominated the Maryland political campaign. Believing that electoral success again depended on a strong stand in favor of election reform, Democrats pledged in their state platform to enact laws to preserve "the purity of the ballot box" by preventing bribery, fraud, and corruption. Republicans found it necessary to concede in their own platform, adopted the following week, "that the great bulk of our Democratic fellow-citizens" desired election reform but denied that "their party leaders share this desire, or propose voluntarily to relinquish the unworthy practices to which they have so often owed their retention of power." Thus they too endorsed ballot reform as did the Independent Democrats in their platform.[31] Uncomfortable with the prospect of significant electoral reform, however, Gorman also sought to emphasize the reactionary purposes of the Independent Democrats, whom he attacked as "selfish men, identified with corporate greed." The fusion movement, Senator Gorman maintained, was "a corrupt scheme of Mr. Cowen's to get possession of the Legislature in the interest of the B&O R.R. Company, and to prevent its tax exemptions from being interfered with."[32]

Gorman's lack of commitment to the party's campaign pledge for election reform was dramatically revealed after the 1889 election gave the Democrats solid control of the new legislature to meet in 1890. Calling the state's Democratic editors to a meeting in Baltimore, Gorman denounced the Australian ballot as a threat to the party, saying it should be titled "A bill to throw the Democratic party in the rear," and urged the editors to oppose the measure. Some editors agreed. The Cumberland Times, for example, ardently argued Gorman's position in an editorial entitled "Ballot Reform—Its Real and Its Apparent Friends." Declaring that Americans were more united on the necessity of election reform than any other subject, the Times insisted that Gorman favored ballot reform but not the Australian system. Gorman's opposition, the paper asserted, stemmed from "the extreme liability of the illiterate and unfortunately educated voter to practical disfranchisement under the provisions for secret voting and an absolute and exclusively official ballot" and from his concern to protect the political

rights of the common people. Gorman himself declared, "the system that re-
moves the voter from the influences of men of intelligence to a box leaves him to
the danger of the money power. You pay a voter, if you pay him at all, in secret.
By the [Australian] system he is exposed to the corrupt influences of bribery
more than ever."[33]

Most Democrats, however, rejected Gorman's position. The *Hagerstown
Mail, Salisbury Advertiser, Cecil Democrat,* and other newspapers insisted that
the party fulfill its campaign pledges and enact the Australian system to prevent
bribery and fraud. "Then, and not until then, will we cease to hear of independent movements and fusion with Republicans." Democratic rallies throughout
the state also revealed rank-and-file support for the Australian ballot. In Hagerstown, for example, a rally "representing every shade of opinion in the Democratic party" unanimously demanded the Australian ballot and sent delegations
to Annapolis to lobby the Democratic legislators to fulfill their pledges. As for
workers, labor organizations sharply rejected Gorman's expressed concerns. The
Baltimore Critic reminded Gorman that the Knights of Labor were among the
most vociferous advocates of the Australian system, and another labor editor
declared that by "men of intelligence" Gorman meant "ward boss, foreman,
and superintendent": Gorman sought not to protect workers' political rights but
to retain Democratic control of Baltimore.[34]

Having failed to divert popular sentiment for the Australian system, Gorman
and the regular Democratic organization next attempted to use their control of
the legislature to frustrate it. The senate elections committee put aside the numerous Australian bills introduced and reported a "sham bill," which the *Hagerstown Mail* declared should have been titled "A bill to protect the Bosses in
suppressing the voice of the people." This measure, endorsed by Gorman and
other regulars who had earlier announced their opposition to the Australian
system, provided for separate ballots for each party rather than a blanket ballot. It
failed in so many other respects to provide for the Australian system that one
reporter described it "as full of loopholes as a shad seine."[35] Again there was a
popular reaction. The *Critic* described the senate committee bill as "a farce and
a fraud," and labor organizations took the lead in demanding an authentic Australian system. The Knights' District Assembly denounced the legislature for
considering this "miserable substitution" and demanded enactment of their own
ballot bill. "Never did public sentiment appeal more unanimously for a law,"
concluded a reporter for a New York newspaper. Democratic regulars retreated,
reviving the Australian ballot bill prepared by the Democratic Business Men's
Association, which they amended and promptly enacted into law. Although it
applied to only fourteen of Maryland's counties, it represented the adoption of
the state's modern system of voting.[36]

Significantly, however, the Republican legislators, after clamoring for the
Australian ballot, voted against the measure while regular Democrats supported
its passage—suggesting that in their amendments the Democrats had learned

how to shape the Australian system to their own purpose. Indeed, it is inaccurate to conclude, as some political scientists have done, that the adoption of the Australian ballot ended the previous practice of manipulating the electoral framework for partisan purposes. Although labor reformers, mugwumps, conservative businessmen, and political radicals had led the movement for ballot reform, the actual law was shaped and enacted by practical politicians who understood the electorate and how election machinery influenced political outcomes. The law derived from political conflict; not surprisingly, it also reflected it. "In matters of [electoral] legislation," one newspaper later concluded, "the 'professionals' beat the amateurs every day."[37]

In the first place, the legislature attempted to retain some of the familiar partisan features of the old ballot system while providing the secret and official characteristics of the new. Rather than adopting an office-bloc ballot format, which would minimize partisanship and encourage split-ticket voting, the Maryland law adopted the party-column format. This grouped candidates by parties in parallel columns, at the head of which appeared party vignettes to enable the voter to distinguish the separate party slates. The new law, moreover, provided that a single mark by a vignette would constitute a vote for the entire party ticket, and thus it facilitated straight-ticket voting and minimized the demands placed upon the partisan voter.[38]

Second, the law attempted to promote the particular interests of the dominant Democratic party. It authorized the governor, rather than county commissioners, to appoint a Board of Election Supervisors in each county. Although such three-member boards were to have minority representation, this measure gave the Democrats control of the election machinery in every county, including those which formerly had been controlled by Republicans because of local political alignments. Next, the law authorized the appointment of state election police equal to the number of federal supervisors and deputies at each polling place. Regarding the federal election officials as "merely Republican hustlers," the Democrats seized the chance to offset them with state-appointed Democratic hustlers. But, of course, as the *Civil Service Reformer* observed bitterly, the Australian system was purportedly designed, by providing for public distribution of tickets, to eliminate hustlers, not to provide for them legally and at public not party expense. Since no qualifications, not even residency, were required of such election police, this provision seemed to improve Democratic opportunities to control voting while shifting party campaign expenses to the public. Another provision of the new law also seemed to provide opportunities for Democratic party workers to continue to influence voters. This authorized foreign-born voters (but not illiterate blacks likely to vote Republican) to be accompanied by a friend at the polls. Not only Mugwumps and Republicans but many Democrats viewed this provision as a means to facilitate vote-buying and other fraud.[39]

Nor were third parties like the Prohibitionists altogether pleased with the legislation they had long demanded. Although it did authorize each party to have a challenger in the polling room, it also explicitly excluded third parties from being represented among the ballot clerks and practically excluded them from serving as election supervisors and judges by not explicitly providing for them. Moreover, while the law mandated printing and distributing ballots at public expense, thereby removing one of the major difficulties third parties had faced under the former ballot system, it also established rules for parties to gain access to those ballots. For existing parties, the rules were nominal but still restrictive: such parties must have received one percent of the vote in the preceding election. For new parties or independents, however, nomination and placement on the legal ballot required filing with public officials a petition of registered voters, with the number of signatures necessary ranging from two hundred to five hundred depending upon the office sought. An inability to meet those requirements, because of time, organization, or finances, effectively eliminated such citizens from equal participation in Maryland's elections, for the Australian ballot law prohibited the resort to ballots not sanctioned and issued by the state. One of Gorman's Democratic followers had earlier objected to the Australian system because it involved ''the imperial coercion by the State of the voter's will in requiring the use of a single form of ballot.'' Such rhetoric reflected the Democratic image as the party of ''personal liberty,'' but the practical effect of this concern would be felt by citizens of other partisan inclinations.[40]

Finally, the Australian law also assigned to the state other powers of ''coercion'' over matters that formerly had been left to political parties or individual citizens. It authorized election supervisors to decide which group was entitled to party names and ballot vignettes when claimed by more than one group. This served to regularize the electoral process by removing some of the confusion possible under the old system and limited the possibility that a bolting faction of a party—such as the Independent Democrats—would be able to appropriate the advantages of the party's traditional symbolism. The law also discouraged factionalism and strengthened the regular party machinery by requiring that the nomination papers of candidates be signed by the regular officers of the party convention. By preventing the printing and issuance of ''bogus tickets,'' moreover, the Australian system gave the regular party organization increased control over local party officials and the ability to impose its will on conflicting groups, an instance of the law's ability to strengthen the ''machine.''[41]

Republicans, Independents, and laborites were not satisfied with this ballot legislation but did support it as a great improvement over the previous system. The depth of Republican discontent was revealed, however, during the fall campaign when party officials filed suit against the law, challenging its constitutionality on technical grounds related to the circumstances of its passage and because it did not apply to all counties. Their real objection, however, was against the provision that empowered the governor to choose election supervisors. Under the previous arrangement of having the county commissioners appoint election judges, Republicans had controlled the election machinery in several counties, particularly in Western Maryland. Expediently employing traditional Democratic rhetoric in an effort to protect this partisan advantage, Republicans condemned this new provision as a "flagrant act of centralization and partisanship" which "cheated the people by robbing the counties of their right of self-government." The Democratic State Committee retained counsel to assist the state's attorney general in defending the law before the courts. Mugwumps and Democrats of all opinions were appalled at "the Republican assault" upon the Australian ballot, regarding the matter as "a political case, instituted for party purposes strictly," and revealing "a good deal of hypocrisy in this Republican cry for ballot reform." The *Sun* insisted that Republicans relied on bribery and intimidation to retain the votes of blacks and Western Maryland miners, respectively, and therefore opposed secret voting. "Yoked in an unholy alliance with the employing corporations, the Republican party is opposed to the enfranchisement of the workingman, the freedom and secrecy of the ballot."[42]

Maryland's courts also rejected Republican arguments and upheld the Australian ballot law, clearing the way for the first election to be held under its provisions. To prepare the electorate for the new style of voting, both Democrats and Republicans organized campaign schools to instruct voters in the use of the new ballot. Party officials taught voters to select the right column by recognizing the party vignettes—the Democratic rooster, liberty tree, or Andrew Jackson portrait, depending on the voting district; the various pictures of Lincoln used by the Republicans; the Prohibitionist rose or flag. They carefully explained how to mark the ballots, a voter's task that had been not only unnecessary but actually discouraged under the party-ticket system. Finally, to overcome popular apprehension about being "shut up in a box" to vote, both major parties constructed voting booths and carried them around the state to illustrate the new system of voting at each political rally. Party newspapers also used the campaign to educate the voters, printing facsimiles of the official ballot and detailed directions on how to vote.[43]

The 1890 election itself brought general satisfaction with the new system. Although many voters approached the Australian ballot experience and especially the booths "with trepidation," most were pleased. The major complaint in Baltimore was about the smallness of the voting compartments. "But even the worst booth," declared the *Baltimore American,* "was a great advance over the old system, where the voter was assailed by [party] workers and crowded by ticket holders and made generally uncomfortable." Because the law prohibited electioneering within sixty feet of the polls, moreover, "it was one of the most quietly conducted elections ever held in Baltimore." In the counties, voters and observers also rejoiced over the new system of voting. "It is the first time a poor and timid man could go up and vote as the equal of the greatest," announced one Western Maryland newspaper. "It is the first time there was no collaring or hustling or intimidating. The vote is a free and true expression of the popular will.'' The *Hagerstown Mail* concluded, ''The most popular institution in Maryland at this time is the Australian ballot law.''[44]

There remained problems, of course. Secret voting did not altogether end election bribery but merely required a change in tactics. Because the briber could no longer be assured that the vote was delivered, he now bribed opposing voters *not* to vote. ''This method of bribery is rendered necessary by the Australian Ballot law,'' declared one observer, and the cost increased to $7–10 per voter.[45] In ''the Bohemian districts'' and other ethnic precincts in Baltimore, moreover, there was little secrecy in voting, and often Democratic workers still guided voters to the polls and controlled the conduct of the election. Labor groups, especially the Knights of Labor, complained that the voting compartments were too small to adequately shield the voter from observation and immediately began to lobby for larger and improved booths in order to prevent observation and guarantee secrecy in voting.[46]

Because of popular satisfaction with the Australian system, Democratic Governor Elihu Jackson recommended in 1891 that the law be extended to all counties with proper revisions to accommodate the complaints. The Democratic-dominated Maryland legislature of 1892 promptly adopted legislation accomplishing these purposes but also seized the occasion to make further revisions in the ballot law that again demonstrated both the law's ability to achieve partisan purposes and the ironic effects of ballot ''reform'' upon its original advocates. Whereas ballot reformers had viewed the Australian system as a way to facilitate independent and third-party nominations and to guarantee independence to the voter, the Democrats now used the law to prevent both objectives.[47]

These revisions reflected political developments in the 1891 campaign. The first was the unprecedented political activity of Maryland's farmers, organized into the militant Farmers' Alliance. They were largely responsible for the Democratic gubernatorial nomination of Frank Brown over Gorman's opposition and were determined to control the legislature to enact taxation reform. Newspapers described the Alliance activity as ''a cause of anxiety to the leading Democrats.'' Most alarming was the possibility that the Alliance might even join with Baltimore's labor groups to form a radical new party—a specter raised by Alliance state president Hugh Mitchell of Port Deposit when he assailed both major parties for rejecting Alliance demands. Democratic leaders decided that ''delicate and ingenious'' steps were needed to control the Alliancemen within the party.[48] Gorman's command of the party and state politics was also threatened from the right by the Independent Democrats, and their actions in the 1891 campaign provided the incentive for a second electoral change by the 1892 legislature. As in the past, they fused with the Republicans, doing so under the new Australian system by filing petitions to place their joint nominees on the ballot under the heading of ''Independent Democrats'' as well as in the Republi-

Figure 5.6. Partially mutilated sample ballot under the Australian system, permitting the voter to select from the available parties and nominees in the secrecy of a voting booth. (Collection of the Maryland Historical Society.)

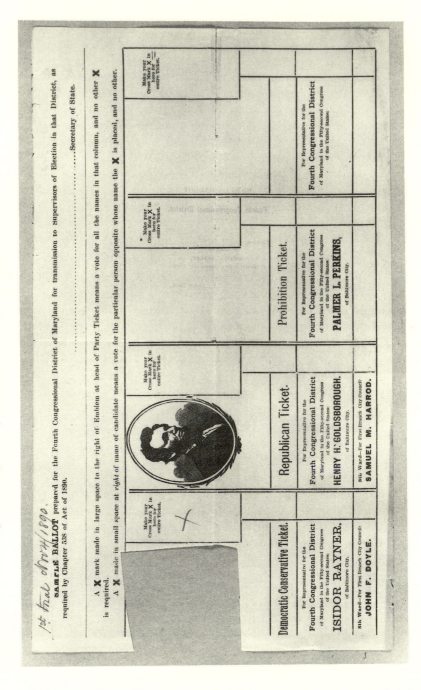

can column. This enabled them to vote for the fusion candidates as Democrats rather than as Republicans, a disagreeable prospect in such a partisan age. Gorman, a firm believer in party government, denounced the possibility of independent success as "more objectionable even than Republican success."[49]

In the 1892 legislature, then, Democrats attempted to constrain voters within the partisan harness by amending the ballot law. Their objective, as the *Sun* observed, was to "limit, if not destroy, the possibility of any independent action in politics by multiplying difficulties in the way of independent nominations," either as independents or as new parties. One new law prohibited listing again on the ballot any candidate nominated by petition if he were already listed as the nominee of a party. Henceforth, Independent Democrats would have to sacrifice their partisan identifications and vote as Republicans or else lose the effectiveness of a fusion campaign. State control of the electoral process thus restricted the electoral possibilities which had been available under the party-ticket system and worked to the advantage of the dominant party.[50]

More immediately controversial was a second new law. Dubbed the Carter amendment, after Gorman's House leader, this measure applied only to Baltimore and made major changes in the process of nomination by petition. Rather than permitting petitions to be circulated freely, it required citizens to go in person to Baltimore City Hall to sign the petition papers before the Board of Election Supervisors and to swear and sign an affidavit that they were registered voters, intended to support the candidate, desired to have him elected, and would not aid any other candidate. This law prevented citizens from signing petitions simply to give everyone an opportunity to vote for the candidate of their choice by assisting in placing his name on the ballot; it would also cause petitioners to lose at least half a day's work and pay; and by requiring them publicly to swear their voting intentions, it violated their voting privacy, effectively nullified the concept of a secret ballot, and subjected them to possible intimidation. It was expected that the difficulty, inconvenience, and expense would persuade most people not to try to nominate independent candidates. An attempt to organize a new party able to compete fully in Baltimore would be frustrated by the need for at least 4,400 voters, evenly distributed across the city's twenty-two wards, who were willing to make such personal sacrifices. Mugwump reformers, who often had organized independent candidacies in the past, condemned the Carter amendment as "a plan for making the nomination of any but machine candidates for the [City] Council almost impossible."[51]

Baltimore's labor organizations were even more vociferous in their opposition. Electrical Assembly 6280 of the Knights of Labor, one of the earliest and most active supporters of the Australian reform system, denounced the Carter amendment as destructive of popular rights, and other local assemblies as well as the Baltimore District Assembly 41 passed ardent resolutions against the measure. The Knights also sent delegations to Annapolis to lobby against this "disfranchising" measure. The *Critic* titled the measure "A bill to suppress independent candidacies in the city of Baltimore" and declared that it made the Australian ballot "an instrument of oppression, instead of one of freedom, which it was intended to be."[52]

Democratic politicians agreed that the amended ballot law would "prevent any more independent candidates" and enjoyed the naiveté of their opponents. "No matter how often we fool the businessmen and innocent mullets," said one Baltimore machine politician, "they are always ready to be fooled again."[53]

The political effect of the new ballot law was promptly demonstrated in the fall campaign when it effectively suppressed the new People's Party. Organized in August by members of the Farmers' Alliance and directed toward the labor organizations of Baltimore, the new party secured the necessary five hundred petitioners in each of the first, second, and fifth districts to nominate candidates for Congress and presidential elector but was prevented by the new law from nominating candidates in the two districts in Baltimore. "This law was passed after our party had obtained a foothold in other states, in order to keep us out of Maryland," charged Populist State Chairman Nelson Dunning of Sykesville. "It is a Democratic force bill to keep the People's Party out of this state." Dunning maintained that the Democrats themselves would find it difficult to make nominations under the legal restrictions but wisely noted "they were making laws for others, instead of themselves." He estimated that the ballot restrictions disfranchised five thousand voters in Baltimore, and the *Critic* agreed: "Many old labor men were in the party and are, no doubt, much discouraged. The so-called Australian ballot law militated against them very largely."[54]

Thus the achievement of the Australian ballot "reform" and its extension to the whole state by 1892 did not end the partisan use of the electoral structure, and subsequent revisions in the election law would often follow the same pattern. Rather than weakening the machine or facilitating independent nominations and voting or fostering third parties, ballot legislation often had the opposite effect, at least in the short run. What ballot laws really accomplished was the expansion of the role of the state in the political process, and that expansion, in turn, permitted the politicians in power to use state authority to promote self-serving conditions of order. The Baltimore *Sun* noted this ironic consequence of electoral reform when it concluded that the Australian ballot law had become "an engine in the hands of those who at first dreaded and opposed its enactment, and against whose influence the law was intended to operate as a barrier and a safeguard."[55]

Notes

1. See Paul Kleppner, *The Third Electoral System, 1853–1892: Parties, Voters, and Political Cultures* (Chapel Hill: University of North Carolina Press, 1979); Albert C.E. Parker, "Beating the Spread: Analyzing American Election Outcomes," *Journal of American History* 67 (1980): 61–87; Jean H. Baker, *Affairs of Party: The Political Culture of*

Northern Democrats in the Mid-Nineteenth Century (Ithaca: Cornell University Press, 1983).

2. *Laws of Maryland, 1874*, chap. 229; *Laws of Maryland, 1876*, chap. 223; *Civil Service Reformer* (Baltimore) 2 (1886): 6 and 3 (1887): 25; *Baltimore American*, 26, 27, October 1886.

3. *Laws of Maryland, 1874*, chap. 490; Baltimore *Sun*, 20 August 1885.

4. *New York Times*, 7 May 1880.

5. Baltimore *Sun*, 11 September 1879; *Civil Service Reformer* 2 (1886): 5, 77–79.

6. *Revised Code of the Public General Laws of Maryland, 1878*, Art. 5, pp. 46–47. See Baker, *Affairs of Party*, pp. 306–11, for a useful description of voting in Baltimore County in 1864. Despite the beliefs of several historians, Maryland apparently never prohibited colored ballots.

7. *Baltimore American*, 2 November 1886; *Cumberland Daily Times*, 5 November 1888, 2 November 1889; *Baltimore American and Commercial Advertiser*, 27 October 1875; Baltimore *Sun*, 7 November 1879.

8. *Baltimore American and Commercial Advertiser*, 4 November 1875. The judge's dexterity was necessary for Maryland attempted to prohibit pudding tickets by providing that multiple ballots found "deceitfully folded together" in the ballot box should be rejected. *Maryland Code, 1860*, Art. 35, p. 262.

9. Elihu S. Riley, *A History of the General Assembly of Maryland* (Baltimore: Nunn & Co., 1905), p. 389; Baltimore *True Democrat*, 26 October 1875; *Baltimore American and Commercial Advertiser*, 28 October 1875; *Citizen* quoted in Baltimore *Sun*, 8 November 1879.

10. *Hagerstown Mail*, 29 November 1889. For an excellent account of this practice in New Jersey, see John Reynolds, " 'The Silent Dollar': Vote Buying in New Jersey," *New Jersey History* 98 (1980): 191–211.

11. Albie Burke, "Federal Regulation of Congressional Elections in Northern Cities, 1871–1894" (Ph.D. diss., University of Chicago, 1968); *Ex parte Siebold*, 100 U.S. 371 (1880).

12. *Hagerstown Mail*, 11 April 1890; Burke, "Federal Regulation," ii; *Laws of Maryland, 1872*, chap. 208, *1874*, chap. 61 and 361, *1880*, chap. 375.

13. For a description of "army-style" campaigns, see Richard Jensen, "Armies, Admen, and Crusaders: Types of Presidential Election Campaigns," *History Teacher* 2 (1969): 33–50.

14. *Laws of Maryland, 1874*, chap. 250, *1884*, chap. 190, *1886*, chap. 189. Such restrictions had been decreed for Baltimore in 1860. *Maryland Code, 1860*, Art. IV.

15. *Appleton's Annual Cyclopedia, 1879* (New York: D. Appleton, 1880), 596, *1881* (New York: D. Appleton, 1882), 534; *Baltimore American*, 23 October 1886.

16. The best study of the mugwumps remains John Sproat, *"The Best Men": Liberal Reformers in the Gilded Age* (New York: Oxford University Press, 1968). For Baltimore, see *Civil Service Reformer*, passim, and Eric F. Goldman, *Charles J. Bonaparte, Patrician Reformer* (Baltimore: Johns Hopkins Press, 1943).

17. Charles J. Bonaparte to James H. Raymond, 14 May 1895, Bonaparte Papers, Library of Congress; *Civil Service Reformer* 2 (1886): 6, 21–22 and 4 (1888): 39; *Baltimore American*, 30 October 1886; James B. Crooks, *Politics and Progress: The Rise of Urban Progressivism in Baltimore* (Baton Rouge: Louisiana State University Press, 1968), 14.

18. *Civil Service Reformer* 3 (1887): 11–12, 23–31; John R. Lambert, *Arthur Pue Gorman* (Baton Rouge: Louisiana State University Press, 1953), 135; R.E. Wright, "Some Problems in City Government," *An Address to the Landlords Mutual Protective Association*, 26 November 1889; Margaret Law Callcott, *The Negro in Maryland Politics, 1870–1912* (Baltimore: Johns Hopkins University Press, 1969), 42.

19. *Civil Service Reformer* 5 (1889): 140; C.K. Yearley, *The Money Machines: The Breakdown and Reform of Governmental and Party Finance in the North, 1860–1920* (Albany: State University of New York Press, 1970), 174–175.

20. Baltimore *Critic*, 16 June 1888; *Civil Service Reformer* 4 (1888): 7; *Baltimore American*, 2, 3, 5 November 1886.

21. Baltimore *Sun*, 27 October 1877, 11 September 1879; *Baltimore American*, 28, 29, 31 October 1886.

22. *Baltimore American*, 25 October, 1 November 1886; Baltimore *Critic*, 9 June 1888.

23. *Appleton's Annual Cyclopedia, 1887* (New York: D. Appleton, 1888), 457.

24. Ibid.; *Civil Service Reformer* 4 (1888): 34.

25. *Civil Service Reformer* 4 (1888): 30, 18; *Laws of Maryland, 1888*, chap. 155, 104, 112.

26. *Civil Service Reformer* 4 (1888): 39, 42–43, 76; 5 (1889): 7.

27. Ibid., 4 (1888): 7; *Hagerstown Mail*, 3 January 1890.

28. Baltimore *Critic*, 14, 21 July 1888; Baltimore *Sun*, 18 March 1892.

29. *Civil Service Reformer* 4 (1888): 21 and 5 (1889): 19, 138–39; *Appleton's Annual Cyclopedia, 1889* (New York: D. Appleton, 1890), 533. The Knights were insistent that the voting rights of illiterates be protected and proposed the use of party vignettes on the ballot for that purpose. The Reform League's proposal caused its members to be castigated as "pseudo reformers." The Reform League, declared the *Port Tobacco Times*, an organ of the regular Democracy, "is always careful that none of its alleged reforms shall in any way impinge upon the ignorant colored vote." "This great league has always directed its energies at the white Democrats," the *Times* continued. "It would not have mattered that a few illiterate white Democrats should have been disfranchised by the system." *Port Tobacco Times*, 27 December 1889.

30. *Civil Service Reformer* 5 (1889): 107–9, 145; *Hagerstown Mail*, 13 December 1889.

31. *Hagerstown Mail*, 31 January 1890; *Appleton's Cyclopedia, 1889*, 533; *Civil Service Reformer* 5 (1889): 138–139.

32. Callcott, *The Negro in Maryland Politics*, 50; *Civil Service Reformer* 5 (1889): 137–38.

33. Baltimore *Critic*, 4 January 1890; *Cumberland Daily Times*, 11 January 1890; *Journal of the Knights of Labor* (Philadelphia), 23 January 1890.

34. *Hagerstown Mail*, 15, 22 November 1889; 3, 31 January, 21 February 1890; Baltimore *Critic*, 4 January 1890; *Journal of the Knights of Labor*, 23 January 1890.

35. *Hagerstown Mail*, 14 March 1890; *New York Times*, 17 March 1890.

36. Baltimore *Critic*, 1 March 1890; *Journal of the Proceedings of the Senate of Maryland, 1890* (Annapolis: George Melvin, State Printer, 1890), 463, 1073; *New York Times*, 17 March 1890.

37. Baltimore *Sun*, 8 March 1892.

38. *Laws of Maryland, 1890*, chap. 538.

39. Ibid.; *Hagerstown Mail*, 11 April 1890; *Civil Service Reformer* 6 (1890): 30; *New York Times*, 17 March 1890.

40. *Laws of Maryland, 1890*, chap. 538; *Cumberland Daily Times*, 11 January 1890.

41. *Laws of Maryland, 1890*, chap. 538. For this feature of ballot legislation, see John Reynolds and Richard L. McCormick, "Outlawing 'Treachery': Split Tickets and Ballot Laws in New York and New Jersey," *Journal of American History* 72 (1986): 839–58.

42. Baltimore *Sun*, 22, 23 October 1890; *New York Times*, 28 August 1891; *Congressional Record*, 51st Cong., 1st sess., 1890, 21, pt. 7:6676; *Hagerstown Mail*, 12 September 1890; Baltimore *Critic*, 29 March 1890.

43. Baltimore *Sun,* 22 October 1890; *Lankford v. County Commissioners of Somerset County,* 73 Md. 105; *Hagerstown Mail,* 31 October 1890; *Baltimore American,* 1, 4 November 1890.

44. *Baltimore American,* 5 November 1890; *Hagerstown Mail,* 7 November 1890.

45. *Hagerstown Mail,* 17 October 1890. For this type of "deflationary" fraud, see Gary W. Cox and J. Morgan Kousser, "Turnout and Rural Corruption: New York as a Test Case," *American Journal of Political Science* 25 (1981): 646–63.

46. *Baltimore American,* 5 November 1890; Baltimore *Critic,* 26 March 1892.

47. *Appleton's Annual Cyclopedia,* 1891 (New York: D. Appleton, 1892), 495.

48. *New York Times,* 20 July, 12 August 1891.

49. *Baltimore American,* 22, 24 October 1891.

50. Baltimore *Sun,* 8 March 1892; *Laws of Maryland, 1892,* chap. 236. This was not as strong a ballot restriction as the anti-fusion legislation enacted elsewhere, for the Maryland law still permitted a candidate nominated by two parties (as legally defined) to have his name listed in the ballot columns of each party; it simply restricted the freedom of "independents." For this other legislation, see Peter H. Argersinger, " 'A Place on the Ballot': Fusion Politics and Antifusion Laws," *American Historical Review* 85 (1980): 287–306, reprinted in this volume as chapter 6.

51. *Laws of Maryland, 1892,* chap. 205; Baltimore *Sun,* 8, 24 March 1892; *Civil Service Reformer* 8 (1892): 32.

52. Baltimore *Critic,* 12, 19, 26 March 1892; Baltimore *Sun,* 18 March 1892.

53. Baltimore *Sun,* 15 March 1892.

54. *Baltimore American,* 28, 30 October 1892; Baltimore *Critic,* 5, 12 November 1892; Baltimore *Sun,* 11 August 1892.

55. Baltimore *Sun,* 8 March 1892. Subsequent revisions in Maryland's election laws can be traced in Callcott, *The Negro in Maryland Politics,* and Crooks, *Politics and Progress.* For suggestive comments about the long-run effects of the Australian ballot in weakening party dominance in the electoral system, see John F. Reynolds, "Testing Democracy: Electoral Behavior and Progressive Reform in New Jersey," *Historian* 48 (1986): 231–54.

6

"A Place on the Ballot": Fusion Politics and Antifusion Laws

Only in recent years have historians seriously investigated the institutional framework of the American electoral system and begun to examine the political effects of ballot forms, voting systems, and suffrage requirements. In particular, some scholars have sought to explain the dramatic changes in political behavior that occurred around the turn of this century as "unintended consequences" of reforms in the structural properties of the electoral system rather than as a reflection of any larger development. While illuminating the political results of such institutional changes, these scholars have largely ignored the political context within which the changes evolved. Thus, they have regarded those structural modifications as essentially apolitical or nonpartisan and have sharply rejected any view that change stemmed from an "antidemocratic conspiracy" to control the political system.[1] Yet, at least one little-known development in the electoral reform of the 1890s involved a conscious effort to shape the political arena by disrupting opposition parties, revising traditional campaign and voting practices, and ensuring Republican hegemony—all under the mild cover of procedural reform. This development was the adoption of so-called antifusion laws, which also altered the political behavior characteristic of the Gilded Age, with varying effects on the role of third parties, modes of political participation, and the electoral process itself.

Fusion, or the electoral support of a single set of candidates by two or more parties, constituted a significant feature of late nineteenth-century politics, partic-

From Peter H. Argersinger, " 'A Place on the Ballot': Fusion Politics and Antifusion Laws," *American Historical Review,* vol. 85 (April 1980), pp. 287–306. Reprinted with permission of the American Historical Association.

A preliminary version of this article was presented at the annual meeting of the American Historical Association in Dallas, December 28–30, 1977. I wish to thank the principal commentator at that time, Howard W. Allen, for his helpful criticism. I also wish to express my appreciation to Jo Ann E. Argersinger for advice and assistance.

ularly in the Midwest and West, where full or partial fusion occurred in nearly every election. Such fusions customarily involved a temporary alliance between third parties and the weaker of the two major parties, usually the Democrats in the Midwest and West. In the 1878 congressional elections, however, Indiana Greenbackers fused in one district with Democrats and in another with Republicans. That fusion often seemed to have a life of its own was evident in the Greenback effort of 1884 to arrange fusions in each state with whatever party was in the minority.[2] Fusion plans were generally undertaken, nevertheless, to promote the needs of the major party and were generally initiated or avoided according to the calculations of its politicians rather than those of the leaders of the evanescent third parties. Thus, the Republicans sometimes arranged fusions in the South but retreated whenever their participation in such a campaign might work against the Democratic divisiveness they sought to exploit. Similarly, in the West, Democrats repeatedly fused *on* third party tickets even over the bitter opposition of independents—that is, any third party followers in the nineteenth-century usage—who feared absorption by the major party or accusations of ideological betrayal. But, if fusion sometimes helped destroy individual third parties, it helped maintain a significant third party tradition by guaranteeing that dissenters' votes could be more than symbolic protest, that their leaders could gain office, and that their demands might be heard. Most of the election victories normally attributed to the Grangers, Independents, or Greenbackers in the 1870s and 1880s were a result of fusion between those third-party groups and Democrats. That some politicians regarded fusion as a mechanism for proportional representation is not surprising.[3]

Fusion was a particularly appropriate tactic given the period's political culture. Voter turnout was at a historic high, rigid party allegiance was standard, and straight-ticket voting was the norm. Partisanship was intense, rooted not only in shared values but in hatreds engendered by cultural and sectional conflict. Changes in party control resulted less from voter conversion than from differential rates of partisan turnout or from the effect of third parties. Although the Republicans continued to win most elections, moreover, the era of Republican dominance had ended in the older Northwest by 1874 and had been considerably eroded in the states farther west by the 1880s, so that elections were bitterly contested campaigns in which neither major party consistently attracted a majority of the voters.[4] Minor parties regularly captured a significant share of the popular vote and received at least 20 percent in one or more elections from 1874 to 1892 in more than half of the non-Southern states. Even where their share was smaller, it represented a critically important proportion of that electorate. Between 1878 and 1892 minor parties held the balance of power at least once in every state but Vermont, and from the mid-1880s they held that power in a majority of states in nearly every election, culminating in 1892 when neither major party secured a majority of the electorate in nearly three-quarters of the states.[5] By offering additional votes in a closely divided electorate, fusion became a continuing objective not only of third party leaders seeking personal advancement or limited, tangible goals but also of Democratic politicians interested in immediate partisan advantage. The tactic of fusion enabled Democrats to secure the votes of independents or disaffected Republicans who never considered voting directly for the Democracy they hated; it permitted such voters to register their discontent effectively without directly supporting a party that represented negative reference groups and rarely offered acceptable policy alternatives.

The use of separate party ballots constituted another feature of the political culture of the Gilded Age that facilitated fusion. Each party printed and distributed its own ballot, without the necessary involvement of either state officials or the candidates themselves. The ballots, or tickets, were strips of paper on which only the names of the candidates of that party appeared. The individual voter could remain ignorant of the nominees of other parties; he merely had to deposit his party ticket in the ballot box, without studying or, in some states, even marking it. This election system allowed partisans of fusing parties to cast their votes without explicitly acknowledging their shared behavior or its significance, and it enabled a party to pursue fusion with an unwilling partner.

Given their vulnerability to fusion politics, Republicans continually sought to prevent cooperation among their opponents. Repeatedly, they pointed out the contradictions in the platforms of the different groups contemplating fusion and urged members of each to adhere to their own principles rather than to fuse with groups holding obviously different aims. Although the Republican motive was transparent, the argument held considerable force, particularly for conservative Democrats, for those Democrats and third party followers who believed in the representative nature of parties and nominations (not uncommon among minority political groups), and for those third party supporters who were interested in the development of their party and realized their reform goals required more than just immediate and perhaps counterproductive electoral victories.[6] At times Republicans tried to encourage these antifusion elements among their opponents by going beyond such attempts to incite partisan prejudice and actually subsidizing their activities and party newspapers. In 1878 Indiana Republicans even underwrote a separate campaign by the Greenbackers, hoping thereby to draw votes from the Democrats. One final, if perhaps unofficial, tactic to sabotage fusion was demonstrated in Michigan's legislative elections of 1884, when Republicans distributed ''bogus tickets calculated to deceive the greenbackers and democrats'' by substituting the names of the Republican nominees for the fusion candidates on what otherwise appeared as a regular, fusion-party ballot.[7]

The effectiveness of this type of ballot trickery in disrupting fusion was easily surpassed by the possibilities inherent in the Australian ballot system. The presidential election of 1888, with its widespread incidents of bribery, intimidation, and fraudulent voting, provoked a reaction against the partisan excesses possible in the party-ballot system of voting and helped spur most states toward adopting the Australian ballot, long advocated by a number of disparate groups. This system did more than merely ensure secrecy for the voter. It also provided for an official ballot printed at public expense and distributed only by public election officers at the polling place. The system featured a blanket ballot, moreover, which contained the names of all of the candidates legally nominated by any party. The candidates' names were arranged on the ballot in one of two general patterns, the office-bloc or the party-column format. On the office-bloc ballot, candidates were grouped under the name of the office sought and their partisan affiliations were shown. The voter made his choice for each office by marking a square corresponding to the appropriate candidate. On the party-column ballot, candidates were grouped by party and listed in parallel columns. In some states the ballot laws even placed emblems or vignettes at the head of the columns to enable the voter to distinguish more easily the separate parties. Finally, lawmakers frequently added to the ballot a device to facilitate straight-ticket voting, a party circle, which, when marked, constituted a vote for the entire party ticket. These developments represented legislative efforts to retain some of the familiar, partisan features of the old ballot system while providing the secret and official characteristics of the new.[8]

By providing for public rather than partisan control over the ballots and by featuring a blanket ballot, the Australian system opened to Republicans, given their dominance in state governments, the opportunity to use the power of the state to eliminate fusion politics and thereby alter political behavior.[9] The Republicans' modifications of the Australian ballot were designed to take advantage of the attitudes and prejudices of their opponents and were based on a simple prohibition against listing a candidate's name more than once on the official ballot. This stipulation, Republicans believed, would either split the potential fusion vote by causing each party to nominate separate candidates or undermine the efficacy of any fusion that did occur, for in this time of intense partisanship many Democrats would refuse to vote for a fusion candidate designated "Populist" and many Populists would feel equally reluctant to vote for a "Democrat."[10] Related regulations could restrict straight-ticket voting by fusionists or even eliminate one of the fusing parties, antagonizing its partisans and causing them either to oppose the fusion arrangements or to drop out of the electorate altogether. Given the closely balanced elections of the late nineteenth century, the elimination of even a small faction of their political opponents because of ideology, partisanship, or social prejudice would help guarantee Republican ascendancy. Although other ballot adjustments increased its effectiveness, this simple prohibition against double listing became the basic feature of what the Nebraska supreme court described as a Republican effort to use the Australian ballot as a "scheme to put the voters in a straight jacket."[11]

Publicly, Republicans defended this prohibition as necessary for achieving equal treatment, efficiency, and an end to political corruption, and they insisted that technically it did not interfere with nominations or voting. But, given what one Wisconsin judge called "the strength of party ties" and the reality that "political rights are universally exercised through party organizations," the logic of the law lay in his conclusion that "its only purpose is to prevent fusion." The law, he continued, "will prevent no illegal vote from being cast, nor will it stop any corrupt practice, nor in any way preserve the purity of the ballot." It was designed, instead, to interfere with "the freedom of action of the party . . . [and] of the citizens who compose that party." The Republican judicial rejoinder, of course, was that "mere party fealty and party sentiment, which influences men to desire to be known as members of a particular [political] organization, are not the subjects of constitutional care."[12] The law, then, was intended to promote the dissolution of party ties while giving Republicans the residual benefits of them.

The possibilities of adjusting the ballot system in this direction became evident during the 1892 presidential campaign, the first held under the original Australian ballot system. That campaign marked as well the initial national appearance of the most important third party of the late nineteenth century, the People's Party, which had its greatest appeal to economically distressed farmers in the Western states, traditionally controlled by Republicans. In an effort to increase the electoral chances of its presidential candidate, Grover Cleveland, the Democratic National Committee urged party officials in several Western states to withdraw their nominees for the electoral college and fuse on the Populist nominees, thereby denying Republicans the electoral votes that Cleveland would be unable to capture for himself.

The responses in Oregon and Minnesota proved most significant. Both states were controlled by Republicans although the GOP represented only a minority of voters in each. Hoping to arrange a successful fusion, Democratic officials withdrew one of their four nominees in Oregon and four of their nine nominees in Minnesota, replacing them with candidates nominated by the Populists. In both states many Populists denounced the Democratic maneuver, worrying that, as one Minnesota Populist elector said, the tactic "will hurt the People's Party rather than help it, as a great many in that party were formerly Republians, and . . . will have a tendency to drive them back to the old party." Many Democrats also complained of the arrangement, but gradually most concluded that, although fusion with the Populists was distasteful, "in the present case, the end justifies the means," as the Oregon state chairman observed.[13] The initial Republican reaction to these fusion arrangements also followed the customary pattern. To their own partisans Republican leaders stressed two contradictory conclusions: fusion was a confession of Democratic weakness, but Republicans would have to turn out in greater numbers to vote it down. To Democratic and Populist voters, the Republican leaders appealed separately, insisting that fusion required their party to subordinate its own sacred principles and able candidates to those of the other party.[14]

These fusion campaigns differed from previous ones, however, because of the Republicans' partisan implementation of the Australian ballot law, which both states had enacted in 1891. In adopting the office-bloc form of ballot, the Oregon legislature had also prohibited the name of any candidate from appearing more than once on the ballot. Perhaps this provision had seemed a logical corollary to the ballot type, for it excited no comment at the time. When in 1892 Democratic officials recognized the implications of that clause for their fusion plans, they argued that another provision, which permitted the names of electoral college candidates to be grouped by parties, allowed the fusionist elector, Nathan Pierce, to be listed with Democrats as well as with Populists on the ballot. Republicans countered that Pierce's name could be listed only once and identified as a "Populist" or at most "Populist-Democrat," expecting that the word "Democrat" would be a signal to Republican-Populists to scratch the name and that the Populist designation would alienate some Democratic voters: "a very pretty jungle," in the words of one Republican editor.[15]

The question of ballot form appeared so late in the campaign that there was no time to secure a legal decision, and county clerks turned to party leaders for guidance in printing the official ballots. The ballot devised by the Democratic state committee and subsequently copied by Democratic county clerks listed Pierce's name in both the Democratic and Populist groupings, while those county clerks who followed the instructions of the Republican state chairman listed Pierce only among the Populist nominees, though designating him with both party affiliations.[16]

Because of this singular ballot situation, Oregon's election results revealed both the value of fusion and the effect of ballot format in shaping electoral outcomes and disrupting fusion coalitions. The Republicans won three of the four electoral votes, averaging 35,000 votes for their candidates. The straight Populist candidates averaged 27,000 and the straight Democrats 14,000. Had Pierce received the full vote of both parties he would have been an easy victor with approximately 41,000 votes, but he squeaked through with only 35,811. Regression analysis indicates that in those counties in which his name was listed under both Democratic and Populist groupings virtually all Populists voted for their fellow partisan, while 92 percent of the Democrats also supported Pierce, an indication of some hostility to fusion but also of a general willingness to vote the Democratic ticket and all who were designated on it. But, in those counties in which Pierce's name was listed on the ballot only once (under the Populist group), 9 percent of the Populist voters refused to support a Populist who was also labeled a Democrat, although he was identified as a Populist and listed with the other Populist electors. And 29 percent of the Democrats refused to vote for a Democratic candidate who was also listed as a Populist.[17] Republican expectations as to voter behavior had proved accurate.

While Oregon provides the most revealing evidence of the effect of ballot format on voting behavior and fusion politics, events in Minnesota proved more immediately influential for electoral reform. Like that in Oregon, the ballot law in Minnesota also established the office-bloc format, but without the restriction on listing candidates' names more than once. In preparing the official ballot for 1892, however, the Republican secretary of state simply proceeded as though that were a legal requirement, grouping the five straight Democratic electors separately and scattering the four endorsed Populists among the five other Populists, though designating them as both Populist and Democratic. Democratic officials charged that the Republican ballot design was constructed to "render it more difficult for the voter to cast his vote according to his preference" and sought a court order to compel the double listing of fusion electors. Democratic lawyers argued that, as drawn up, the official ballot would disfranchise twenty thousand voters. But, since the ballots were already printed, the court was confronted with a Republican *fait accompli,* the reversal of which would have required a postponement of the election itself, and accordingly the court judiciously ruled that it had no jurisdiction in the matter.[18]

Ignoring their own structural revolution, Republicans crowed that "the court and secretary of state do not propose to become the cat's paws of the fusion schemers and turn the ballot upside down to suit their political ends." Democrats found consolation in the publicity their court case had engendered: it called voter attention to the structure of the ballot and indicated how Democrats would have to vote. Indeed, even Republicans argued that repeated instruction in "the science and art of casting a ballot under the Australian system" would be more valuable than "profound dissertations on the tariff and the currency." The election results validated that estimate of the importance of the ballot. The straight Democratic electors averaged 101,000 votes and the straight Populists 29,000; their combined total would have easily defeated the Republicans' 113,000. Yet the four fusion electors received only 110,000 votes, the drop of 20,000 that Democratic officials had predicted, which allowed the minority Republicans to sweep to complete victory.[19]

The massive vote differentials in these states were largely a function of institutional change in the voting system, but they also involved a behavioral component, for the ballot arrangements were advertised and explained extensively, and voters could have selected the fusion candidates if they had been willing to vote with a different party. That some voters were obviously unwilling to ally themselves even symbolically with another party testifies again to the nature and strength of partisan affiliation in the political culture of the time. In evaluating the decline in the fusionists' votes, one Minnesota election judge observed, "It matters not whether this was the result of sharp practice or not, the fact remains . . . they were cheated out of their votes" by the "system of voting."[20] But, significantly, the decline was not an "unintended consequence" of ballot change but rather resulted from "sharp practice." The institutional change had been purposely designed to exploit the observed behavioral patterns in the political culture and did not represent some abstract or disinterested impulse toward "reform."

This basic reality became increasingly obvious from the reactions in other states to the Minnesota experience. Neighboring Wisconsin, traditionally Republican, had gone Democratic in 1892 because of local circumstances. Fusion had occurred at several levels and, as one Republican editor complained, "the labor party, or people's party, or Farmers' Alliance, assisted to place in power" the Democrats, and "without those voters the democratic party is in a minority in the state." To protect these voters and their own new position, Democratic legislators amended the election law in 1893 specifically to provide for dual ballot listings in the event of fusion nominations.[21]

By 1893, Michigan had perhaps experienced more consistent fusion politics than any other state, and the new, Republican legislature decided to revise the Australian ballot law that had been enacted by its Democratic predecessor. Although there was considerable discussion about the need "to purify elections and prevent fraud thereat," the GOP's objective clearly was, as one Democrat observed, to "purify elections according to the Republican idea of purity, and prevent frauds by all other parties." One Republican legislator, at least, was candid: "We don't propose to allow the Democrats to make allies of the Populists, Prohibitionists, or any other party, and get up combination tickets against us. We can whip them single-handed, but don't intend to fight all creation."[22] The Republicans' solution was ballot manipulation, a tactic they first applied retroactively by unseating non-GOP legislators whose names had been listed upon more than one ticket. The presiding officer refused even to entertain Democratic protests against this "revolutionary action," but the state supreme court partially restrained the Republican majority by upholding the legality of ballots with dual listings. The Republicans then countered by moving to amend the state's election law by prohibiting double listing of candidates' names on the ballot. This effort also failed, but by only three votes. All forty-eight votes in favor of the bill were Republican; all Democrats and Populists voting opposed the measure.[23]

This Republican attempt to unseat legislators reveals an important aspect of the movement for the legal disruption of fusion politics. Fusion occurred most often in local and state-legislative contests, where the candidates' personal popularity was more likely to displace partisan issues in determining voters' preferences. In Michigan, for example, fusion did not materialize in the presidential race of 1892, and the Populists made a negligible showing. But Populist strength was regional and often proved decisive in local contests. In the legislature of 1893, which first debated the issue, twenty-one of the thirty-one Democratic and Populist state representatives had been elected through fusion, while twenty-six Republican representatives had been elected over fusion opponents. At least twenty more Republicans were elected only by plurality votes and would have been defeated if their opponents had successfully fused. Thus, a major object of antifusion legislation was at times local, not national, politics. When Michigan did, in fact, later enact an antifusion law, its passage owed some of its immediate support to a pending special congressional election in southwestern Michigan, where Populists were strongest and where the Republican candidate, the presiding officer of the state senate, was opposed by the fusion nominee of Populists, Prohibitionists, Silverites, and Democrats. This local nature of fusion was what prompted interest in antifusion legislation in those states where, at the aggregate level, it did not seem necessary or important. But a focus on the small total number of Populists in large industrial states like Michigan or Wisconsin is misleading in other ways as well. While Michigan Populists polled only 4.3 percent of the total state vote in 1892, that proportion gave them the balance of power in the closely contested electorate; when delivered to Democratic candidates through fusion, as in the contest for attorney general, it sufficed to bring about the only Republican losses on the state ticket.[24]

South Dakota succeeded where Michigan failed in 1893 in passing the first explicitly antifusion law.[25] Constituting only a minority of the voters, the state's Republicans had apprehensively watched developments in Minnesota and devoted their own 1892 campaign "almost exclusively to the business of preventing a fusion" between Populists and Democrats. In 1893 they carried this objective into the legislature and enacted a number of changes in election laws. The most important simply provided that "the name of no candidate shall appear more than once on the ballot for the same office." Related changes similarly designed to frustrate fusion included a prohibition against the withdrawal of candidates shortly before elections, called "the Minnesota plan" of fusion; a provision to treat fusing parties as a single party when appointing election judges; and the replacement of the office-bloc with the party-column format, containing a party circle provision for straight-ticket voting.[26] This last modification made more effective the prohibition against double listing, for by requiring party columns a candidate could be identified with only one party affiliation, unlike candidates on the Oregon and Minnesota ballots, and the second party to nominate a candidate would appear on the ballot as having no nominee for that office at all. Those wishing to fuse would thus lose the symbolic protection of voting for their own party and be required to vote as members of another party. When fusion did not involve whole tickets, which was the usual case, fusion voters would also lose the advantage of the party circle and have to check each individual name—a provision that was certain to complicate voting and lead to the invalidation of ballots through improper marking.[27]

The effects of these new ballot provisions were felt in the state's elections in 1893 and 1894, when, as Republicans observed, they served as a "stumbling block" to their opponents. Populists and Democrats named separate state tickets in order to maintain their parties' organization and independence, though each party conceded that such separation would lead to a Republican victory. The weaker Democrats, in particular, feared that under the new law cooperation with Populists would be "not fusion but absorption." Although fusionist leaders made some local efforts at fusion, they predicted that at least 20 percent of the

Democrats would refuse to vote outside their party name, a fall-off that spelled defeat in a close election. After the expected Republican victory, one Democratic party official observed, "Under the present system of voting as arranged by the Republican party, fusion results in confusion to Democracy."[28]

Nationally, the Republican success in 1894 led to the passage of antifusion laws by other states in 1895. Oregon Republicans, who had captured a majority in the legislature with only a minority of the popular vote, formally enacted an antifusion statute.[29] In neighboring Washington, after successfully campaigning against "fusion schemes," the Republicans applied the force of the one-listing provision in the party-column format to the office-bloc ballot by stipulating that only one party affiliation could be designated for any candidate.[30] Michigan Republicans, now in complete control of the legislature, reintroduced their anti-fusion bill of the previous session and pushed it into law. Although some judges described it as "unconstitutional" and "revolutionary," the state supreme court upheld the measure in the same partisan spirit in which it had been enacted—four Republican judges in the affirmative, one Democrat in dissent.[31] The Ohio legislature, meeting in 1896, concluded this first legislative flurry with the so-called Dana law, an elaborate measure based upon the customary antifusion ballot requirement. In Ohio, the local focus of antifusion legislation seemed particularly evident, at least initially. In the recent Cincinnati mayoral election, the Republican machine of "Boss" George Cox and Joseph B. Foraker had been challenged by a fusion coalition of Populists, Socialists, laborites, and dissident Republicans that had nearly received the Democratic endorsement as well. The regular Republicans had reacted "as if civilization were at stake." Some legislative observers regarded the subsequent Dana bill, prepared by a Foraker Republican, as primarily designed to prevent just such unified popular revolts against machine rule in municipal elections. Indeed, the Republican legislative majority, so large as to be "dangerous," according to one editor, voted down a proposed amendment to exclude municipal elections from the antifusion provisions.[32]

The larger political importance of these new antifusion laws was promptly demonstrated in the presidential election of 1896, the pre-eminent fusion campaign of the late nineteenth century, when Democrats, Populists, and Silver Republicans fused on the candidacy of William Jennings Bryan. In those antifusion states, like Ohio, in which Democrats constituted by far the major portion of Bryan's supporters, the Populists were sacrificed in a way that not even middle-of-the-road Southerners anticipated when they opposed the Populist endorsement of Bryan.[33] Ohio state election officials announced that the Dana law would eliminate a Populist national ticket from the ballot and, through its party-column and marking procedures, might invalidate ballots that tried to combine support for Bryan with a state or local Populist ticket. To avoid that outcome, Democratic and Populist leaders reluctantly also agreed to fuse on complete state and local tickets. The Democratic state committee withdrew the Democratic nominees for several offices and substituted Populist nominees in exchange for Populist acceptance of the remaining Democratic candidates. All candidates were listed on the ballot only under the Democratic heading. Many Populists, however, were loath to become even nominal Democrats and objected to these arrangements in which their party "was left without a place on the ballot." Defiance County Populists even advocated rescinding Bryan's nomination in order to protect their own party, while other Populists refused to withdraw their nominations. Ultimately, in addition to the designated Democratic ticket, composed of both Democrats and Populists, the official ballot *did* list a severely truncated Populist ticket after all, so that a Populist could not easily vote a straight ticket.[34]

A second antifusion provision of the Dana law threatened even the Democrats' ability to cast a straight ticket by prohibiting the entry of nominees on one party's ticket when they were certified as members of another party. Accordingly, the secretary of state prepared to split the arduously constructed composite ticket into separate columns after all. Thus, Populist nominees had to declare themselves as Democrats, causing still more disaffection, for the Populists announced that they had "already gone much further than they had wished in order to effect the fusion agreement" and were reluctant "to declare that they are Democrats and thereby destroy absolutely the individuality of the party organization they have been striving to represent." Finally, the Populist state chairman ignominiously had to assert that the Populists had not really made any nominations and to withdraw their certificates; election officials then placed the fusion slate on the ballot as the Democratic ticket.[35] Though the fusionists' troubled campaign ended in defeat, the straight Populists fared even worse with the election law. Their officially disavowed ticket failed to attract enough votes to entitle the party to be on the Australian ballot in the future, except by petition. As one Populist disconsolately wrote his national chairman, "We have now in Ohio no People's party, but simply scattered organizations here and there."[36]

In antifusion states where Populists constituted the majority of Bryan's supporters, roles were reversed but the same difficulties developed. In Oregon, Democrats had to withdraw their electors and accept the Populist ticket as their own. The Populist state chairman explained the result: "Under our statute they surrendered their legal autonomy by this act, so that we have but two parties in this state." The further consequence was that, whereas the Populists and Democrats running separate tickets had together captured 53 percent of the votes in the June state election on much the same issues, Democratic fall-off permitted them to attract only 48 percent of the vote in November under this rankling arrangement.[37] In Washington as well, after a committee of lawyers examined the "cunningly devised" election law, the Democrats felt forced to accept the Populist name for the fusion ticket. The outcry against sacrificing the party name was so great, however, that, to the end of the negotiations, it seemed likely that the Democrats would repudiate the plan, thereby defeating Bryan in a state where victory would have been easy under previous electoral rules.[38]

Similarly in South Dakota, Democrats recognized that under the ballot law they had to sacrifice their party's organization to secure the state's electoral votes for their party's nominee. Accordingly, they canceled their state convention and adopted the ticket and the name of the People's Party. At the county level, however, Democratic opposition to voting under the Populist name frequently led to a compromise name of "Free Silver" for the local fusion ticket. But this ran afoul of the party-column and party-circle provisions of the ballot law and made it difficult for fusionists to cast a straight ticket for both state and local offices. The likely result under the ballot law, one newspaper predicted dryly, was "the loss of numerous votes for one ticket or the other or . . . loss of both tickets."[39]

Michigan, with its fusion tradition and moderately strong third parties, furnished the final experience among antifusion states in 1896. Both Populists and Democrats objected to accepting the others' name and, unable to fuse in the customary fashion, therefore dropped all old party names to adopt a new collective one for the purpose of the ballot: the Democratic-People's-Silver Union. But even this stratagem had a weakness, for the state supreme court ruled that by entering the DPSU the regular Democratic organization had abandoned the name "Democrat." The court therefore awarded that designation on the ballot to a ticket named by bolting anti-Bryan gold Democrats, a decision that the Democratic state chairman understandably denounced as "an attempt to mislead the people."[40]

The Michigan and Ohio experiences were not lost on Republicans in Indiana, the state in which Mark Hanna feared fusion most.[41] Hoosier Republicans made two unsuccessful efforts during the campaign to secure the effects of antifusion legislation without actually having such a law. When the Populists and Democrats agreed on a common electoral ticket to appear on the ballot under both the Democratic rooster and the Populist plow and hammer vignettes, the Republicans sought to enjoin the fusionists from filing dual nomination papers. Populists were alarmed that, if this tactic succeeded, "a large proportion of our voters will be practically disfranchised." One Populist, who wrote his national chairman seeking legal assistance, expressed his fear that they would "have trouble in Ind. & perhaps all other states that have accepted the Australian system of ballots to get our fusion tickets on the official ballot." The Republican state chairman also instructed Republican election judges to separate fusion votes into Democratic and Populist totals, as though the parties had different candidates. Though both of these maneuvers failed, after the election the Republicans made immediately clear, as the *Chicago Tribune* reported, their intention "to amend the election law so as to prevent fusion like that perpetrated in the last campaign."[42] The bill, involving the customary prohibition against double listing, was drawn up by the Republican state committee and then passed in the legislature by a vote of 83 to 58, all Republicans in favor, all Democrats and Populists opposed.[43]

The lessons learned in, and the opportunity presented by, the sweeping 1896 Republican victory led Republican-dominated legislatures in many more states to enact antifusion laws quickly. Republican legislatures passed antifusion laws in 1897 in Illinois, Iowa, North Dakota, Pennsylvania, Wisconsin, and Wyoming as well as in Indiana. As Republicans gained sufficient legislative control elsewhere, the law spread still further: California and Nebraska in 1899; Kansas, Minnesota, and South Dakota in 1901; Idaho in 1903; and Montana in 1907.[44]

Ending the effective cooperation of Democrats and third party groups was both the primary goal and the major result of these efforts. As the attorney general of one state noted, the antifusion law should have been renamed "an act to keep the populists in the middle of the road." Any cooperation that did take place under the new electoral rules involved a sacrifice of voters that rendered the whole less than the sum of its parts. If forced to vote for fusion as Democrats, many Populists declared, they would prefer to return to the GOP or simply not vote at all.[45] Analysis of the Kansas election returns of 1902 confirms this. Under the 1901 antifusion law, the fusion vote declined drastically from that of 1900. Those Populists who had voted for a fusion ticket under their own heading in 1900 proved little more likely to vote for a fusion ticket under a Democratic heading in 1902 (45 percent) than actually to vote Republican (40 percent), and, when confronted with that choice, a sizable minority either voted for a symbolic third party or dropped out of the electorate altogether.[46] This last course proved even more agreeable to South Dakota Populists. The proportion of original Populists willing to support fusion fell by two-thirds between 1900, when they could vote under their own heading, and 1902, when they were required to vote as Democrats following the Republican enactment of the antifusion law in 1901. And three-fourths of that shift was accounted for by a huge increase in those who simply refused to vote at all.[47]

By preventing effective fusion, antifusion laws also brought an end to another major characteristic of late nineteenth-century politics—the importance and even existence of significant third parties.[48] Whether such legislation split the GOP's opponents or encouraged attenuated new combinations, the same result obtained: the non-viability of third parties. A Populist explained the dynamics involved with these words: the law "practically disfranchises every citizen who does not happen to be a member of the party in power. . . . They are thus compelled to either lose their vote (as that expression is usually understood), or else unite in one organization. It would mean that there could be only two parties at one time."[49] Political realities, moreover, dictated that those two parties would be the existing major ones. Because the adoption of a new composite name left the Democratic name, with all of its appeal and tradition, to be used by minority factions as in Michigan in 1896, because of even more grotesque ballot complications under the laws of some states,[50] or merely because their greater national strength gave them an advantage in all electoral contests, the Democrats were ultimately able to insist successfully that the name "Democrat" be adopted by all fusionists. In Michigan, for example, the charade of maintaining three separate conventions ended in 1899, and in 1901 the DPSU became simply the Democratic Party. Similarly, in Washington the fusionists joined in a union convention in 1900 and agreed to the Democratic name. A Detroit newspaper alluded to this logical tendency of the antifusion law when it renamed the legislation "the law providing for the extinction and effacement of all parties but the Democratic and Republican."[51]

Antifusion legislation also undermined the People's Party by exacerbating the existing fratricidal split within the party between the middle-of-the-roaders and fusionists. As one Indiana Populist immediately recognized of the antifusion law, "an element of discord has been introduced by the dominant party which is expected to rend the populists' ranks and remove all doubts from future contests."[52] The usual mid-road arguments against fusion, based on the necessity of maintaining the party's identity and organization, acquired new and intense meaning in a legal situation that, as one judge phrased it, "says to the party, and through the party to the electors composing it: 'You shall not endorse candidates of any other party, except on condition that you surrender your existence as a party and lose your right of representation upon the official ballot in the future.' "[53] Antifusion legislation thus required those Populists interested in preserving their party's integrity to attack fusion ever more vigorously. As one Minnesota mid-roader noted, such laws would otherwise eliminate the Populists in every state where they did not outnumber the Democrats and thereby end any semblance of a national People's Party. But fusionist Populists countered that the mid-road position, in combination with the Republican "ballot law plot," would itself "divide and disfranchise populists and aid the monopoly and gold standard power." They argued that third parties had had their practical importance primarily as members of fusion coalitions and that "fusion, in the manner it has been had before on the official ballot, is no longer a possibility."[54] The logic of their position, then, required fusionists to merge the People's Party into the Democratic ranks. Limited to a ballot choice between Democrats and Republicans, some Populists voted Republican while others dropped out. The mid-roaders, though legally a bolting minority, issued their own Populist ticket, which after lengthy court battles between the two Populist factions invariably failed to attract enough support to guarantee the party a position on the ballot in the future.[55] In either case the People's Party ceased to exist.

In some measure, then, the People's Party died not only from prosperity and psychic collapse but also from ballot restrictions deliberately imposed by partisan legislatures in a movement that cannot accurately be said to have "scrupulously" preserved "all the forms of political democracy."[56] Some Populists vigorously attempted to amend the ballot laws, but others, recognizing that the Australian ballot itself had opened politics to "the dictation of state authority," argued for its repeal. "If 'amendment' is insisted upon," wrote one Iowa Populist, "let it be in the style of the farmer who amended his worthless dog's tail by letting the cleaver fall just behind the cur's ears."[57] Other Populists in antifusion states began to push for electoral change to protect the existence of third parties: proportional representation.[58] That those efforts failed is hardly surprising.

Nor did the effects of antifusion legislation end with the destruction of the People's Party. Obviously, these laws contributed to the widely observed decline in party competition in the "System of 1896." It is reasonable to assume, moreover, that demoralized former Populists, whether they were forced into the Democratic or Republican Party, became more "peripheral" than "core" supporters of their new parties and were less likely to vote and, when they did, were more likely to engage in the split-ticket, drop-off, and roll-off tendencies characteristic of the electorate after the crisis of the 1890s.

Certainly, antifusion laws were not solely or even primarily responsible for those tendencies, which appeared throughout the political system. But the time has surely come to discard the notion that political effects were "unintended consequences" of nonpartisan institutional reforms. Such alterations in electoral law must be viewed within a larger political context and not treated as "uncaused causes" of the transformation of voting behavior.[59] These laws were enacted by politicians who deliberately sought to protect or advance their own interests by manipulating the rules of the game. That their interests corresponded in some respects to decreased political participation, particularly by the more democratic elements of the population, and a consequent circumscription of public policy only adds to the poignancy of the process. Obviously, it is not true that electoral "reform," as one political scientist has claimed, "ended the earlier party practice of using the institutional framework for its own benefit."[60] Indeed, antifusion laws, as one dissident observed in 1895, were "a step toward making the Australian ballot system a means for the repression instead of the expression of the will of the people."[61] As for whether there was a "conspiracy," the Populists, who have often been charged with paranoia and conspiracy-mindedness, might have appreciated today's graffiti—"even paranoids have real enemies."

Notes

1. For present purposes, this "legal-institutionalist" school is best approached in terms of the reaction to Walter Dean Burnham's "The Changing Shape of the American Political Universe," *American Political Science Review*, 59 (1965): 7–28. Burnham argued that sharp declines in turnout and increases in split-ticket voting and other indexes of partisan volatility and voter marginality reflected the establishment of corporate political hegemony in the realignment of 1896 and a consequent breakdown in party organization and competition coupled with a rise in voter alienation. For major rejoinders, see Jerrold G. Rusk, "The Effect of the Australian Ballot Reform on Split Ticket Voting, 1876–1908," *ibid.*, 64 (1970): 1220–38; and Philip E. Converse, "Change in the American Electorate," in Angus Campbell and Philip E. Converse, eds., *The Human Meaning of Social Change* (New York, 1972), 263–337. For the continuing controversy, see Burnham, *Critical Elections and the Mainsprings of American Politics* (New York, 1970); Burnham and Rusk, letters in *American Political Science Review*, 65 (1971): 1149–57; Burnham, "Theory and Voting Research: Some Reflections on Converse's 'Change in the American Electorate,' " *ibid.*, 68 (1974): 1002–23; Converse, "Comment on Burnham's

'Theory and Voting Research,' '' *ibid.,* 1024–27; Rusk, "Comment: The American Elec-
toral Universe: Speculation and Evidence," *ibid.,* 1028–49; and Burnham, "Rejoinder to
'Comments' by Philip Converse and Jerrold Rusk," *ibid.,* 1050–57. John J.
Stucker, like
Rusk a former student of Converse at the University of Michigan, has joined Rusk in two
further contributions to the legal-institutional theory of electoral change: "The Effect of
the Southern System of Election Laws on Voting Participation: A Reply to V.O. Key,
Jr.," in Joel H. Silbey *et al.,* eds., *The History of American Electoral Behavior* (Princeton,
1978), 198–250; and "Legal-Institutional Factors in American Voting," in William
Crotty, ed., *Political Participation and American Democracy* (Westport, Conn., forthcoming). For Burnham's most recent and developed statement, see his "The System of 1896:
An Analysis," in Paul Kleppner *et al., The Evolution of American Electoral Systems*
(Westport, Conn., 1981), 147–202. Finally, for an evaluation of the behavioral and legal-
institutional positions in light of the decline in voter turnout in the early twentieth century,
see Paul Kleppner and Stephen C. Baker, "The Impact of Registration Requirements on
Electoral Turnout, 1900–1916: Multiple Tests of Competing Theories," paper delivered
at the annual meeting of the American Political Science Association, Washington, D.C.,
August 1979. Converse has noted that Burnham's "conspiratorial interpretation"
prompted his own work: "Comment on Burnham's 'Theory and Voting Research,' ''
1024. Much of Rusk's work seems similarly motivated; see his "Comment: The American Electoral Universe," 1045–46. In 1974 Burnham backed away from suggestions of a
conspiracy; "Theory and Voting Research," 1022. In one prominent exception to the
"nonpartisan" thesis of the legal-institutionalist school, however, J. Morgan Kousser has
argued that "the cross-fertilization and coordination" between Democratic movements to
quash political opposition legally in the South "amounted to a public conspiracy"; see
Kousser, *The Shaping of Southern Politics: Suffrage Restriction and the Establishment of
the One-Party South, 1880–1910* (New Haven, 1974), 39. Rusk was prepared to "find a
conspiracy which used legal means to control the system" within the Democratic South
but strongly denied that one existed among Republicans in the North. He quite rightly
recognized that the "paramount" issue in determining the nature of electoral change is
that of "legislative intent"—"*who* urged the passage of these laws and *why?*" See his
"Comment: The American Electoral Universe," 1045–46. The present essay will con-
centrate on those two questions in explaining one particular Northern electoral development.

2. *Appleton's Annual Cyclopedia, 1878* (New York, 1879), 443; *Chicago Daily Tribune,* September 4, 1884; and Fred E. Haynes, *Third Party Movements since the Civil
War* (1916; reprint ed., New York, 1966). An extreme example of the complexity of
fusion politics came in North Dakota in 1890 when the Independents fused with the
Prohibitionists to nominate candidates for governor and auditor, after which this coalition
fused *on* Republican nominees for lieutenant governor and congressman and Democratic
nominees for secretary of state and attorney general. *Appleton's Annual Cyclopedia, 1890*
(New York, 1891), 629.

3. *New York Herald,* March 12, August 13, 1892; *Chicago Daily Tribune,* September
2, 1884; and Haynes, *Third Party Movements.* Also see Lee A. Dew, "Populist Fusion
Movements as an Instrument of Political Reform, 1890–1900" (M.A. thesis, Kansas State
Teachers College, Pittsburg, 1957). Fusion was not, of course, always successful, but it
did offer the best chance of overcoming the Republicans. As one South Dakota Republican observed, "No fusion means Republican victory"; *Brookings County* (S.D.) *Press,*
September 29, 1892. Even when defeated the policy of fusion caused a great deal of
uncertainty within Republican ranks. In 1884, for instance, Republican Senator William
B. Allison of Iowa warned party "managers in the East that this fusion of the Democrats
with [Benjamin F.] Butler's forces in the West would require some attention and that we

could not afford to rest on our oars with the field combined against us''; *Chicago Daily Tribune*, September 7, 1884.

4. For general discussions of the period's political culture, see Burnham, "Changing Shape of the American Political Universe"; Paul Kleppner, *The Cross of Culture: A Social Analysis of Midwestern Politics, 1850–1900* (New York, 1970) and *The Third Electoral System, 1853–1892: Parties, Voters, and Political Cultures* (Chapel Hill, 1979); and Melvyn Hammarberg, *The Indiana Voter: The Historical Dynamics of Party Allegiance during the 1870s* (Chicago, 1977).

5. These conclusions as to the political importance of minor parties are derived from data that Paul T. David recorded for gubernatorial and presidential elections in the thirty non-Southern states; see his *Party Strength in the United States, 1872–1970* (Charlottesville, Va., 1972), 102–286. Even these statements underestimate the role of minor parties, because David systematically adjusted his data to discount the minor parties precisely when they engaged in fusion. I have made allowances for this adjustment only in a few obvious instances, as in the 1892 presidential returns for North Dakota or Wyoming. I have focused on state elections here, because electoral laws were a function of individual state legislatures. Paul Kleppner emphasized the same point from a wider perspective when he wrote, "The mean vote cast for minor parties in both the 1876–88 and 1876–92 sequences of biennial elections exceeded the major-party mean partisan lead in the Midatlantic, the East North Central, the West North Central, and the Western regions of the country, as well as in the United States as a whole"; *The Third Electoral System*, 239.

6. For examples of such Republican appeals, see the *Portland Morning Oregonian*, October 25, 26, 27, 28, 1892; and the *Minneapolis Tribune*, October 12, 20, 21, 1892. For an examination of the issue of representativeness in parties, see Austin Ranney, *Curing the Mischiefs of Faction: Party Reform in America* (Berkeley and Los Angeles, 1975).

7. *Detroit Evening News*, November 1, 1884. Morton Keller, *Affairs of State: Public Life in Late Nineteenth-Century America* (Cambridge, Mass., 1977), 282; and Des Moines *Farmers Tribune*, August 18, 1897.

8. The scholarly literature on the development of the Australian ballot is surprisingly thin and analytically unsophisticated. But see L.E. Fredman, *The Australian Ballot: The Story of an American Reform* (East Lansing, Mich., 1968); and Eldon C. Evans, *A History of the Australian Ballot System in the United States* (Chicago, 1917).

9. It is not asserted here that Republicans enacted the Australian ballot in the first place for such partisan purposes, and Rusk's attempt to deny the partisan effect of the Australian ballot by noting that both Democrats and Republicans voted for the initial reform in state legislatures is unsatisfactory. Rusk, "Comment: The American Electoral Universe," 1045. The law itself and its basic provisions for a secret, public ballot did not become the object of contention (except in rare cases as in New York) so much as the modifications of the Australian ballot system and the use that could be made of them did. As one opponent of subsequent Republican ballot changes in South Dakota said, "The real trouble is the change from the law as it originally stood." Another Dakota correspondent noted that each legislature after the one that had enacted the Australian ballot "has been tinkering at the law, and . . . wrapped the ballot in technicalities." After a Populist governor urged "that the old safe-guards which have been one-by-one repealed since the passage of the original law be reinstated," a Populist legislature adopted a law providing "for a return to the method when the Australian system was first adopted." Sioux Falls (S.D.) *Argus-Leader*, January 11, 1895; *Chicago Daily Tribune*, January 4, 1897; *South Dakota Senate Journal* (Pierre, 1897), 43–44; and Yankton (S.D.) *Press & Dakotan*, February 11, 1897. For opposition in New York to the Australian ballot itself on practical, ideological, and partisan grounds, see the discussion in Herbert J. Bass, *"I Am a*

Democrat'': The Political Career of David Bennett Hill (Syracuse, 1961), 96–101, 128–30, 133–35, 147–48, 151–53.

10. It was "well known," one newspaper observed, that many voters would not vote for a candidate unless he were listed on their ticket. "This may be a prejudice, but it is not an unworthy one in a community where party government is recognized." *Detroit Free Press,* March 15, 1895. An Ohio Greenbacker had made the same point earlier and more graphically: "Men would as soon cut off their right hands almost as vote a Democratic ticket." *Cincinnati Enquirer,* August 22, 1877, as quoted in R.C. McGrane, "Ohio and the Greenback Movement," *Mississippi Valley Historical Review,* 11 (1925): 535.

11. *State v. Stein* (Neb.), 53 N.W. Rep. 999.

12. *State v. Anderson* (Wisc.), 76 N.W. Rep. 482.

13. *Minneapolis Tribune,* October 13, 19, 24, 1892; and *Portland Morning Oregonian,* October 28, November 2, 1892.

14. *Portland Morning Oregonian,* October 25, 26, 27, 28, November 2, 1892; and *Minneapolis Tribune,* October 12, 20, 21, 1892.

15. *Portland Morning Oregonian,* October 27, 28, 30, 1892.

16. *Ibid.,* October 28, 30, 1892.

17. *Appleton's Annual Cyclopedia, 1892* (New York, 1893), 615; and *Portland Morning Oregonian,* November 11, 1892, January 6, 1893. Estimates of voter behavior were derived from ecological regressions calculated for those twenty-seven (of thirty-two total) counties for which firm evidence exists as to the ballot format employed. For the best introduction to this technique, see J. Morgan Kousser, "Ecological Regression and the Analysis of Past Politics," *Journal of Interdisciplinary History,* 4 (1973): 237–62; and W.P. Shively, " 'Ecological Inference': The Use of Aggregate Data to Study Individuals," *American Political Science Review,* 63 (1969): 1183–96.

18. *Minneapolis Tribune,* October 16, 18, 19, 1892.

19. *Ibid.,* October 10, 19, 1892. John D. Hicks, "The People's Party in Minnesota," *Minnesota History Bulletin,* 5 (1924): 545.

20. *Minneapolis Tribune,* November 17, October 19, 1892.

21. Madison *Wisconsin State Journal,* January 3, 1893; and *The Registry and Election Laws of the State of Wisconsin* (Madison, Wisc., 1894), 26.

22. *Detroit Free Press,* February 1, January 5, 1893.

23. *Ibid.,* January 4, 19, February 15, 16, 25, 1893; *Journal of the House of the State of Michigan, 1893* (Lansing, 1893), 697, 1031; and *Official Directory and Legislative Manual of the State of Michigan, 1893–4* (Lansing, 1893), 706–11.

24. Richard Harvey Barton, "The Agrarian Revolt in Michigan, 1865–1900" (Ph.D. dissertation, Michigan State University, 1958), 125–51; *Kalamazoo Weekly Telegraph,* October 19, 1892, March 20, 1895; *Official Directory and Legislative Manual of Michigan, 1893–4,* 593–625; and *Appleton's Annual Cyclopedia, 1892,* 467.

25. The Oregon law of 1891 cannot be so considered for it was passed without apparent recognition of its significance, was still open to contrasting interpretations, and preceded a formal antifusion law enacted in 1895. Both Kentucky and Indiana had early laws that contained provisions resembling those characteristic of antifusion laws but that were really designed to deal with the possibility of nonpartisan nominations by petition rather than with party action. In practice, moreover, their election laws were not interpreted in a fashion to prevent fusion. For a discussion of the local political context surrounding the development of antifusion legislation in South Dakota, consult my " 'Confusion to Democracy': Ballot Laws and Politics, 1890–1902," paper delivered at the thirteenth annual Northern Great Plains History Conference, Fargo, N.D., October 27, 1978, pp. 2–6.

26. *New York Times,* October 21, 1892; *South Dakota House Journal* (Pierre, 1893),

862; *South Dakota Senate Journal* (Pierre, 1893), 58, 283–86, 1006; and Yankton (S.D.) *Press & Dakotan,* March 9, 23, 1893.

27. See Sioux Falls (S.D.) *Argus-Leader,* November 4, 1893; Yankton (S.D.) *Press & Dakotan,* November 24, December 8, 1892; and DeSmet *Independent,* as quoted in *Brookings County* (S.D.) *Press,* November 2, 1893.

28. *Brookings County* (S.D.) *Press,* October 19, 1893; and Sioux Falls (S.D.) *Argus-Leader,* August 3, 29, September 5, 6, November 13, 1894.

29. *Appleton's Annual Cyclopedia, 1894* (New York, 1895), 636; *Appleton's Annual Cyclopedia, 1895* (New York, 1896), 632; *Oregon House Journal* (Salem, Oreg., 1895), 1007–08; and *Oregon Senate Journal* (Salem, Oreg., 1895), 631, 640.

30. *Spokane Spokesman-Review,* November 1, 10, 1894; *House Journal of the State of Washington, 1895* (Olympia, Wash., 1895), 667–72; and *Senate Journal of the State of Washington, 1895* (Olympia, Wash., 1895), 709. Republican legislators backed this "reform" by a vote of 68 to 1, while Populists opposed it by a margin of 17 to 3.

31. *Journal of the Senate of the State of Michigan, 1895* (Lansing, 1895), 112, 373–74, 457, 775–78; *Journal of the House of the State of Michigan, 1895* (Lansing, 1895), 961; *Kalamazoo Weekly Telegraph,* March 20, 1895; *Detroit Free Press,* March 26, 1895; and *Todd v. Election Commissioners,* 104 Mich. 474, 486 (1895).

32. Zane L. Miller, *Boss Cox's Cincinnati: Urban Politics in the Progressive Era* (New York, 1968), 89; *Cincinnati Enquirer,* November 7, 1895; *Cleveland Plain-Dealer,* April 9, 1896; *The Journal of the Senate of the State of Ohio, 1896* (Norwalk, Ohio, 1896), 399–400; and *The Journal of the House of the State of Ohio, 1896* (Norwalk, Ohio, 1896), 689.

33. The following discussion involves only those developments that stemmed from antifusion legislation and does not cover any of the quite different difficulties with respect to fusion that Robert Durden has already described well; see his *The Climax of Populism: The Election of 1896* (Lexington, Ky., 1966). The phrase "mid-road," or "middle-of-the-road," referred to those Populists who opposed fusion or cooperation with either major party, which they regarded as being in the gutters of the political system—on each side of those who kept clean and pure in the middle of the road.

34. *Bowling Green* (Ohio) *Daily Sentinel,* July 17, 28, August 28, September 16, 23, 1896; *Cincinnati Commercial Tribune,* August 8, 12, October 21, 1896; and Columbus *Ohio State Journal,* October 20, 24, 1896.

35. *Cincinnati Commercial Tribune,* October 3, 4, 6, 7, 8, 1896.

36. Hugo Preyer to Marion Butler, March 19, 1897, Marion Butler Papers, Southern Historical Collection, University of North Carolina Library; and *Bowling Green* (Ohio) *Daily Sentinel,* November 10, 1896. This dissolution of Ohio's Populist party demonstrates the destructive effect on smaller parties of the interaction between the antifusion law and another standard provision of the Australian ballot system. The adoption of the Australian ballot meant of course that disgruntled citizens could no longer simply organize themselves spontaneously and enter the political arena independently by issuing their own party ticket. The use of an official, blanket ballot required the state to establish procedures to regulate the appearance of parties and their candidates on the ballot. This regulation usually involved, *inter alia,* defining a party that could appear on the ballot in terms of its percentage of the total vote in the preceding election. Manipulation of the minimum required percentage often reduced the number of minor parties by directly limiting their ability to present themselves for voter consideration. Petitioning provided an alternative method for gaining party access to the ballot. But, again, some states required unreasonably large numbers of signatures—or even specified a particular geographical distribution of the petitioners—so that, in practice, the candidates would be confined to the larger parties. Once parties were stricken from the ballot (through their candidates) by

the operation of the antifusion law, they legally ceased to exist until their partisans successfully petitioned to secure ballot consideration again. Even the Democratic Party had no standing in those states where it fell victim to antifusion regulations; see below. But small and poor or loosely organized parties faced particular difficulty in regaining an opportunity to appear on the ballot. Members of all political parties were extremely sensitive to this possible consequence of the interaction of the antifusion and other ballot provisions of the electoral law. Unfortunately, not even some of the Populists themselves could resist this legal opportunity to obstruct possible opponents by keeping them off the ballot in the first place. In Kansas, for instance, the regular Populists, after being troubled by a radical (middle-of-the-road) Populist separate ticket in 1896, amended the state's Australian ballot law in the 1897 legislature to quintuple the number of signatures required to gain a ballot position through petition and thereby keep "small bodies of reformers out of politics." Only rarely, of course, were Populists in a position to manipulate the legal parameters of politics, a point perhaps underlined by this same legislature's simultaneous ability to *defeat* an antifusion bill—on a strict party vote, all Republicans in favor, all Populists and Democrats opposed. *Dubuque* (Iowa) *Herald,* February 17, 1897; and *Senate Journal: Proceedings of the Senate of the State of Kansas* (Topeka, 1897), 787, 884–85, 1111, 1201. For examples of the more typical major party effort to obstruct new parties through the requirement of an extraordinary number of petition signatures, see Erik Falk Petersen, "The Struggle for the Australian Ballot in California," *California Historical Quarterly,* 51 (1972): 239; and Charles Chauncey Binney, "Merits and Defects of the Pennsylvania Ballot Law of 1891," *Annals of the American Academy of Political and Social Science,* 2 (1892): 751–71, esp. 757n, 758n. Beyond mandating procedures for securing a position on the ballot, the "infamous" Missouri election law required a party to receive one-third of the total votes cast or be "disbarred from all privileges and representation" in the appointment of election judges and clerks. *Kalamazoo Weekly Telegraph,* April 15, 1891. For a striking example of the local exclusion of small parties through legal regulations, see *Bowling Green* (Ohio) *Daily Sentinel,* March 27, 1896.

37. John C. Young to Marion Butler, March 22, 1897, Butler Papers; and *Appleton's Annual Cyclopedia, 1896* (New York, 1897), 628.

38. *Spokane Spokesman-Review,* August 15, 18, 22, 1896; and Winston B. Thorson, "Washington State Nominating Conventions," *Pacific Northwest Quarterly,* 35 (1944): 104–05.

39. *Sioux City* (Iowa) *Journal,* October 17, 1896; and *Appleton's Annual Cyclopedia, 1896,* 707–08.

40. *Detroit Free Press,* November 1, 1896; *Kalamazoo Weekly Telegraph,* August 26, September 2, 1896; and *Baker v. Board of Election Commissioners* (Mich.), 68 N.W. Rep. 752.

41. James S. Clarkson to H.G. McMillan, October 5, 1896, James S. Clarkson Papers, Library of Congress.

42. Lew W. Hubbell to Marion Butler, September 13, 1896, Butler Papers; *Chicago Daily Tribune,* January 4, 27, 1897; and *Cincinnati Commercial Tribune,* October 28, 29, 1896.

43. *Indianapolis Journal,* January 15, 1897; *Journal of the Indiana State Senate, 1897* (Indianapolis, 1897), 592; and *Journal of the Indiana House of Representatives, 1897* (Indianapolis, 1897), 967–68.

44. *Appleton's Annual Cyclopedia, 1897* (New York, 1898), 395, 419, 574, 664; New York State Library Bulletin, *Summary of Legislation* (Albany, 1897), 519; *Appleton's Annual Cyclopedia, 1901* (New York, 1902), 702; and Arthur C. Luddington, *American Ballot Laws* (Albany, 1911), 15, 39, 43, 78. South Dakota's law of 1901 followed the Populists' repeal in 1897 of the original antifusion legislation of 1893. Republican legis-

lators had passed an antifusion bill in 1899, only to have it vetoed by the Populist governor. This pattern of ballot legislation suggests the partisan motivation involved and indicates the common conviction of the law's political effects. See Argersinger, " 'Confusion to Democracy,' " 11. In addition, the Democratic legislatures of three Southern states also enacted antifusion legislation in the early 1900s, and controversy over the law actually provoked a riot in the Kentucky legislature. Thus, while the focus here has been on Northern Republicans, the law was obviously regarded as serving the interests of the dominant party wherever it was enacted. Antifusion legislation was of minor importance in the South because the passage of more blatantly partisan electoral legislation obviated the need for subtler controls; see Kousser, *The Shaping of Southern Politics*. Antifusion laws were more appropriate to the more closely balanced North, where slight alterations in the electorate were sufficient to guarantee partisan control. Some Northern Republicans, however, likened their antifusion legislation to the South's repressive legislation. See, for example, Des Moines *Iowa State Register*, February 19, 1897.

45. *Detroit Evening News*, March 16, 1895; *New York Times*, April 6, 1900; and Des Moines *Farmers Tribune*, August 3, 1897.

46. Based on an ecological regression calculated over those sixty-nine counties for which 1900 fusion votes were separately returned according to their Populist and Democratic components. This 1902 election, moreover, finally marked an approximate return to the state's pre-Populist political alignments: the Republican vote correlated significantly with the Republican vote of the 1880s for the first time in more than a decade and the Democratic vote correlated significantly with the Democratic vote of the 1880s (as the fusion votes of 1896, 1898, and 1900 had not).

47. Based on ecological regression involving 1890, 1900, and 1902 South Dakota voting results; also see Sioux Falls (S.D.) *Argus-Leader*, November 6, 7, 8, 1902. Original Populists are here defined as those who voted the Independent ticket in 1890. Clearly, this is an incomplete measurement, for it provides no information concerning those who joined the People's Party in, say, 1894. This is only part of the difficulty in trying to measure the effect of antifusion legislation. The general question is the counterfactual one: how would things have been different if they had not been as they were? One major consequence of antifusion legislation of course could be what did *not* happen, as in those instances in which fusion was avoided. The common failure of election boards to report disaggregated partisan votes for fusion candidates, except for the partial Kansas case analyzed above, prevents a careful calculation of effects when fusion did take place. Ideally, that determination also requires consecutive fusion elections with low issue-salience, a condition that did not obtain in the 1890s. The 1892 Oregon contest thus assumes great significance in establishing the political importance of an antifusion ballot.

48. Third parties did, of course, appear in subsequent years, but with the exception of the Socialists they were generally expressive rather than instrumental. Those with any great support were short-lived and often based on the appeal of a dominant personality, like the Roosevelt Progressives of 1912 or the La Follette Progressives of 1924. Certainly, such parties rarely had, over time, the characteristics of late nineteenth-century third parties: local organization, voter identification, mass support in some areas and generalized regional strength, and especially tangible electoral success.

49. *Kalamazoo Weekly Telegraph*, March 20, 1895.

50. Following the passage of North Dakota's antifusion law in 1897, Independents (Populists) and Democrats, each opposing incorporation under the other's banner, combined into a new organization and adopted the title Independent-Democratic Party "as a party name . . . under which both Democrats and Populists can fight." But the imaginative Republican secretary of state interfered with this new-style fusion by ruling that the candidates of the Independent-Democratic Party could not be permitted on the Australian

ballot at all, for such a party had not received the legal minimum of 5 percent of the vote in the preceding election—when, of course, it had not yet existed. Furthermore, he ruled, since the separate Independent and Democratic parties had formed a new party, they had ceased to exist themselves and therefore could not *regain* a ballot position, leaving the Republicans the only party on the ballot. See *Winterset* (Iowa) *Review,* March 31, 1897; *Bismarck* (N.D.) *Daily Tribune,* October 28, 31, November 2, 1898; and *State v. Falley* (N.D.), 76 N.W. Rep. 996. This action seemed to answer an earlier Populist who wondered, after the passage of an antifusion law, "why [the legislature] did not go on a little further and say there shall be but one ticket allowed on the ballot, and that must be the Republican ticket." Des Moines *Farmers Tribune,* March 17, 1897. For similar comments, see *Kalamazoo Weekly Telegraph,* March 20, 1895; and *Spokane Spokesman-Review,* August 18, 1896. Wyoming simply prevented the creation of any new-style fusions such as the DPSU or the Independent-Democratic Party by adding to its antifusion ballot amendment a requirement that the names of political parties not exceed *one* word. New York State Library Bulletin, *Summary of Legislation,* 519.

51. *Detroit Evening News,* March 20, 1895; Arthur Millspaugh, *Party Organization and Machinery in Michigan since 1890* (Baltimore, 1917), 19, 55; *Spokane Spokesman-Review,* August 30, 1900; and Des Moines *Iowa State Register,* May 13, June 24, 1897.

52. Quoted in Des Moines *Farmers Tribune,* March 17, 1897.

53. *State v. Anderson* (Wisc.), 76 N.W. Rep. 482.

54. Des Moines *Farmers Tribune,* March 17, June 23, 1897. Also see O.D. Jones to Marion Butler, April 21, 1897, Butler Papers.

55. In particular, see the Iowa experience in the *Winterset* (Iowa) *Review,* July 28, September 9, 1897; Des Moines *Farmers Tribune,* June 30, September 15, November 10, 1897; Des Moines *Iowa State Register,* August 19, 20, September 4, 8, 1897; and *Dubuque* (Iowa) *Herald,* October 17, 22, 28, 1897.

56. Also see Burnham's larger statement that it "is difficult to avoid the impression that while all the forms of political democracy were more or less scrupulously preserved, the functional result of the 'System of 1896' was the conversion of a fairly democratic regime into a rather broadly based oligarchy." Burnham, "Changing Shape of the American Political Universe," 23.

57. *Sioux City* (Iowa) *Journal,* May 26, 1897; and Des Moines *Farmers Tribune,* February 17, 1897, January 5, 1898.

58. William E. Lyons, "Populism in Pennsylvania, 1892–1901," *Pennsylvania History,* 32 (1965): 55; and *Bowling Green* (Ohio) *Daily Sentinel,* August 12, 1897.

59. Burnham, "Rejoinder to 'Comments' by Converse and Rusk," 1054.

60. Rusk, "Comment: The American Electoral Universe," 1049.

61. *Kalamazoo Weekly Telegraph,* March 20, 1895.

7

Regulating Democracy: Election Laws and Dakota Politics, 1889–1902

In recent years, legal historians have widened their frames of reference to investigate new areas, particularly the interplay of law and society, in order to understand, as James Willard Hurst has put it, "how law has really worked in social experience."[1] But while research in legal history, by expanding its focus beyond the earlier emphasis on courts and the judicial process to include legislative, administrative, and other legal agencies, has illuminated topics as diverse as economic development, technology, and the environment, other relevant subjects have been neglected. Surprisingly, one of these is the political arena and the relation between election law, itself a product of politics in America, and the rough-and-tumble world of parties and politicians.[2] While historians may describe and analyze elections in terms of the political issues or constituencies involved, the contests themselves took place within and were shaped by the parameters of election laws regulating parties, nominations, ballots, and voting. Although historians ignore or take for granted many of these now standard electoral parameters, they were often matters of major concern at the time of their adoption and during political campaigns that followed. For, as one political scientist has observed, "decisions on rules are never politically neutral. . . . In politics as in all other forms of human conflict, the rules make a difference in determining who wins and who loses."[3] However equitable procedures might seem, they are rarely impartial in their effects within a specific political context. An examination of the early development of election laws in two states, North Dakota and South Dakota, reveals the partisan motivation and consequences of election laws and emphasizes the role of ballots, courts, and election officials in political history.

From Peter H. Argersinger, "Regulating Democracy: Election Laws and Dakota Politics, 1889–1902," *The Midwest Review,* vol. 5 (Spring 1983), pp. 1–19. Reprinted with permission.

The basic and most important election law established the Australian ballot system. Before its adoption, citizens voted openly, using separate party ballots— strips of paper printed and distributed by the party itself and listing the names of its candidates. At times, moreover, each party printed its ballots on distinctively colored paper so that the voter's choice of party was readily apparent. Under these circumstances, there was considerable opportunity for fraudulent voting and intimidation. Eventually laws required all ballots to be printed on white paper of uniform size. Even so, according to one observer of elections in Dakota Territory, "bribery was then open at the polls, and ballot-box stuffing was often resorted to."[4]

It was to prevent such abuses that both North and South Dakota adopted the Australian ballot system in 1891.[5] In addition to providing secrecy for the voter, this system mandated that ballots be printed at public expense, that they be distributed by public officials, and that they contain the names of all candidates. One Dakota correspondent of the *New York Times* explained that "the Australian ballot law will restrain corrupt or fraudulent voting" by depriving "the purchaser of a vote of the satisfaction of knowing whether he will get what he pays for or not."[6] But in enacting the Australian system for such purposes, lawmakers necessarily had to consider other subjects, such as the structure of the ballot, the question of who could be listed on the ballot, and the rules for registering nominees, printing ballots, and so forth—all of which heretofore had been left up to the parties. In establishing these procedures, politicians responded to political conditions and manipulated the rules to achieve partisan ends.

There were two general types of ballots. One, initially adopted by both North and South Dakota, was the office-group ballot, which listed candidates in blocs according to the office sought and required the voter to sort through the various candidates to find his choice. Though partisan affiliations were indicated, the "pure" office-group ballot minimized partisanship by depriving the voter of an opportunity to cast a straight-ticket with a single mark. The second general format was the party-column ballot. This grouped candidates by parties in parallel columns. Most states added to this ballot a provision for voting a straight-ticket with a single mark, usually in a "party circle" at the head of the party column. The political effect of using this ballot was to promote straight party voting. Although both Dakotas established the office-group ballot, North Dakota provided a circle for straight-ticket voting, and many South Dakota politicians favored switching to the party-column format in their state to facilitate partisan voting.[7]

Regardless of ballot format, most states required newspapers to print voting instructions and sample ballots before election day to acquaint voters with the task before them. Additionally, in North Dakota many candidates had printed in newspapers, as paid political advertisements, that portion of the ballot which contained their names, coupled with an explanation of how to vote for them. Some observers argued that practical demonstrations of voting would be more helpful than merely providing printed instructions, and in both Dakotas political parties soon organized campaign schools to teach their followers how to mark their ballots, while party headquarters distributed sample ballots for practice voting. Even so, voting errors were common in the first election under the Australian system. Ballots were frequently incompletely or imperfectly marked or even deposited entirely blank, reflecting voter continuity from the past when party ballots required no marking. Listing a series of such errors, the Mandan *Times* announced that "a large majority of the people are ready to admit that the Australian voting law is a nuisance."[8]

There were other difficulties arising from the new system. Necessarily, the ballot law had to establish rules for the size, number, and placement of voting booths and the amount of time a voter was to be permitted within one. In some areas, according to one observer, "many voters through ignorance or timidity would not venture into the booths under the new law."[9] There were other problems as well. South Dakota, for instance, established so many specifications for printing ballots that in 1892 only one printing firm in the state was qualified to do the work, and that company stalled for better terms, leading state officials to fear that no ballots at all would be available on election day. North Dakota legislators also devoted considerable effort to such details only to realize on the eve of the 1892 campaign that they had made no arrangements for choosing presidential electors or canvassing election returns. The governor had to call a special session of the legislature to remedy the problem.[10]

The new laws led to one of the most anomalous situations in the history of the electoral college. In North Dakota Democrats and Populists nominated a joint electoral ticket in the 1892 election, and their three candidates for elector, on the face of the returns, narrowly defeated the Republican nominees. But the new state board of canvassers, controlled by Republicans, rejected some of the returns and declared one Republican elected by eight votes. Democratic State Chairman Daniel Mara brought suit against the board and secured a court ruling that the board had to accept all returns as submitted. While Democrats and Populists celebrated the court's order, giving them the full electoral vote, Republican Governor Andrew Burke ignored the decision and issued a certificate of election to the Republican candidate, declaring that the time permitted under the election law to contest the voting results had expired even as the court ruled. In the end, then, North Dakota cast one vote for each of three different Presidential candidates: Democrat Grover Cleveland, Populist James B. Weaver, and Republican Benjamin Harrison.[11]

Other provisions of the new ballot laws had consequences just as serious and more enduring. Election legislation had to detail the procedures by which candidates could gain a place on the ballot. Generally, the law provided that a political party securing a certain percentage of the total vote in the preceding election could have its nominees listed on the official ballot. North Dakota's 1891 law, for example, authorized printing the names of, and limiting straight-ticket voting privileges to, those parties that had received at least 5 percent of the total vote in the preceding election. This rule bestowed benefits on the major parties that were not immediately available to the frequent but evanescent third parties of the period. In 1892 the Republican *North Dakota Capital* enjoyed the irony that reformers "now find that the Australian system of voting which they asked for . . . is something of an obstruction to the launching of the new people's party, as it is not entitled to a place in the heading of the ticket."[12] The implications of legally subordinating the Populists to the old parties were not only politically but also ideologically significant. Indeed, the California supreme court in 1892 invalidated that state's identical ballot provision for voting a straight party ticket with the statement that "it is an attempt to discriminate against classes of voters, and its effect . . . would be to subject such classes to the alternative of partial disfranchisement or to the casting of their votes upon more burdensome conditions than others no better entitled . . . to the free and untrammeled exercise of the right of suffrage."[13]

A second method by which candidates could secure a place on the ballot was by petition of interested citizens. While some states made this process difficult by demanding large numbers of signatures, South Dakota's ballot law initially made the appearance of new candidates extremely easy by requiring the signatures of only 20 voters to nominate a candidate. According to the Sioux Falls *Argus-Leader,* this led to placing numerous candidates "in the field not with the idea of winning but solely to kill off some others."[14] This practice undermined partisan regularity and gave rise to demands to increase the number of required petitioners in order to limit voters' options and protect the regular parties.[15]

However candidates qualified for the ballot, they still had to follow detailed regulations for filing their official nomination papers. Generally state candidates were required to file their certificates of nomination with the secretary of state, and local candidates with their county auditors. Even years after the passage of the law, candidates failed to file their certificates or did so with the wrong office or after the specified deadline and were accordingly disqualified from the election. The 1891 South Dakota ballot law required nomination papers to be certified thirty days before election and to state the candidate's name, occupation, home and business addresses, and the office sought. In some cases, still more information was required. These regulations often proved burdensome to parties lacking professional officials or regular legal counsel. This was demonstrated in 1892 when the Prohibition party failed to adhere strictly to these regulations, filing its certificates late and omitting some of the required information. Republican state officials refused to place the Prohibition party on the ballot, a decision sustained by the state supreme court after the Prohibitionists filed suit to compel acceptance of their nominations. Observers recognized that this disqualification benefited the GOP. As the *Brookings County Press* put it: "there are 3,000 or 4,000 Prohibitionists who will [now] have to vote the Republican ticket, and as the Republican majority would have been rather small these votes will be hailed with delight."[16]

Republican realization that election laws could provide partisan advantages soon produced an important and enduring innovation in ballot legislation, the so-called antifusion law. This legislation was fraught with serious implications for a democratic polity. The law became so widely adopted in other states—and so useful politically to the dominant party—that its provisions came to be seen as logically necessary and unexceptionable. But in the 1890s, the law was a source of great controversy and its implementation fundamentally changed the existing political process.

Fusion was the term applied to the common nineteenth-century practice by which two or more political parties attempted to combine the votes of their followers by naming the same candidates to their tickets. Fusion typically involved a third party cooperating with the weaker of the two major parties, in opposition to the stronger major party, in the hope of sharing political influence that would otherwise be denied to both when acting separately. In an electorate of multiple parties, fusion helped to prevent plurality rule, promoted majority rule, and protected the minority's access to power.

In the Dakotas during the 1890s, fusion usually involved the Democratic party and the radical Populist or People's party. The Populists first appeared in South Dakota in the 1890 election when they captured nearly a third of the vote and displaced the Democrats as the chief opposition party. So many Republicans joined the People's party that the GOP lost its majority status and retained political control of the state by only a plurality. It seemed clear that if the Populists and Democrats could fuse in 1892, victory would be theirs, a conclusion that seemed confirmed when legislators of the two parties cooperated in 1891 to replace Republican Senator Gideon Moody with Populist James Kyle. One alarmed Republican wrote privately after Kyle's election: "I predict that the parties who elected him will dominate state politics for the next five years."[17] Conversely, as another Republican put it, "No fusion means Republican victory."[18]

Party managers made their plans accordingly. The fusionist plans, however, were complicated by the intensity of partisan identification, which prompted many Democrats to insist on their own ticket, their own candidates, and their own principles. Partisanship also caused former Republicans now in the Populist ranks to oppose any cooperation with their traditional Democratic adversaries. As one Populist editor maintained, "We did not leave the corrupt Republican party to hobnob with the rotten Democratic party."[19] Thus even though partial fusions were arranged in many counties on local races, Populists rejected state-wide fusion in South Dakota at their 1892 state convention. Delegates to the Democratic state convention also spurned a fusion proposal to endorse the Populist nominees and instead nominated a straight ticket of their own. However, the convention did authorize the Democratic State Committee to remove candidates from the ticket if such action would promote the party's interests: an implicit offer of partial fusion. Democratic officials promptly maneuvered toward fusion. Their plan called for each party to withdraw two of its four candidates for presidential elector and fuse on the other party's remaining two. The Democratic National Committee endorsed this plan, hoping to gain six electoral votes. As a Brookings editor explained, "The republicans would lose four votes they count on while the democrats would gain two they never expected to get."[20] Unofficial committees representing the two parties tentatively accepted this plan in September.

Many South Dakota Republicans concurred with the warning issued by Minnesota Senator William Washburn to South Dakota Senator Richard F. Pettigrew. "I don't see how you're going to save yourselves," he said, "if the Democratic fusion scheme is carried out."[21] Indeed, Pettigrew, the Republican state boss, was greatly distressed at the prospect of a Populist-Democratic fusion. Because of their minority status and consequent vulnerability to fusion, South Dakota Republicans devoted their political efforts, according to one political correspondent, "almost exclusively to the business of preventing a fusion."[22] To their relief, the tentative fusion agreement collapsed in October when Populist State Chairman A.L. Peterman refused to convene his state committee to ratify the plan. By late October, with the expiration of the time during which tickets could be amended, the possibility of fusion had ended, and Republicans felt confident of success.[23]

The possibility of arranging fusion by revising party tickets already filed was called "the Minnesota plan." In that state, Democratic officials had pursued the tactic by withdrawing four of their nine candidates for elector and endorsing four Populist nominees. If the Democrats would not directly benefit from this maneuver, at least it promised to injure their major national opponent, and the Democratic National Committee had endorsed the plan. Because of the similarity of their political situations, South Dakotans closely followed developments in Minnesota.[24]

In preparing the official ballot under the state's Australian ballot law, Minnesota's Republican election officials ingeniously countered this fusion scheme. Though designating the four endorsed electors as both Populists and Democrats, the election officials refused to group them with the five remaining Democratic electors, scattering them instead among the other Populist candidates. Democratic leaders, fearful that their partisans would not support the fusion candidates if required to vote with a different party, charged that the Republican ballot design was constructed to "render it more difficult for the voter to cast his vote according to his preference."[25] However, they failed to secure a court order compelling the fusion electors to be listed with the Democrats as well as with the Populists. The election results confirmed Democratic fears, for the fusion candidates ran far behind the combined totals of straight Populist and Democratic candidates, allowing the minority Republicans to win by a plurality.[26]

This legal disruption of fusion was instructional to South Dakota Republicans, for they too polled a minority of votes and carried the election only because their opponents had failed to fuse for their own internal, and perhaps temporary, reasons. Other neighboring states also seemed to offer lessons. In North Dakota, Democrats and Populists had fused on a state ticket and easily prevailed over the GOP. The Republicans' only victor was their congressional candidate, who was elected by a minority vote when his Populist and Democratic opponents failed to fuse.[27] To the south, in Nebraska, Republicans triumphed on the state and electoral tickets in the absence of fusion but lost a number of legislative elections to fusion opponents. Several of the defeated Republicans filed suit to secure election certificates anyway on the grounds that the ballots were deceptive in listing fusion candidates twice, once as Democrats and once as Populists, thereby attracting votes from Democrats who would not have voted Populist and from Populists who would not have voted Democratic. Nebraska's ballot law, however, did not explicitly forbid printing nominees' names twice, and the state supreme court rejected the argument as an effort to use the law for partisan purposes and allowed the election results to stand.[28]

South Dakota Republicans already had learned of the political uses of a ballot law, for in the recent campaign the disqualification of the Prohibitionist party had apparently contributed substantially to the narrow Republican margin of victory. After the election Republicans suggested that the 1893 legislature revise the ballot law to promote other political goals. Many favored making independent nominations more difficult and facilitating straight-ticket voting. The major objective, however, was to use the Australian ballot for partisan ends and prevent fusion by legislative enactment. Led by State Senator Robert Dollard, who, as attorney general, had figured in the decision to keep the Prohibitionists off the ballot, the Republican majority revised the election law to provide that "the name of no candidate shall appear more than once on the ballot for the same office." This simple provision came to be known as the antifusion law. Related revisions also framed to obstruct fusion included prohibiting the withdrawal of nominees shortly before elections—thus blocking the Minnesota plan; treating fused parties as one party in the appointment of election judges; and replacing the office-group with the party-column format, accompanied by a party-circle for straight-ticket voting.[29]

This change in ballot format made more effective the ban against double-listing candidates' names. The party column format meant that a nominee could be designated with but one party affiliation and the second party to nominate a candidate would appear on the ballot as having no nominee for that office at all. Those wishing to fuse would thus be deprived of the symbolic comfort of voting for their own party and be forced to vote as members of another party. The ultimate consequence of fusion for the second party, moreover, would be the sacrifice of its legal identity and existence, for by not having candidates on the ballot it would be unable to poll the minimum percentage of the vote required for legal recognition as a political party and a position on the ballot in subsequent elections. When fusion did not encompass complete tickets, fusionists would also be denied the very real benefit of the party circle—becoming subject, in the words of the California court, "to the alternative of partial disfranchisement or to the casting of their votes upon more burdensome conditions than others"—and instead be required to mark each individual name. This requirement was certain to complicate voting and cause the invalidation of ballots through improper marking.[30]

The political significance of these new ballot regulations in South Dakota became evident in the 1893 and 1894 elections. Populists and Democrats tried in several ways to evade the anticipated effects of the law but met with little success. On the local level, they attempted to cooperate in order to gain control of the next legislature and repeal the antifusion law, although they recognized that their cooperation would necessarily disrupt party organization by sacrificing the legal identity of the second party nominating a candidate. Indeed, in some areas the parties competed to schedule their conventions first, each hoping to arrange fusion on its own terms at the fatal expense of the other. In other instances, politicians attempting to promote local fusion accepted both nominations and then withdrew from one after the legal deadline for nominating anyone else. These efforts frequently produced bitterness and competition among groups trying to cooperate.[31] On the state level, Populists and Democrats felt compelled to nominate separate tickets to maintain their parties' legal existence, even though acknowledging that this would lead to Republican victory. Populists did hope, however, that Democrats would endorse their congressional nominees and thereby end what one Populist termed the Republicans' success "in preventing a united front against them."[32] But the Democratic state convention rejected all fusion proposals. The delegates believed, according to one reporter, that under the ballot law any cooperation would involve "not fusion but absorption" and that the party organization required a separate ticket which admittedly would "stand no chance to win."[33]

The Sioux Falls *Argus-Leader,* South Dakota's leading Democratic newspaper, demonstrated the difficulties of conducting a campaign constrained by the ballot law, partisan loyalties, and political necessities. Advocating faithful support of a Democratic state ticket that it conceded would be easily defeated, the newspaper also urged its Democratic readers to support a local fusion ticket which would appear on the ballot under the Populist heading but which the *Argus-Leader* referred to as simply "The County Ticket." The paper printed not only the Democratic platform at the head of its columns but also the Populist platform, which it carefully abridged to exclude the national demands that would surely antagonize the more conservative Democrats. But even with a common enemy and only local issues involved, fusion leaders predicted that at least 20 percent of the Democrats would refuse to vote in the Populist column, a fall-off that in a close election could result in defeat.[34]

Republicans also anticipated that fusion candidates, as the *Brookings County*

Press reported, would "lose many . . . votes by having their names printed only once on the official ballot instead of once under each party name," but of course they welcomed the "serious complications" the ballot law imposed on their opponents.[35] Moreover, the Republican-dominated judiciary in South Dakota obstructed those who did not vote the single-party straight ticket. Rejecting the argument that "the intention of the voter" should determine the counting of his ballot, Supreme Court Justice Dighton Corson disallowed numerous ballots that told of painful efforts to construct a personally satisfactory ticket. Corson announced disdainfully that "if the elector does not take interest enough in his vote to follow these simple and easily understood rules, he can complain of no one if his vote is not counted."[36] The courts even invalidated ballots on which the voter had written, in his own party column, the name of a candidate of another party. The courts held that the 1893 law prohibited the second appearance of a candidate's name, even if added by an individual voter attempting to create a political coalition while voting as a member of his own party. It is little wonder that after the Republicans swept the elections the demoralized Democratic State Chairman E.M. O'Brien surveyed the results and concluded, "Under the present system of voting as arranged by the Republican party fusion results in confusion to Democracy."[37]

Democratic difficulties under the election law dramatically increased in 1896 when both the Democratic and Populist national conventions nominated William Jennings Bryan for the presidency. This necessarily imposed a fusion policy on the state parties. Numerically weaker, the Democrats in South Dakota recognized that under the ballot law they would have to sacrifice their party's organization to secure the state's electoral votes for their party's nominee. Accordingly, the Democratic state committee cancelled the party's convention and adopted the ticket nominated by the Populists.[38]

Many Democrats, however, reacted angrily to this decision to drop their party from the ballot. The editor of the Kimball *Graphic* deplored the "killing of his party's organization."[39] Conservative Democrats, who might have loyally voted for Bryan as the party's nominee despite their hostility to his ideas, complained of being disfranchised by the surrender to Populism required by the ballot law. Some decided to vote Republican or not at all rather than vote as Populists. At the county level, in fact, Democratic opposition to voting under the Populist name, even among silver advocates, was so strong that in many instances a compromise name of "Free Silver" had to be given the local fusion ticket. But this ran afoul the party column and party circle provisions of the 1893 ballot law, for, with the fusion state ticket printed under the Populist heading, the Free Silver local ticket had to be placed in a separate column. If the silver voter marked both party circles, reasoned one paper, "there would be no conflict in the names voted for, as the corresponding spaces in the different columns are left blank." But the courts held that crosses in the party circle of two or more columns neutralized each other, so the effect would be to leave the ballot as though no party circle had been marked, thereby eliminating the fusionist's vote altogether unless he also had voted separately for each individual office. This inability to effectively cast a straight-ticket fusion ballot, the Sioux City *Journal* concluded, would "result in the loss of numerous votes."[40]

Under these circumstances, the fusionists were able to eke out only a narrow victory in South Dakota. Moreover, although the famous campaign had been debated in the most enthusiastic language, the actual outcome was shaped not merely by ballot regulations but by election procedures generally. Members of all parties charged their opponents with illegal voting, bribery, colonization of voters from outside the state, and illegal acts by election judges and poll-watchers. A widespread demand developed in the aftermath of the election for revision of the state's election laws to prevent such occurrences in the future.[41]

The fusionists, in fact, planned radical changes in South Dakota's election laws now that they controlled the legislature. They were determined to punish bribery at elections, to enact a registration law, to make politicians report election expenses, and to require that ballots be counted according to the voter's intention regardless of compliance with the marking regulations. Fusionist legislators also intended to abolish the antifusion provisions, not only the prohibition against double-listing candidates' names but the party circle as well, for it encouraged straight-ticket voting to the detriment of fashioning a ticket out of candidates in separate columns. A legislative correspondent for the *Chicago Tribune* reported from Pierre that the Populist goal was to eliminate the Republican "technicalities" enacted in 1893 that had "so wrapped the ballot . . . that to deviate from a straight ticket the voter is very likely to transgress so that his ballot will be worthless."[42] Similarly, Populist Governor Andrew E. Lee recommended that "the old safeguards which have been one by one repealed since the passage of the original law be reinstated," that the party circle provision be rescinded, and that all parties be represented among the election judges.[43] The House Elections Committee drafted a bill embodying these provisions, and by strict party votes the Populists forced it through the legislature over Republican opposition.[44]

Another section of the Populist election reform law prohibited voters from receiving assistance in marking their ballot except in cases of physical disability. Republicans maintained that the political effect of this clause was to disfranchise several thousand German, Russian, and Scandinavian immigrants who were unable to read English. Populists countered that their intention was merely to prevent ballot fraud, for they believed that local Republican election judges disregarded these voters' wishes and marked their ballots Republican. The new law seemed to support the Populist rebuttal by also providing for the distribution of sample ballots in several different languages so that foreign-language voters would be able to prepare their ballots to reflect their own wishes, not those of the election judge.[45]

To cap their electoral reform, the Populists also passed two measures authorizing amendments to the state constitution, subject to voter approval in the 1898 elections. The first of these established woman suffrage, a Populist objective intended to democratize the political process. The second amendment, also viewed as a step toward greater popular democracy, provided for the nation's first initiative and referendum system, a famous construct that in practice was less important in defining the political process than the simple ballot laws the Populists were fighting.[46]

Ironically, at the very time that South Dakota Populists repealed their state's antifusion law, neighboring states under Republican control were copying those provisions into their own election codes. North Dakota, Iowa, and Wyoming passed laws in 1897 to prohibit candidates' names from appearing on the ballot more than once. North Dakota also revived a procedure for voting a straight ticket with a single mark, thereby benefiting the Republicans while further obstructing fusionists. If they attempted to fuse despite the new law, they would have to vote in different columns and would thereby be denied the advantage of the party circle.[47]

North Dakota's opposition political parties now went through the same convolutions that South Dakota's had suffered earlier. The state committees of the Democratic and Populist parties met to decide upon a course of action under the restrictive new election laws. With daring and imagination, they sought to circumvent the partisan law and create a new form of fusion. Their plan was to evade the divisive implications of the party column ballot and to gain access to the party circle by finding a party name acceptable to both Democrats and Populists. In 1898, the state conventions of the two parties decided to drop their separate names and adopt that of "Independent-Democrat" for the ballot; they then nominated a common ticket to appear under that heading. But equally imaginative Republican officials used the ballot law to frustrate this new style of fusion. Secretary of State Fred Falley ruled that the candidates of the new Independent-Democratic party would not be permitted on the ballot, for such a party had not attracted the required 5 percent of the vote at the preceding election—when, of course, it had not existed. And since the old Independent (Populist) and Democratic parties had formed a new party, Falley ruled, the two former parties had ceased to exist and also could not have a ballot position, leaving only Republican candidates on the ballot.[48]

Although the North Dakota supreme court partially invalidated this ruling, lower courts accepted such reasoning in other electoral disputes. In one county the district court forced the fusion nominees to be listed on the ballot simply as Democrats, producing a Populist fall-off and contributing to what the Bismarck *Tribune* called "a complete revolution" in local politics as the entire Republican ticket won for the first time in the county's history.[49] In other counties, the courts issued restraining orders keeping fusion candidates off the ballot altogether because of legal technicalities occasioned by the difficulties the two parties encountered in holding a common nominating convention. Subsequent fusionist attempts to secure a place on the ballot by petition failed either because of insufficient signatures or because the deadline set for filing petitions had already passed. The Republican secretary of state disqualified one petition effort by ruling that the fusion candidate, having tried to gain a ballot position through a convention nomination, had forfeited his right to a nomination by petition. Even some Republicans denounced this "forcing [fusionists] off the printed ticket" as "disgraceful" and "manifest scoundrelism," but the result remained that, in some localities, no Independent-Democratic candidates were on the ballot.[50]

The battered and demoralized North Dakota fusionists were not only crushed in the election but subsequently suffered the defection of Populists, who announced that rather than be subsumed in an organization under the Democratic name they would return to the GOP. Democrats also abandoned the coalition, complaining that the response to the antifusion law had eliminated their traditional party. By shattering the opposition, North Dakota's ballot laws helped set the stage for twentieth-century Republican hegemony in the state.[51] The 1901 legislature strengthened the restraints by providing that no party could be represented by more than one list of nominees on the ballot. This prevented the recognition of minority or bolting factions, such as the mid-road Populists who had been on the ballot in 1900, and still further restricted the democratic electoral spontaneity which had been possible before the Australian ballot law. The 1901 law also insured that any factionalism within the GOP itself would not lead to the party's defeat.[52] Finally, in a related development, Republican domination was enhanced in 1907 by North Dakota's adoption of the direct primary, which, however much it widened popular participation in the nominating process, effectively stripped other parties of their remaining role of controlling the political opposition. By regularizing intraparty competition within the GOP, the primary minimized the possibility of a realignment of parties that would topple the Republicans from power.[53]

Republicans soon turned electoral legislation against their opponents in South Dakota, too, and Populist success in reforming that state's election laws in 1897 proved as short-lived as Populist success in the wider political arena. Though the traditional form of fusion was revived in 1898 when Populists, Democrats, and Silver Republicans met in three simultaneous conventions and nominated a joint ticket to appear on the ballot in each of three party columns, the GOP nonetheless carried the legislature and all state offices except that of governor, which Andrew Lee narrowly retained. Both Lee and his Republican opponent Kirk Phillips ran well ahead of their tickets, reflecting voter roll-off and the absence of a party circle on the new ballot. Republicans, however, were more concerned with other aspects of the 1897 ballot law. They charged that Lee owed his victory to the legislation, which, according to the *Brookings County Press,* was "never designed for anything except to promote fusion."[54] The *Press* even claimed that Populists voted for Lee on each of the three tickets listing his name and that partisan election judges counted each mark as a separate vote for Lee.

The newspaper insisted that a fair count would find Phillips the winner. Others maintained that ballots with multiple marks should not be counted even once for Lee because such marks, however much they might suggest the intention of the voter, might also constitute what the Valley Springs *Vidette* called distinguishing signs revealing a voter's attempt to sell his vote and "let the purchaser know, by his markings on the ballot, that he had performed his part of the bargain."[55] If those ballots were thrown out altogether, the election of Phillips would be easily secured. Some Republicans, in attacking the Populist emphasis on the intention of the voter when counting ballots, even argued that "instead of officially interpreting the mind of ignorant voters it would be . . . more in the interest of good government if a strict educational qualification was required."[56]

The Republican claims of fraudulent voting were apparently unfounded, and the official canvass of returns certified Lee's victory. Soon thereafter Phillips dropped his plans to contest the outcome, citing imperfect procedures for such action. The new Republican legislature, however, moved quickly in 1899 to advance the party's position in future elections. First, the legislature resurrected the 1893 law by again prohibiting multiple listing of candidates and by restoring the party circle. In another attempt to prevent fusion, Republican legislators enacted a "pure caucus bill," forbidding voters from attending the caucus or convention of more than one party, thereby inhibiting the necessary consultation between parties contemplating fusion. To minimize the adoption of what one Republican termed "undesirable constitutional amendments," a reference to the recent voter approval of the initiative and referendum, they passed an act requiring that ballots for constitutional amendments be separate from those for the election of public officials.[57] To satisfy other Republican grievances from the 1898 election, the legislature also passed an act establishing procedures for contesting election results, a registration law to prevent the importation of illegal voters into the state, and a bill enabling voters who did not read English to obtain assistance from election judges in marking their ballots.[58]

Governor Lee tried to defend the Populist position on election law. He vetoed the bill for voter assistance, maintaining that it would increase ballot fraud and that existing law provided sufficient protection for the voting rights of illiterates. He vetoed the antifusion bill, describing it as an attempt to "disfranchise political parties" and frustrate majority rule. Lee also vetoed the caucus bill, which, he said, should have been titled "a bill to destroy political independence." Republicans had described the measure as reform legislation, designed to prevent fraudulent voting at primaries, but Lee argued that it was an attempt to "prevent men by force of law and under penalty from changing their political allegiance."[59] Lee's vetoes did not surprise Republicans, for they admitted that their election legislation was designed to destroy the means by which their opponents had been elected.[60]

Lee's vetoes only postponed the final Republican triumph. After the GOP swept South Dakota's 1900 elections, the 1901 legislature re-enacted the antifusion law, demonstrating again the Republicans' conviction of the efficacy of such ballot regulations in protecting their hegemony. Several Democrats also voted for the bill this time, perhaps anticipating that their party would benefit by attracting Populists whose own party would be eliminated through the operation of the law.[61]

The new ballot legislation dominated the next election campaign. The 1902 Populist platform did not focus on the party's original issues of money, land, and transportation but on the election laws which threatened the party's ability to present a reform alternative on such policy issues. Meeting in Huron, the Populists adopted a platform which assailed the state supreme court for a decision emasculating the initiative and referendum, condemned one Republican election law for its undemocratic motive and effects, and denounced the ballot law as a partisan attempt to violate "the right of every citizen to cast his vote as his conscience dictates." The Populist convention then considered its options under that law and reluctantly dissolved into the Democratic state convention, meeting simultaneously in Huron. The joint convention named a ticket to appear on the ballot under the Democratic heading and issued a final blast at the legislature for "confining the number of parties represented on the ballot."[62]

Without admitting their own legal complicity, Republicans welcomed what they termed this Populist "suicide." One Sioux Falls editor pointed out that the Huron arrangements differed from previous fusions in that the delegates "extinguished the populist name and . . . agreed to leave the name 'democratic' as the sole appellation of the fusion idea." He concluded that "South Dakota gave birth to the populist party in 1890. It now sees its final extinguishment."[63]

Thus, although the People's Party had clearly declined from its peak influence, its actual demise was not mandated by the electorate but was legally imposed by the state. While Populists did not have to accept the Democratic name, it was their only practical course if they wanted any political influence. Fusion had provided for minority participation in politics and had been the primary avenue of success for third parties. Under the new legal conditions, a separate party would represent only a symbolic gesture. Those willing to accept that type of limited political participation turned to the new Socialist party, which polled 3.5 percent of the 1902 vote. Some Populists returned to the GOP rather than vote under the Democratic name, as Republicans had predicted. Other Populists, especially former Democrats, did move into the Democratic party, but large numbers simply dropped out of politics altogether. Unwilling either to vote as a member of the "corrupt" old parties or to cast a futile vote for a symbolic third party, they were citizens legislated out of the effective electorate.[64]

Their party's ascendancy assured, Republicans henceforth fought among themselves, safe in the realization that they operated in a closed system, and one faction made South Dakota a leading state in Progressivism. But Progressive reform often differed markedly from the reform impulses of the 1890s and took place within a truncated electorate. Indeed, the regulation of elections had established the legal parameters within which other subjects would be considered. Further electoral "reform" legislation, such as the introduction of the direct primary, merely fastened Republican control more tightly upon the state. In any event, in legislating the end to disruptive fusion, Republicans had demonstrated an early instance of the now familiar Progressive use of state power to promote self-serving conditions of order.

The 1901 Republican legislature demonstrated that practice in another instance as well. Spurred on by Governor Charles Herreid, who as Republican state chairman in 1898 had been especially interested in the operation of election laws, the legislature passed a law requiring county commissioners to be elected on a county rather than a district basis. Fusionists opposed the measure as partisan legislation designed to use the larger electorate to overcome local pockets of resistance to Republican domination. Indeed, the law represented the rural analogue to the simultaneous "reform" in Progressive municipal government so well described by Samuel P. Hays: the shift from ward to city-wide elections in order to limit "the expression of grass-roots impulses and their involvement in the political process."[65] The South Dakota legislature, moreover, went beyond this practical restriction of political representation by also requiring that local elections coincide with general elections, the larger turnouts of which could be expected to overwhelm dissidents even on issues of intense interest to certain communities. Not surprisingly, the Populists, in their final platform, denounced this law as "denying the minority in each county from any representation whatever."[66]

Finally, completing the structure for political stability, South Dakota's Republican-controlled supreme court in 1901 sanctioned an extraordinary legal restriction on the rights and freedom of the individual voter. Building on Judge Corson's earlier rulings, the court prohibited write-in votes on the grounds that writing the candidate's name constituted placing a "distinguishing mark" on the ballot. One judge dissented by raising the larger issue of voters' rights against this procedural concern. Denying Corson's contention that prohibiting write-in votes did not violate constitutional rights, Judge Howard Fuller argued that it was "neither plausible nor reasonable to say that the right of suffrage can be freely, equally, and independently exercised under a statute which merely gives to qualified electors an option to vote for persons whose names are printed on the official ballot, or not to vote at all." The majority opinion meant that "the sovereignty of the nation no longer resides in the people" and that "there is nothing left worthy of the name of the right of suffrage."[67]

But Fuller stood along in his concern for the undemocratic consequences of ballot legislation. Indeed, Republican judges in North Dakota had already dealt with the issue, holding that a consequence of denying citizens their suffrage could not serve as an argument against election legislation. Ruling that "the very franchise is subject to legislative control," they found perfectly acceptable "many regulative provisions in election statutes" that "deprive voters of their privilege."[68]

Thus, in scarcely a decade from the original enactment of the Australian ballot system, the political arena in the Dakotas had been significantly altered through the adoption of legal procedures regulating parties, ballots, nominations, and voting. The open and democratic, if sometimes disorderly, polity of earlier years had given way to one in which, by law, it was more difficult to organize new parties, to secure representation, to act with spontaneity or without special counsel, to cooperate politically with other citizens, to vote independently, or to express political dissatisfaction other than by dropping out. Now public officials talked casually of disfranchisement and, as one observer said, "idly trifled with . . . serious matters" reaching to the heart of the democratic process. Considering the political effects of such regulations, together with their partisan and ideological origins, one might wonder whether, as one judge wrote, "the boasted free ballot becomes a delusion."[69]

Notes

1. James Willard Hurst, "Old and New Dimensions of Research in United States Legal History," *American Journal of Legal History*, XXIII (January, 1979), 20.
2. One scholar has even argued that the special characteristic of legal historians is their "insistence on a radical separation between law and politics." See Morton J. Horwitz, "The Conservative Tradition in the Writing of American Legal History," *ibid.*, XVII (July, 1973), 281.
3. Austin Ranney, *Curing the Mischiefs of Faction: Party Reform in America* (Berkeley, 1975), 61, 74.
4. Minneapolis *Tribune*, October 23, 1892.
5. Actually, North Dakota's constitution required the Australian ballot, and its first legislature passed an Australian ballot bill in 1889, but the bill was stolen before it reached the governor for his signature—indicating very serious opposition to the measure.
6. *New York Times*, October 25, 1892.
7. *Laws Passed at the Second Session of the Legislative Assembly . . . of North Dakota . . . 1891* (Bismarck, 1891), ch. 66, 171–184; *Laws Passed at the Second Session of the Legislature of . . . South Dakota . . . 1891* (Pierre, 1891), ch. 57, 152–166; Yankton (S.D.) *Press and Dakotan*, October 20, November 12, November 17, 1892; *Brookings* (S.D.) *County Press*, October 13, 1892.
8. Mandan *Times* quoted in Jamestown *North Dakota Capital*, November 18, 1892; Jamestown (N.D.) *Daily Alert*, October 20, 1892; Yankton *Press and Dakotan*, October 20, October 29, November 3, November 24, 1892; *Brookings County Press*, November 3, 1892; *Fargo Forum*, November 8, 1892.
9. Yankton *Press and Dakotan*, October 20, 1892, November 16, 1893.
10. Des Moines *Iowa State Register*, October 12, 1892; *Laws Passed, North Dakota, 1891*, 178; Jamestown *North Dakota Capital*, May 6, May 13, June 3, 1892.
11. *New York Times*, December 15, December 29, 1892; Bismarck *Daily Tribune*, December 27, December 28, 1892.
12. Jamestown *North Dakota Capital*, March 18, 1892; *Laws Passed, North Dakota, 1891*, ch. 66. The Jamestown *Daily Alert* reacted to this plan to " 'monkey' with the ticket" by describing it as an "injustice," although conceding that the partisan "tempta-

tion to juggle with the Australian ballot is great.'' See issues of September 30, October 13, and October 14, 1892.

13. *Eaton v. Brown*, 31 Pacific Reporter 250. The North Dakota attorney general ruled, however, that the Populists could appear on the 1892 ballot under the heading ''Independent Party,'' because a party with that name had captured the requisite 5% of the vote in the 1890 election. Jamestown *North Dakota Capital,* March 18, April 8, 1892. In this way the Populists in North Dakota officially became, and subsequently had to remain, the ''Independents.'' For North Dakota's reaction to the California court decision, and recognition of its applicability to the North Dakota ballot, see *ibid.,* October 21, 1892 (misdated October 12, 1892) and Jamestown *Daily Alert,* November 5, 1892.

14. Sioux Falls *Argus-Leader,* November 15, 1892; *Laws Passed, South Dakota, 1891,* 153–154.

15. Yankton *Press and Dakotan,* November 17, 1892, January 12, 1893.

16. *Brookings County Press,* October 20, 1892; *Laws Passed, South Dakota, 1891,* 153–155; Yankton *Press and Dakotan,* October 13, November 10, 1892, October 19, November 2, 1893; Pierre *Daily Capital,* October 11, 1894; *Lucas et al. v. Ringsrud,* 53 Northwestern Reporter 426.

17. Kenneth E. Hendrickson, Jr., ''The Public Career of Richard F. Pettigrew of South Dakota,'' South Dakota Department of History, *Report and Historical Collections,* XXXIV (Pierre, 1968), 217.

18. *Brookings County Press,* September 29, 1892.

19. Clear Lake *Advocate* quoted *ibid.,* November 2, 1893.

20. *Brookings County Press,* September 15, 1892; Yankton *Press and Dakotan,* September 8, September 15, November 3, 1892.

21. *New York Times,* September 19, September 29, 1892.

22. *Ibid.,* October 21, 1892; Hendrickson, ''Pettigrew,'' 222, 233–234.

23. *New York Times,* October 21, 1892.

24. *Ibid.,* October 19, October 25, 1892; *Brookings County Press,* October 13, 1892.

25. Minneapolis *Tribune,* October 16, 1892.

26. *Ibid.,* October 18, October 19, 1892; John D. Hicks, ''The People's Party In Minnesota,'' *Minnesota History Bulletin,* V (November, 1924), 545.

27. Actually, Republicans also elected the secretary of state, but only with the fusion assistance of the Prohibitionists.

28. *State v. Stein,* 53 Northwestern Reporter 999; Lincoln *Nebraska State Journal,* November 15, November 16, November 17, 1892.

29. *Laws Passed at the Third Session of the Legislature of . . . South Dakota . . . 1893* (Pierre, 1893), 137–141; Yankton *Press and Dakotan,* November 17, December 22, 1892, March 9, March 23, 1893; *Brookings County Press,* November 24, 1892; Sioux Falls *Argus-Leader,* November 15, 1892, January 3, 1893; *South Dakota House Journal* (Pierre, 1893), 862, 1113; *South Dakota Senate Journal* (Pierre, 1893), 283–286, 581, 1006.

30. *Eaton v. Brown,* 31 Pacific Reporter 250; Sioux Falls *Argus-Leader,* November 4, 1893; Yankton *Press and Dakotan,* November 24, December 8, 1892; De Smet *Independent,* quoted in *Brookings County Press,* November 2, 1893. In its 1893 legislative session, North Dakota adopted the party column ballot but eliminated the provision for straight-ticket voting, perhaps with the intention of forcing fusionists to confront directly the necessity of voting outside their party, thereby provoking roll-off and scratched tickets. See Jamestown *North Dakota Capital,* November 4, 1892.

31. Sioux Falls *Argus-Leader,* August 3, August 29, 1894; Pierre *Daily Capital,* October 16, October 24, 1894.

32. Sioux Falls *Argus-Leader,* August 18, 1894.

33. *Ibid.,* September 5, September 6, 1894.

34. *Ibid.,* August 29, September 7, September 14, October 23, 1894.

35. *Brookings County Press,* October 19, 1893.

36. *Vallier v. Brakke,* 64 Northwestern Reporter 180.

37. Sioux Falls *Argus-Leader,* November 13, 1894; *Parmley v. Healy,* 64 Northwestern Reporter 186; *McKittrick v. Pardee,* 65 Northwestern Reporter 23.

38. Sioux Falls *Argus-Leader,* August 18, 1896.

39. Kimball *Graphic* quoted *ibid.,* August 25, 1896.

40. Sioux City (Iowa) *Journal,* October 17, 1896; Pierre *Daily Capital,* October 23, 1896; Sioux Falls *Argus-Leader,* August 18, September 1, 1896; *Vallier v. Brakke,* 64 Northwestern Reporter 180; *McKittrick v. Pardee,* 65 Northwestern Reporter 23.

41. Sioux City *Journal,* November 15–21, December 26, 1896; Arthur Brooks, ''The Administration of Andrew E. Lee, Governor of South Dakota, 1897–1901,'' M.A. Thesis (University of South Dakota, 1939), 18–19.

42. *Chicago Tribune,* January 4, 1897; Sioux City *Journal,* November 19, November 30, 1896.

43. *South Dakota Senate Journal* (Pierre, 1897), 43–44

44. *Ibid.,* 1263–1264, 1282–1283; *South Dakota House Journal* (Pierre, 1897), 713, 1275–1280; *Laws Passed at the Fifth Session of the Legislature of . . . South Dakota . . . 1897* (Pierre, 1897), 170–171.

45. *Laws Passed, South Dakota, 1897,* 173–176; Sioux City *Journal,* March 27, April 4, 1897. See also *South Dakota House Journal* (Pierre, 1899), 1283.

46. Yankton *Press and Dakotan,* March 18, May 6, 1897.

47. *Laws Passed at the Fifth Session of the Legislative Assembly . . . of North Dakota . . . 1897* (Bismarck, 1897), 117–119. In another action of political and ideological significance, the 1897 North Dakota legislature repealed the Edwards Precinct Law, which had established rules for allowing citizens to vote despite moving from one local precinct to another. In its place a firm 90-day residence requirement was established, which disfranchised more than a hundred residents of Fargo alone in the next election. See *Fargo Forum and Daily Republican,* November 10, 1898.

48. *Winterset* (Iowa) *Review,* March 31, 1897; *State v. Falley,* 76 Northwestern Reporter 996.

49. Bismarck *Daily Tribune,* November 12, 1898.

50. *Ibid.,* October 23, October 31, November 1, November 2, November 12, 1898; *Fargo Forum and Daily Republican,* November 14, 1898.

51. Bismarck *Daily Tribune,* November 8, 1898; *New York Times,* April 6, 1900.

52. *Appleton's Annual Cyclopedia, 1901* (New York, 1902), 747; Bismarck *Daily Tribune,* March 8, March 9, 1901; *North Dakota Senate Journal* (Bismarck, 1901), 568; *North Dakota House Journal* (Bismarck, 1901), 512.

53. Literature on the primary and its consequences is vast. See especially V.O. Key, Jr., *American State Politics: An Introduction* (New York, 1956).

54. *Brookings County Press,* December 1, 1898; Yankton *Press and Dakotan,* June 30, 1898.

55. Valley Springs *Vidette,* quoted in Sioux Falls *Argus-Leader,* November 19, 1898; *Brookings County Press,* November 17, 1898.

56. *Brookings County Press,* December 1, 1898.

57. Quoted in Sioux Falls *Argus-Leader,* March 7, 1899.

58. Brooks, ''Administration of Lee,'' 48; *Brookings County Press,* December 22, 1898, January 12, January 26, February 9, February 23, 1899; *South Dakota House Journal* (1899), 586, 596–597, 1563–1564; *South Dakota Senate Journal* (Pierre, 1899), 973.

59. *South Dakota House Journal* (1899), 1283, 1562; *South Dakota Senate Journal* (1899), 1508; Sioux Falls *Argus-Leader,* March 7, March 8, March 10, 1899.

60. Sioux Falls *Argus-Leader,* March 8, 1899.

61. *South Dakota House Journal* (Pierre, 1901), 1415; *South Dakota Senate Journal* (Pierre, 1901), 1283.

62. Sioux Falls *Argus-Leader,* June 26, June 28, 1902.

63. *Ibid.,* June 26, 1902.

64. *Ibid.,* June 28, 1902.

65. Samuel P. Hays, "The Politics of Reform in Municipal Government in the Progressive Era," *Pacific Northwest Quarterly,* LV (October, 1964), 169; Sioux Falls *Argus-Leader,* March 4, 1901.

66. Sioux Falls *Argus-Leader,* June 28, 1902.

67. *Chamberlain v. Wood,* 88 Northwestern Reporter 109, 113.

68. *Miller v. Schallern,* 79 Northwestern Reporter 865–866.

69. *Chamberlain v. Wood,* 88 Northwestern Reporter 109, 113–114.

8

Populists in Power: Public Policy and Legislative Behavior

The great historiographical debate over Populism, begun in the 1950s, shows little sign of ending now, three decades later. For a generation historians had generally accepted the picture drawn by John D. Hicks in his classic *The Populist Revolt* (Minneapolis, 1931). The Populists, Hicks maintained, had been earnest farmers responding politically to agricultural difficulties and political indifference by agitating for political and economic reforms. Then in the 1950s a number of scholars, reacting to the tensions of their own times and reflecting different interests, depicted Populists variously as reactionary, nativistic, anti-Semitic, and irrational. This picture, so absurdly overdrawn and poorly substantiated, was in turn countered by a long list of studies that effectively destroyed all the claims of the revisionists. This scholarly debate, however, leaves the student of Populism little more knowledgeable about the subject than at the beginning. As Turner has observed, "Reactionary Populists chased socialist Populists through the learned journals in a quarrel that generated more heat than light."[1]

Two basic problems underlie this impasse. The first is methodological, for too often the historian's position depends on the particular Populists studied—Tom Watson or Jerry Simpson, Texans or Nebraskans—and a blindness to the necessity and the difficulty of determining whether the choice was representative. The second problem evident in Populist historiography is its data base, as scholars continue to comb the same newspapers and manuscript collections, in the belief that (as one maintained) "we have no other sources."[2]

Reprinted from *The Journal of Interdisciplinary History,* XVIII (1987), 81–105, with the permission of the editors of *The Journal of Interdisciplinary History* and the MIT Press, Cambridge, Massachusetts. © 1987 by The Massachusetts Institute of Technology and the editors of *The Journal of Interdisciplinary History.*

An earlier version of this article was presented to the Weingart Social Science History Association conference on "The Variety of Quantitative History," 1983. The author is indebted to Allan G. Bogue, Ballard C. Campbell, J. Morgan Kousser, Martin Ridge, Philip VanderMeer, and James E. Wright for helpful criticism and useful advice.

To resolve this impasse, new approaches and the use of new sources of data seem necessary. Several recent studies have employed quantitative analysis of the statistics of popular voting behavior to describe the constituencies of the Populists and other parties, thereby advancing our knowledge of the mass electorate. But there has been considerably less effort to exploit the data provided by legislative journals, what Bogue has called "the largest body of opinion data, systematically collected and organized, that American society has preserved." Historians have traditionally ignored this information, perhaps because the labor involved is so great and their usual methodological tools have been so limited. And yet systematic analysis of the voting data derived from legislative roll calls can reveal the issues of most interest to the legislators themselves and the relative importance of those issues. It can identify the questions that divide or unite legislators and suggest the ideological parameters of the resultant groups. And by examining the often mundane world of policymaking, roll-call analysis provides a practical perspective on the concerns of Populists not available through either the traditional analysis of campaign speeches or the quantitative investigation of mass politics. Finally, by considering these matters, roll-call analysis allows historians to push beyond the now rather stale question of whether Populism was reactionary or radical and reach a deeper understanding of the movement.[3]

The 1897 Kansas Senate serves as a case study of the value of roll-call analysis. Much was expected of this legislature, which had skilled Populist leadership and a clear Populist majority, the only time Populists controlled both houses in this key state. After the disappointments of the 1893 legislative war and the 1894 election defeat, party leaders had used the silver issue as the catalyst to unite different groups into a successful coalition in 1896. To attract votes from Democrats and Silver Republicans, they had also traded off nominations for other offices in exchange for fusion support of legislative candidates and had nominated to the senate such popular figures as former Congressman William A. Harris and former Governor Lorenzo D. Lewelling to insure that support. Such maneuvering helped place twenty-seven Populists in the senate chamber alongside eleven Republicans and two Democrats.

Operating under intense public scrutiny in this crucial session, nearly all senators actively engaged in legislative business and introduced hundreds of bills reflecting a variety of concerns. Of these, 241 bills were brought to a vote. Excluding roll calls for procedural or personnel matters, local or minor bills provoking neither controversy nor disagreement, perfunctory votes of appreciation, apportionment proposals, repetitive motions, and bills passed unanimously, there were ninety-two substantive roll calls provoking at least some opposition.[4]

Virtually all of this divisive legislative activity—eighty-one roll calls—pertained to the "reform" issues raised in Populist party platforms: railroad regulation, usury and interest regulation, labor legislation, tax reform, stockyard regulation, and so forth. Some Populists demonstrated great ingenuity in devising legislation to implement their national demands at the state level where their limited power applied. To counteract the credit shortage and decrease the influence of moneylenders, one Populist introduced a bill to put the state "into the moneylending business" by lending the principal of the state permanent school fund to individual citizens at low rates and on landed collateral. Another Populist sought to promote monetary inflation and unemployment relief by proposing Coxeyite legislation authorizing townships and cities to employ the jobless and pay them with county-issued notes to be redeemed by the state, a remarkable measure described by its sponsor as a test case for the great question of who controlled and issued money. Populists also enacted laws reflecting Debsian concerns, one providing for jury trials and the restriction of judicial authority in contempt of court cases, and another authorizing municipal ownership of gas, water, and electric plants.[5]

Analysis of senators' votes on such proposals helps reveal the factors that influenced legislative behavior and the lines of division in public policymaking. Legislative analysts have found that voting cleavages often occur along partisan, regional, and occupational lines, thereby suggesting some possible explanations of behavior in the 1897 Kansas Senate. Indexes of cohesion and disagreement are particularly helpful in understanding and describing the behavior of nominal groups, and I used them to determine whether voting patterns followed such divisions.[6]

Not surprising, given the nature of the legislation under consideration, the primary determinant of legislative voting was party. Although there usually was some Republican support for reform proposals, fifty-six of the eighty-one roll calls relating to reform questions and many other roll calls involving procedural, personnel, administrative, and miscellaneous matters resulted in substantial disagreement by party groupings. The partisan splits over reform issues are clearly revealed in the index of disagreement for Populists and Republicans over such issues as the initiative and referendum (100), election legislation (100), free silver resolutions (100, 100), taxation (100, 100, 92, 76, 65), government reform (100, 77), protective labor legislation (100, 83, 82, 81, 60), railroad regulation (94, 68, 64), stockyard regulation (92, 79), municipal ownership (89), interest and mortgage regulation (86, 76, 71, 70, 67, 65, 64), and banking and corporate regulation (100, 82, 66).

Another measure of the partisan division over reform legislation is provided by the calculation of agreement scores for each senator with the reform position for the eighty-one roll calls. On a scale of 0 (indicating opposition to all divisive reform) to 100 (indicating support for all reform), the average Populist scored 83 and the average Republican only 31. Republicans, on the one hand, constituted only 28 percent of all senators but provided 58 percent of all votes in opposition to reform proposals. Populists, on the other, constituted 68 percent of all senators but provided only 36 percent of the negative votes on reform bills. Such data refute the recent claims of one historian that there was no partisan response to such legislative proposals and that Populist legislators were no more inclined to support reform legislation than were members of the major parties.[7] Thus the typical Republican opposed, and the typical Populist endorsed, reform measures. This finding should hardly be surprising, but the necessity of demonstrating it indicates the impasse that afflicts Populist historiography.

The importance of party does not exclude the possibility that other determinants influenced legislative voting patterns in some fashion. Sectional differences, for instance, constituted a logical basis for voting decisions. There had been frequent conflict in Kansas, as in most western states, between the older and more developed eastern region and the remainder of the state, and historians have argued persuasively that the differential pattern of development provoked a political alignment in the 1890s best described as sectional.[8]

But sectional conflict rarely appeared in the 1897 Senate. On fifteen roll calls a majority of eastern senators did oppose a majority of western senators, but in nearly every case the division was merely an artifact of partisan differences and the asymmetrical geographical distribution of Republicans and Populists. The index of disagreement revealed that party rather than region underlay the voting division. Only on two roll calls was this measure higher for regional than for party groupings. Neither of those roll calls dealt with reform issues. One reflected greater western support for, and more eastern opposition to, establishing a normal school in western Kansas. The other indicated that western more than eastern senators favored the death penalty, perhaps an indication of frontier justice but suggestive of little else. Indeed, indexes of cohesion showed little unity in either regional group (24, 26, 6, 75) and neither roll call resulted in substantial regional disagreement (index figures of 34 and 25).[9]

Occupational influences were somewhat more apparent in legislators' voting decisions. Because of the small number of senators in specific non-agricultural occupations, I established nominal groups composed of farmers and non-farmers. Fifteen roll calls produced significant disagreement between these broad occupational groupings. Here, too, most of the apparent disagreement reflected partisan differences and the fact that farmers were disproportionately Populists. Only on a roll call to restrict the power of local governments to borrow money and create indebtedness was the division among legislators along occupational lines clearly distinct from partisan influences. Farmers supported and non-farmers opposed the bill. Such a measure had long been an agrarian demand and represented the rural reaction to the boom mentality of earlier years, when towns and counties had issued bonds to induce railroad construction and promote business enterprise. Many of these projects failed to materialize or collapsed in the subsequent depression, leaving the rural majority paying for the vanished dreams of business promoters. In the 1897 Senate, farmers remembered the past whereas lawyers, bankers, and merchants from the state's towns and villages still hoped to promote a boom for themselves.[10]

Only one other roll call significantly dividing legislators along occupational lines registered higher occupational than partisan disagreement, and it was indirectly related to the same concern. Farmer senators split evenly over a bill to prohibit railroad commissioners from having any personal economic interests in railroads, their cohesion index of 0 indicating the absence of a common farmer perspective on the issue. But non-farmers of all parties unanimously opposed the bill, suggesting again their common interest or involvement in promotional activities. Still, the occupational disagreement index (50) was virtually the same as the partisan one (46), for all Republicans opposed the bill. Three other bills, each reflecting the different economic interests of town and country, also provoked a majority of farmer senators to oppose a majority of non-farmers and at disagreement levels greater than that indicated by partisanship, though slightly lower than herein defined as "significant" (37, 33, and 30). Farmers more generally supported a bill to levy a county rather than a district school tax and two efforts to impose tighter regulations on banking, whereas most non-farmers opposed these measures. On all five roll calls, however, the relatively low level of cohesion among farmers (54, 0, 22, 4, 42) and, frequently, among non-farmers (38, 100, 28, 70, 25) indicates the comparative unimportance of occupational considerations. Again the general conclusion is that party voting predominated in the legislature.[11]

It has often been suggested that Populists were older men, either literally or figuratively belonging to an earlier time. Recent research on the life cycle also suggests that some attention might be fruitfully directed to the connection between age and legislative behavior, a question once phrased by Malin as "At What Age Did Men Become Reformers?" In the 1897 Kansas Senate, Populists were clearly older than members of the major parties, averaging forty-seven years old to forty-two for their opponents. The more appropriate question, however, is to what extent did age influence voting behavior? The answer is: not much. Differences in average "reform" scores over eighty-one roll calls for legislators grouped into quintiles by age merely reflect the distribution of Populists and non-Populists among the quintiles. Agreement scores by individual roll calls for different age groups also reveal the complete insignificance of age as a legislative determinant.[12]

Nor do other individual characteristics of senators, as reported in the legislative directory, provide much insight into their voting behavior. Religion, frequently regarded as of decisive political importance by ethnocultural historians, seems to have had negligible effect on voting patterns. There were only three senators who claimed to be "liturgicals," too few to evaluate with any confidence, but the other senators divided into two large groups composed of pietists and of those who admitted to no religious affiliation at all. The average reform score for pietistic senators was 73.1 compared to 65.6 for the non-religious and only 54.7 for the liturgicals. However, this apparent distinction only reflected the disproportionate Populist strength among the pietists. Religious differences in voting disappeared when party was considered: Populist pietists averaged 84.2 and non-religious Populists averaged 83.4; Republican pietists averaged 29.0 and non-religious Republicans averaged 30.0. Finally, no roll call showed substantial disagreement scores between the two large categorical groups. Even a roll call related to the cultural issue of prohibition failed to produce serious voting divisions along religious lines.[13]

Similarly, categorical groups composed of senators who attended college and those whose education was limited to a common school preparation showed no significant voting disagreement, not even over educational issues, such as establishing normal schools or mandating taxation policy for public schools.[14]

Although party was thus the most important voting determinant, partisan loyalty did not hold all senators with the same strength. Other factors occasionally influenced some legislators and cut across party lines. The saliency of specific voting determinants varied among senators according to the particular content of legislative proposals, and different issues generated different voting alignments. Since political parties tend to be coalitions of varying degrees of unity, it is important to examine the Populist legislative contingent to determine the fault lines within the party and the issues which provoked defection.

The most obvious determinant among Populist senators was their occupational status as farmer or non-farmer. There was substantial disagreement among Populists along occupational lines on twelve roll calls, all focused on economic issues. These included three attempts to regulate interest rates and prohibit usury and one to tax mortgages, with the farmer Populists in favor of such legislation and their non-farmer fellow partisans opposed. At times the disputes between the two groups became heated. One Populist farmer was "proud of the fact that I am not a lawyer"; Populist lawyer W.B. Crossan snapped, "all the honesty of the country is not confined to farmers, and . . . we should have the same friendship for the banking interests as we have for the farming interests." The sharpest disagreements between the two groups (index of 84 and 72) involved two other financial issues, with farmers strongly endorsing efforts to restrict the power of local governments to issue bonds and to have the state lend money to citizens at low rates of interest in order to decrease dependence on eastern capital. Non-farmer Populists firmly opposed each proposal. On three roll calls over banking regulation and two involving railroad regulation, farmer and non-farmer Populists disagreed substantially, with the farmers favoring stronger measures. Finally, Populist farmers favored (and non-farmers spurned) levying a county school tax to equalize spending for town and country school districts.[15]

The greater farmer support for reform measures is also revealed in the average reform agreement scores over eighty-one roll calls. The merchant/lawyer Populists averaged 75.6 to their rural colleagues' 85.1. Constituting only 26 percent of the Populist senators, the non-farmers provided 38 percent of total Populist opposition to reform measures. Moreover, they consistently furnished disproportionate opposition regardless of the type of issue involved, although their opposition increased as the issues approached the classical Populist ones: 33 percent of all Populist opposition to labor reform legislation, 37 percent of Populist opposition to railroad regulation, and 50 percent of all Populist opposition to interest and moneylending legislation.

Some historians have argued that the previous party affiliation of Populists influenced their political attitudes. Roll-call analysis offers limited confirmation. On eleven roll calls there was significant disagreement between groups of Populists divided along lines of partisan antecedents. Some of these voting alignments overlapped with, and are better explained by, the occupational divisions already noted. But several others are suggestive of possible important differences within the Populist coalition. On two of these roll calls, Populists of traditional third-party origins demonstrated far more support for railroad regulation, particularly for maximum freight-rate legislation, than Populists of major-party antecedents, the majority of whom opposed such legislation. Populists of third-party antecedents also significantly disagreed with Populists of major-party antecedents by supporting several bills that sought to regulate activities of local elites, particularly one that prohibited county commissioners from depositing county funds in any bank in which they held an interest.[16]

Perhaps these votes by Populists of third-party antecedents reflected their traditional outsider status, but they were also consistently more reformist than their colleagues. For all eighty-one roll calls, the Populists of Union Labor and Greenbacker origins had an average reform agreement score of 86.7, whereas former Republicans averaged 81.6 and ex-Democrats 76.5. The differential was even greater in certain areas of traditional reform concern. On roll calls involving both railroad regulation and interest and moneylending questions, third-party Populists averaged 18 points higher than Republican-Populists and 23 and 26 points higher, respectively, than Democratic-Populists. Perhaps Populists of third-party antecedents had been correct to doubt the commitment of latecomers to reform.

At times Populist senators also divided along sectional lines. On six roll calls there was substantial sectional disagreement between eastern and western Populists. Several of these votes did not involve reform issues, including those that most polarized the Populists by sectionalism. On three different measures western Populists favored establishing normal schools in western Kansas, whereas eastern Populists, with a normal school already in their region, opposed establishing more schools and called them unnecessarily extravagant in hard times. Even among themselves, however, the western Populists demonstrated that local boosterism underlay attitude divisions on this subject, for only half voted consistently, whereas the others supported bills for normal schools in or near their home towns but opposed bills to establish schools elsewhere in the region. Other apparent sectional differences, especially on roll calls involving railroad regulation, are better explained by the distribution of farmers or traditional third-party men within the two sectional groupings of Populists.[17]

But there also was substantial disagreement between eastern and western Populists, not related to underlying occupational or political factors, on a deed of trust bill, reducing the redemption period and permitting sales of property without foreclosure by judicial proceedings. Regarded as "always . . . a Republican measure," it now was also supported by a majority of eastern Populists, who represented a well-settled area with relatively little mortgage debt and hoped to promote economic development by making conditions more attractive to potential investors. However, Populists from western Kansas, where mortgage indebtedness was extensive, overwhelmingly rejected the bill as harmful to their constituents' interests.[18]

Other individual characteristics of Populist senators had little apparent influence on their voting decisions. Divided into thirds by age, the Populist contingent showed no difference in supporting reform measures, each group averaging 83 percent over the eighty-one roll calls. Nor was education a measurable voting determinant. Categorical groups of Populists with a college background and those with only a common school education never substantially disagreed on any roll call, not even those dealing with educational issues. Religion also had little apparent influence. Nominal groups of pietistic Populists and those Populists not claiming any religious affiliation differed insignificantly on roll calls.

Constituency characteristics represent another possible influence on legislators' voting patterns. Correlations between legislative voting and measurable characteristics of Populists' respective districts shed some light on this type of determinant. The common perception of Populists as the farmers' representatives in politics was corroborated by the +.522 Pearson correlation coefficient between Populists' reform voting over eighty-one roll calls and the proportion of families in their districts that were engaged in agriculture. That is, the more rural the district, the more reformist was the voting behavior of its Populist senator. This relationship also held for subsets of issues. For instance, Populist reform voting on interest and mortgage legislation correlated at +.513 with this indicator of rural constituency. But correlations between Populists' reform voting in the senate and various indexes measuring the economic distress of their districts, although positive, were of marginal or no significance.

The voting decisions of Populist senators were, however, related to certain political characteristics of their constituencies. The stronger the Populists were in a district (measured by 1896 election results), the more reformist was their senator in his legislative votes, a correlation of +.301. A senator with strong popular support was less inclined to compromise Populist principles than one whose district was less unified. This tendency is also revealed in the much stronger correlation (+.544) between Populist senators' reform voting and the proportion of their districts' Populist strength that was *not* composed of Democrats in the 1896 fusion campaign. The less dependent were the Populist senators upon Democrats or Democratic-Populists in their district electorate, the more reformist were their votes. This pattern reflects the greater conservatism of the Kansas Democrats and of their former partisans within the People's Party and suggests the larger importance of political maneuvering among the factions of the People's Party.[19]

Thus far analysis has been limited to categorical or nominal groups such as Populists and Republicans, farmers and non-farmers. This approach involved classifying legislators on the basis of shared characteristics determined on an a priori basis. Although this procedure proved enlightening, another approach must be employed in order to understand legislative behavior. The second form of analysis involves empirically defined groups—legislators who by regularly voting together demonstrated in their legislative behavior shared attitudes. This mode of inquiry is particularly important because of the earlier use of reform agreement scores. The latter measure can mask as well as reveal relationships: two senators each scoring 50 on such a scale could in fact disagree on every roll call and, despite identical scores, hardly represent a shared attitude.

One technique to determine empirically based groups is cluster-bloc analysis, which requires the calculation of indexes of interpersonal agreement for all possible pairs of legislators over the full gamut of roll calls. Arrangement of these scores in a matrix reveals clusters or blocs of senators who vote together. This technique requires specifying the minimum level of agreement in order to establish the limits of the cluster. The higher the minimum, the smaller and fewer any blocs will be, but progressively relaxing the minimum will expand the cluster. Thus the bloc structure will vary at different levels of agreement.[20]

Several striking facts emerge from this analysis. First, the majority of Populist senators were in accord at such high levels that to make useful distinctions I set the minimum level of agreement initially at ≥ 90 percent. This step revealed a cluster of four Populists, all farmers from western Kansas. Sixteen Populists agreed with at least one other Populist at ≥ 90 percent; no Republicans or Democrats agreed with anyone at that high level. Relaxing the agreement level to 85 percent doubled the size of the bloc to eight Populists, with an additional six Populists on the fringe, agreeing at that level with more than half but not all the members of the bloc. All fourteen of these Populists were farmers, ten from western Kansas.

Second, the non-farmer Populists not only failed to register high levels of agreement with their rural colleagues, they also failed to agree with each other at high levels. No bloc begins to emerge from their ranks until the agreement level is reduced to 80 percent, and then only three of them cluster. At 75 percent another merchant and a farmer join this small bloc, but Populist agreement at that level is so generalized (the average interpersonal agreement score among Populists was 77.5 percent) that little further insight is gained, for the larger bloc contains virtually all remaining Populists. The tendency was for deviant Populists to agree strongly with no one at all, their voting patterns reflecting idiosyncratic factors. But although these Populists did not always vote with their fellow partisans, they were still less likely to vote with Republican senators.

Third, the Republicans demonstrated neither the high levels nor the range of interpersonal agreement apparent among the Populists. No Republicans voted together at a 90 percent rate. Not until an agreement level of 80 percent do even three Republicans emerge in a cluster, but at 75 percent all Republicans are in

Table 8.1

Average Agreement Scores 1897 Kansas Senate

	Majority Populists	Minority Populists	Republicans
Majority Populists Cooke Forney Lupfer Pritchard	92.3		
Minority Populists Crossan Hanna Ryan Shaffer	64.8	75.5	
Republicans Battey Hessin Lamb Morrow	25.0	48.7	76.3

the cluster or at the fringe. At 65 percent all Republicans agree. Significantly, not one Populist agreed with even one Republican at that level, let alone approached inclusion into the Republican bloc by agreeing with all of them. One historian's recent argument that Populists and Republicans generally voted together on reform issues is invalid.[21]

Table 8.1 illustrates these points by summarizing the voting behavior of several groups of senators over the set of eighty-one roll calls. The first group represents the majority element of the Populists, the second includes Populists on the margin of Populist agreement, and the third contains a sample of Republicans. The percentages represent the means of all appropriate interpersonal agreement scores. Neither Populist faction voted at high levels of agreement with the Republicans but instead voted more with each other; the minority Populists agreed considerably less among themselves than did the other Populists; and the Republicans showed virtually the same solidarity as did the Populist minority.

Although cluster-bloc analysis can reveal the existence and cohesion of groups, as well as the distance between them, other techniques are more helpful in identifying the attitudes and values around which grouping occurred. Guttman scale analysis is such a technique, designed to isolate groups on the basis of shared attitudes. The use of Guttman scaling assumes that, as Bogue has written, "legislators will vote for measures which in their minds represent only half a loaf because half is, after all, better than none." This is not always the case, particularly among ideological legislators. The only Populist to oppose the maximum freight rate bill in the 1895 Senate, for example, explained his vote by declaring that he "did not believe there was any way of reaching the railroads except by . . . government ownership." But as a rule, the assumption seems a safe one.[22]

Guttman scale analysis involves examining the patterns formed by legislators' responses to a set of intercorrelated roll calls and classifying legislators in terms of the extent of their support for the measures under consideration. The roll call with the fewest positive votes isolates the senators with the most extreme or radical views on the subject; the roll call with the largest number of positive votes reveals all senators with any sympathy toward the subject, while identifying the remainder as the most conservative senators who voted against all proposals. Numerous positions between the extremes are possible. Although Guttman scales are commonly constructed by determining the scalability of all roll calls sharing an apparent common issue, such as railroad legislation, those roll calls may be linked to others focused on different issues. Thus the common policy dimension as understood by the legislators themselves could escape notice. To eliminate this possibility and to test the likelihood that senators, rather than considering each roll call in isolation, shared general attitudes which regularly influenced their voting behavior, I determined scalability by calculating Yule's Q for each possible pair of roll calls, regardless of apparent issue content, and required each roll call to have a coefficient $\geq .90$ with every other one in the set.

Table 8.2 presents the results of this analysis. It is a skeletal representation of a Guttman scale fitting twenty-five roll calls and tapping a policy dimension among legislators that can best be described as a reform ideology. The roll calls that fit into this scale range over an apparent variety of issues: railroad, interest, bank, and stockyard regulation; taxation reform; prohibition of labor blacklisting; election reform; municipal ownership; and consumer protection. The significant features of this table are several. First, each Populist registers at a more "radical" scale position than any Republican or Democrat, voting the reform position on all or most roll calls from the least controversial to the most. Second, all Populists on scale type 8, reflecting the most radical group, are farmers, whereas the non-farmer Populists dominate scale positions 3 and 4. Third, in light of this evidence of Populist factionalism, it is important to note that the most radical scale position contains more than a third of all Populists; this was an irreducible core on all reform roll-call votes, and they were usually joined by most other Populists. The full scale shows relatively little voting differentiation across the complete set of twenty-five roll calls: most Populists consistently demonstrated a reformist ideology toward all issues. Fourth, most Republicans were as consistent in making their voting decisions from a shared perspective of hostility to reform. Never supporting any of these diverse issues, most belonged to scale type 0, the most conservative position. Finally, the Democrats appear on the scale between the Populists and the Republicans, as might be expected from

Table 8.2

Radical–Conservative Continuum: Scale on Reform Issues

Senator	Party type	Scale 1 (Y)	2 (Y)	3 (N)	4 (Y)	5 (N)	6 (Y)	7 (Y)	8 (Y)	1 (N)	2 (N)	3 (Y)	4 (N)	5 (Y)	6 (N)	7 (N)	8 (N)
Benson	Pop	8	+	e	+	+	+	+	+	+								
Cooke	Pop	8	+	+	+	+	+	+	+	+								
Forney	Pop	8	+	+	+	o	+	+	+	+								
Hart	Pop	8	+	+	+	+	+	+	+	+								
Householder	Pop	8	+	+	o	+	+	+	+	+								
Lupfer	Pop	8	+	+	+	o	+	+	+	+								
Mosher	Pop	8	+	+	+	+	+	+	+	+								
Pritchard	Pop	8	+	+	+	+	+	+	+	+								
Sheldon	Pop	8	+	+	+	+	+	+	+	+								
Titus	Pop	8	+	+	+	+	+	+	+	o								
Braddock	Pop	7	+	+	+	+	+	o	+	o	−							
Caldwell	Pop	7			+	o	o	+	+	+	o							
King	Pop	7		+	+	o	+	o	+	+	−							
Campbell	Pop	6			+	+	+	+	+	+	−	o						
Helmick	Pop	6			+	e	+	+	+	+	−	−	−	x				
Young	Pop	6			+	+	+	+	+	+	−	−	−					
Helm	Pop	5				+	+	+	+	+	e	−	−					
Jumper	Pop	5	x					+	+	o	−	−	−					
Reser	Pop	5				+	o	o	+	o	o	−	o	−				
Armstrong	Pop	4				+	+	+	+	+	−	−	−	−				
Hanna	Pop	4					+	+	+	+	o	−	o	−				
Ryan	Pop	4					+	+	+	+	−	−	−	−				
Shaffer	Pop	4					+	+	+	+	−	−	−	−				
Crossan	Pop	3							+	+	o	−	o	o	o			
Field	Pop	3							+	+	−	o	−	−	o			
Lewelling	Pop	3						+	+	+	o	−	o	o	o			

	Party	Scale	1	2	3	4	5	6	7	8
Farrelly	Dem	2	+	+	−	−	−	o	−	−
Zimmer	Dem	2	+	o	−	−	−	o	−	−
Matthews	Rep	1	o	+	−	−	−	−	−	−
Sterne	Rep	1	+	+	−	−	−	o	−	−
Battey	Rep	0			−	o	−	o	−	−
Coleman	Rep	0			−	−	−	o	−	−
Fulton	Rep	0			−	−	o	−	−	−
Hessin	Rep	0			−	−	−	−	o	−
Johnson	Rep	0			−	−	−	−	−	o
Lamb	Rep	0			−	−	−	−	−	−
Morrow	Rep	0			−	−	−	−	−	−
Stocks	Rep	0			o	−	−	−	−	−
Wallack	Rep	0			−	−	−	−	−	−

+ = reform vote

− = vote against reform

o = absence, non−voting

e/x = error or nonpattern vote

Seventeen more roll calls fit into this scale.

Coefficient of reproducibility = .99

Senator Harris omitted because of excessive absences.

Voting Key:

1. Vote on Titus' amendment, providing for popular election of railroad commissioners, to S.B. 524.
2. Vote on Titus' amendment, establishing maximum railroad freight rates, to S.B. 524.
3. Vote to kill S.B. 8, taxing mortgages.
4. Vote to reconsider killing S.B. 34, regulating interest and prohibiting usury.
5. Vote on amendment, allowing corporations to avoid public scrutiny of their financial records, to S.B. 248.
6. Vote on H.B. 43 to prevent blacklisting.
7. Vote on S.J.R. 1 to amend the state constitution to establish the initiative and referendum.
8. Vote on S.B. 446 to regulate banks.

the fusion politics of the decade. Legislation touching the platform concerns of Populism thus did "activate ideological sensitivities" among senators, and serious ideological differences, not merely rhetorical hyperbole, divided parties over the role of government and the direction of the economy and society.[23]

One final matter for analysis involves the Populists' celebrated failure to enact a significant body of reform legislation in the 1897 Senate. One explanation advanced focuses on their legislative inexperience and alleged lack of unity and skill in the legislative process. Roll-call analysis helps discount this possibility, for cohesion indexes and party support scores reveal that Populist senators demonstrated as much solidarity and unity in voting behavior over the full range of legislative issues as did their opponents. Another reason for Populist failure must be found.[24]

That explanation is suggested by the intra-party variation in party support scores. All Republicans registered scores around their party average, but the standard deviation for Populists was twice as great; although a majority of Populists had extremely high party support scores, a handful had significantly lower ones. These latter Populists were the same senators ranking at the lower positions of the Guttman scale portraying the radical-conservative dimension underlying voting decisions. The crucial importance of this group becomes clear upon examination of the fifteen roll calls in which reform legislation was defeated. On these roll calls, Republicans and Democrats voted as a solid bloc in opposition to the bills, casting only seven reform votes out of a possible 195. When joined by the small group of conservative Populists, this bloc constituted a majority of the senate and defeated the proposed legislation. This Populist faction consisted largely of merchants and lawyers, although one lawyer and one editor generally supported the proposed reforms and a few Populist farmers (usually representing, however, the least rural constituencies of the farmer legislators) often voted against the legislation. This pattern suggests that ideological considerations—shared attitudes—rather than a narrow occupational identification determined legislative behavior, although ideology was itself in some fashion influenced by the rural perspective.[25]

Roll-call analysis also identifies the issues over which the Populist coalition splintered and thereby helps to explain the party's peculiar course and its ultimate demise. Populists in the Kansas Senate were most unified when voting on national issues, such as resolutions in favor of free silver or a federal income tax; on state issues affecting all of them equally, such as the establishment of the initiative and referendum; or on issues affecting virtually none of them directly, such as prohibiting labor blacklisting. But divergent groups emerged when the issues narrowed to specific programs of immediate relevance. These divisions among Populists appeared primarily over certain questions of economic activity at the state and local level. It would be more incomplete than inaccurate to characterize these disagreements as simply a split between radicals and conservatives, for the latter supported a variety of economic and political reforms and stood sharply to the left of their contemporaries in the major parties. The conflict would be better described as a division between those representing what the Populists called the "producing classes" and those interested in promoting economic development. The developers objected to any proposed restrictions on what they perceived as the engines of economic growth: eastern capital investment and the railroads. Bills introduced by producer-oriented Populists to tax mortgages, regulate interest rates, or lend state money to farmers all seemed, to developer Populists as much as to Republicans, to threaten the procurement of eastern capital investment in Kansas.[26]

Developer Populists also joined with Republicans to vote down bills to establish maximum railroad rates, to limit the return on railroad investments, or to prohibit railroad commissioners from having any personal investment in railroads. Similarly, they opposed a bill to restrict the power of local governments to create bonded indebtedness, a power they viewed as a major tool for economic development. The leader of these Populists was Senator William A. Harris, who directed the defeat of railroad regulation and consistently supported the interests of creditors over debtors, arguing the necessity of attracting investment. Thus he helped defeat a bill to prohibit usury by describing it as vindictive toward moneylenders. His own legislation was designed to establish the deed of trust, to reduce the redemption period for property, and generally to "so shape the laws of the state as to protect alike the credit of the state and the money of honest investors."[27]

Many Populists denounced this group of senators for supporting the traditional positions of the major parties. "When Senator Harris favors high interest because he wants to encourage capital to come to Kansas," declared the Norton *Liberator,* "he announces he has not yet divested himself of the swaddling bands of old fogyism." Another Populist newspaper also complained that "Populists of certain districts in Kansas have sent men to the legislature who are more nearly Republicans than Populists." Indeed, most of the Populists who voted with the Republicans on developmental issues were merchants or distinctly entrepreneurial "farmers" like Harris, who was actually a civil engineer and a cattle breeder of national reputation who latter moved to Chicago as president of the American Shorthorn Breeders' Association. Their producer-oriented opponents among the Populists were nearly all farmers. Advocates of the developer point of view tried to ridicule such farmers as ignorant and unfit for public office. A newspaper in Harris' Levenworth District, for example, attacked Senator J.N. Caldwell as a Populist "transplanted from his hog pasture in Anderson County and never realizing the change . . . [with] more realization of shovelling corn than he has of law-making." The source of the criticism, however, was not the alleged ignorance nor the real agricultural origins of such Populists, but the fact that they were consciously trying to change the direction of economic legislation.[28]

The importance of this division is clear in Table 8.3, which summarizes the voting behavior of several groups of senators on sixteen roll calls over

Table 8.3

Average Interpersonal Agreement Scores on Development Issues

	Majority Populists	Minority Populists	Republicans	Democrats
Majority Populists Cooke Forney Lupfer Pritchard	95			
average development score: 9				
Minority Populists Crossan Hanna Ryan Shaffer	17	80		
average development score: 90				
Republicans Battey Hessin Lamb Morrow	12	89	93	
average development score: 97				
Democrats Farrelly Zimmer	30	77	83	79
average development score: 80				

"development" legislation. As with Table 8.1, the percentages given are the means of interpersonal agreement scores and the groups represent samples of the majority element of the Populists, the marginal Populists, and members of the older parties. But whereas the earlier cluster-bloc analysis over the full range of legislation indicated that deviant Populists' voting behavior still resembled that of their Populist colleagues more than that of the Republicans, that pattern is sharply reversed in this particular policy area. The majority Populists were closely united in near total disagreement with development policies (an average score of 9 on a scale of 0 to 100) and had little in common with either the minority Populists or the Republicans who voted solidly together and overwhelmingly supported the development position (scores of 90 and 97, respectively). The Democrats voted substantially in favor of development (a score of 80), but less so than the Republicans—as one might expect from a knowledge of general Democratic attitudes in the 1890s. Strikingly, however, the minority Populists were also more pro-development than the Democrats and even agreed with them far more readily than with their fellow Populists.

In sharing these promotional attitudes, and often town and commercial identifications, these Populists represented a bridge to the major parties and their traditional policies. It was through their efforts and persons, for example, that fusion typically was arranged, especially Senators Harris, Lewelling, and W.H. Ryan with the Democrats and Senator Crossan with the Silver Republicans. Moreover, it was these more conservative Populist senators whom the party promoted politically: Harris was elected United States Senator in 1897; Lewelling had been governor from 1893 to 1895; and incumbent governor John Leedy had been a leader of the conservative Populist group in the 1895 state senate. Their political prominence represented Populist attempts to appeal to a wider constituency and thereby achieve electoral success. As one Populist paper observed of these senators, "These 'conservative' Populists are largely composed of men whose political status was a matter of considerable doubt—who had been nominated because of their supposed ability to get votes." This practice, however, undermined rather than promoted the likelihood of securing Populist reform. This dilution of Populism for practical political reasons constituted a central weakness in the People's Party, and the legislative behavior of those so chosen represented a concrete indication of how politics weakened Populism.[29]

This study has determined the practical policy objectives of Populists in power, specified the particular issues that divided legislators, both across and within party lines, and suggested the nature of the different groupings and their implications for the traditional political questions about Populism. Additional research along these lines, particularly of a cross-sessional nature, is obviously necessary, but these findings are suggestive. The majority of Populists worked, against fairly consistent Republican opposition, to fashion a legislative program that would enact their famous platform demands into law. A minority of Populists, sharing with the mass of the party most political and economic attitudes, also was tangentially related to the representatives of the major parties in terms of promotional attitudes and/or occupation and residence. On questions dealing with promoting or restricting economic development — ironically, as one Populist noted, "the things nearest to the Populistic heart" — this Populist minority deserted their party and its expressed principles. Although a minority, they wielded a decisive influence through their leadership positions and their strategic numbers in an electorate where Populists constituted a minority and in a senate chamber where their votes were needed. As one Populist senator complained of Harris, he "did all in his power to turn back the radical measures of his party." The nature and consequences of this division reveal the Populist tragedy that the methods by which they created a political coalition powerful enough to win elections often left it without the power to enact laws.[30]

Notes

1. James Turner, "Understanding the Populists," *Journal of American History,* LXVII (1980), 356.

2. Bruce Palmer, *"Man Over Money": The Southern Populist Critique of American Capitalism* (Chapel Hill, 1980), xvi.

3. Allan G. Bogue, "American Historians and Legislative Behavior," in Lee Benson et al. (eds.), *American Political Behavior: Historical Essays and Readings* (New York, 1974), 109. Bogue's thoughtful essay represents perhaps the best introduction to the historical study of legislative behavior. For useful elaboration, see Lee F. Anderson et al., *Legislative Roll-Call Analysis* (Evanston, 1966). Three important exceptions to the neglect of legislative analysis in Populist historiography are Sheldon Hackney, *Populism to Progressivism in Alabama* (Princeton, 1969); Stanley B. Parsons, *The Populist Context: Rural Versus Urban Power on a Great Plains Frontier* (Westport, Conn., 1973); James E. Wright, *The Politics of Populism: Dissent in Colorado* (New Haven, 1974).

4. Also excluded were roll calls on legislative proposals the actual substance of which could not be determined even after extensive investigation of a large number of newspapers, particularly the various Topeka newspapers which carried lengthy reports of daily legislative activity. By repetitive motions I refer to repeated roll calls raising substantially the same point on the same bill and provoking the same voting alignment time after time. The Republican minority adopted this procedure as a stalling tactic to prevent the Populist majority from acting. See *Topeka Daily Capital,* Feb. 6, 1897.

5. *Topeka State Journal,* Feb. 13, 16, Mar. 4, 6, 1897; *Leavenworth Times,* Mar. 7, 1897; *Kansas Senate Journal, 1897* (Topeka, 1897), 39, 45, 84, 154, 340, 889–896.

6. For excellent recent examples of such suggestive legislative analyses, see Ballard C. Campbell, *Representative Democracy: Public Policy and Midwestern Legislatures in the Late Nineteenth Century* (Cambridge, Mass., 1980); Bogue, *The Earnest Men: Republicans of the Civil War Senate* (Ithaca, 1981).

The Rice index of cohesion ranges from 0 to 100 and is calculated by determining the absolute difference between the percentrage of group members voting yea and the percentage voting nay on any single roll call. The index of disagreement (the obverse of the index of likeness) also varies from 0 to 100 and is the difference between the percentage of yea votes cast by each group on a roll call. Following the example of Bogue, *Earnest Men,* I regard index of disagreement scores > 40 as indicating significant disagreement.

7. For elaboration of this point, see Argersinger, "Ideology and Behavior: Legislative Politics and Western Populism," *Agricultural History,* LVIII (1984), 43–58.

8. See, for example, O. Gene Clanton, *Kansas Populism: Ideas and Men* (Lawrence, Kans., 1969), 28–29. Clanton also emphasizes important differences between central and western Kansas, but by the 1890s western Kansas had become so depopulated that it had virtually no representation in the senate, 1 senator representing 18 counties in the southwest and another representing 13 counties in the northwest, both districts extending into central Kansas. For purposes of analysis, therefore, the 40 senators were grouped into two blocs, 22 representing the more established eastern third and 18 representing the remainder of the state.

9. Senate Bills (S.B.) 129, 153, *Kansas Senate Journal,* 311, 535.

10. S.B. 147, *ibid.,* 291. Kansas had the largest increase in public debt of any state in the 1880s. For aspects of this boom, see James C. Malin, "The Kinsley Boom of the Late Eighties," *Kansas Historical Quarterly,* IV (1935), 23–49, 164–187. Parsons, *The Populist Context,* emphasizes this same conflict between villagers and farmers over questions of economic promotion in Nebraska. For suggestive observations on the legislative reflection of the conflict between developers and producers, see Bogue, "To Shape a Western State: Some Dimensions of the Kansas Search for Capital, 1865–1893," in John G. Clark (ed.), *The Frontier Challenge: Responses to the Trans-Mississippi West* (Lawrence, Kans., 1971), 203–234.

11. Amendment to S.B. 524, S.B. 111, amendments to S.B. 446, *Kansas Senate Journal,* 641, 852, 945–946; *Topeka State Journal,* Feb. 19, 1897.

12. Malin, "At What Age Did Men Become Reformers?" *Kansas Historical Quarterly,* XXIX (1963), 250–266. Malin's clever and imaginative article has a different focus from this essay. He treats "reformers" in the Kansas legislatures simply as members of self-described reform parties and does not examine their actual voting behavior.

13. Although ethnoculturalists focus on the pietist-liturgical dichotomy, they emphasize the pietistic perspective as underlying the "reform" movements of the nineteenth century. Thus the relative absence of liturgical senators should not altogether prevent testing the role of religion. But many of the most evangelical Populists were exceedingly hostile to organized religion, and thus to the problem of possible non-reporting of affiliations must be added the problem of measuring religious attitudes by this method. For Populist views toward religion and churches, see Argersinger, "Pentecostal Politics in Kansas: Religion, the Farmers' Alliance, and the Gospel of Populism," *Kansas Quarterly,* I (1969), 24–35. The prohibitionist roll call was on House Bill (H.B.) 3, *Kansas Senate Journal,* 638–639.

14. Again, as with religion, a substantial number of legislators did not report their educational background, a fact which should suggest caution about any conclusions here.

15. *Topeka State Journal,* Jan. 20, Feb. 10, 19, 1897; *Leavenworth Times,* Feb. 3, 10, 20, 1897; roll calls on S.B.'s 34, 8, 147, 3, 446, 72, 524, 111, *Kansas Senate Journal,* 398–399, 527–528, 569–570, 291, 833, 945–946, 555–559, 371, 641, 852.

16. S.B. 524, S.B. 121, H.B. 442, S.B. 446, *Kansas Senate Journal,* 641, 678, 349, 1126, 555.

17. Eastern Populist opponents of bills to establish additional normal schools believed that the purpose of such legislation was primarily "the aggrandizement of the local representative or senator." *Kansas Senate Journal,* 586–587. In Nebraska, too, legislatures continually wrangled "over new state institutions, especially normal schools, a favorite device to promote community growth." Robert W. Cherny, *Populism, Progressivism, and the Transformation of Nebraska Politics, 1885–1915* (Lincoln, 1981), 72.

18. *Topeka Daily Capital,* Feb. 18, 1897; S.B. 85, *Kansas Senate Journal,* 744. For the advantages of the deed of trust in the creditor's eyes, see Bogue, "To Shape a Western State," 217; *idem, Money at Interest: The Farm Mortgage on the Middle Border* (Ithaca, 1955), 17.

19. For the debilitating effect of Democratic influence and fusion on the People's Party, see Argersinger, *Populism and Politics: William Alfred Peffer and the People's Party* (Lexington, Ky., 1974).

20. The index of interpersonal agreement is the frequency with which each legislator agrees with every other legislator over the roll calls on which they both vote. Thus, absences are excluded from the calculations. Senators absent for more than half the roll calls are omitted.

21. Karel Bicha, *Western Populism: Studies in an Ambivalent Conservatism* (Lawrence, Kans., 1976), 79, 80, 86, 104.

22. Bogue, *Earnest Men*, 350; *Topeka Daily Capital*, Feb. 14, 1895. An incident in the 1897 legislature, involving the same analogy that Bogue employed, supports the validity of this assumption. Forty-four Populists formally protested against a gutted railroad bill but still voted for it after being told by a colleague that if they did not realize "a half loaf is better than none" their constituents would replace them with politicians who did. Clanton, *Kansas Populism*, 204. For an excellent explanation of the logic of Guttman scale analysis, see Bogue, *Earnest Men*, 345–351.

23. The quote is from Bicha's sentence in *Western Populism*, 80, denying what Table 8.2 demonstrates. Thus perhaps there was some truth in the rhetoric of an earlier Republican who concluded that "All Populists are not socialists . . . but all socialists . . . are Populists." *Topeka State Journal*, Jan. 24, 1893.

24. The charge of Populist failure was exaggerated. The 1897 Kansas legislature passed laws providing for stockyard regulation, ballot reform, banking regulation, a state grain inspection department, a school textbook commission, regulation of life insurance companies, taxation of deficiency judgments, municipal ownership, anti-trust legislation, railroad regulation, conservation, and a series of labor protections from anti-Pinkerton and anti-scrip provisions to anti-blacklisting, protection of unions, and improved health and safety conditions for miners. Even so, as Clanton has noted, "the party's supporters had a right to expect greater things": Clanton, *Kansas Populism*, 201, 89, 199, 294n. Bicha, *Western Populism*, 80, 87, 92; Wright, *Politics of Populism*, 162–163. The party support score is the percentage of time a senator voted with his party majority when the parties were polarized at a disagreement index $\geq$ 50. For those 45 roll calls, Republicans averaged 92%; Populist party loyalty was 87%. For all 81 roll calls, Populist cohesion averaged 70.4 to 65.7 for Republicans.

25. The conservative bloc of 9 Populists had an average reform score of only 21 on these crucial questions whereas the other Populists averaged 79.

26. *Topeka State Journal*, Feb. 19, 1897; *Leavenworth Times*, Feb. 3, 10, 20, 1897; S.B.'s 3, 8, 34, *Kansas Senate Journal*, 398–399, 452, 526–528, 570–571, 833.

27. *Topeka State Journal*, Jan. 14, 1897; *Topeka Daily Capital*, Feb. 6, 1897; S.B.'s 524 (and amendments), 147, 85, *Kansas Senate Journal*, 641, 648, 677, 678, 291, 52, 728–730, 744.

28. *Norton Liberator*, Feb. 26, 1897; *Topeka Advocate*, Mar. 3, 1897; *Leavenworth Times*, Mar. 14, 1897. In an important article, Nugent established that, among Kansas politicians in 1891–1893, Republicans and Democrats were much more likely to be urban-oriented than were Populists, who were overwhelmingly farmers. By carefully examining individual mortgage transactions and land purchases, he also demonstrated that Populists, generally, were more "yeoman-like" and less entrepreneurial and speculative than Republicans and Democrats. See Walter T.K. Nugent, "Some Parameters of Populism," *Agricultural History*, XL (1966), 255–270. Nugent's profile of the typical Populist and his economic attitudes seems comparable to the rural orientation and "producer" attitudes that I have attributed to the Populist majority in the 1897 Senate. By adopting more entrepreneurial and pro-development attitudes and by being disproportionately urban-oriented, therefore, members of the Populist minority diverged in significant ways from most Populists and resembled their Republican senatorial colleagues.

29. *Topeka Advocate*, Mar. 24, 1897; for Populist fusion maneuvers involving Harris, Lewelling, Ryan, and Leedy, among others, see Argersinger, *Populism and Politics*, 52, 127–140, 166–178, 267–269, 279–282, 294; for a discussion of the discontinuity between the People's Party and Populism in political rather than legislative behavior, see *ibid.*, 140–142, 179–181, 197, 209, 221–222, 231, 235–236, 262–266, 306–310. The Democrats in the legislature had also been nominated more for their electoral appeal than for their political principles. Elected on Populist fusion tickets, they were termed

"Popocrats" and caucused with the Populists. But their actual policy attitudes and voting behavior, as noted above, often placed them at odds with the majority of Populist legislators, demonstrating that fusionists could not be depended upon to support Populist policy proposals.

30. Wynne P. Harrington, "The Populist Party in Kansas," *Collections of the Kansas State Historical Society,* XVI (Topeka, 1925), 444; *Kansas Semi-Weekly Capital* (Topeka), Oct. 12, 1897.

Index

About the Author

Peter H. Argersinger is Professor of History at the University of Maryland, Baltimore County Campus, and a Senior Fellow at the Woodrow Wilson International Center for Scholars. A graduate of the University of Kansas, he received his Ph.D. degree from the University of Wisconsin. He is the author of *Populism and Politics: William A. Peffer and the People's Party* and numerous articles on American political and social history and was the recipient of the 1990 Binkley-Stephenson Award of the Organization of American Historians.